The Eight

The Eight

The Lemmon Slave Case and the Fight for Freedom

ALBERT M. ROSENBLATT

EXCELSIOR
EDITIONS

Published by State University of New York Press, Albany

Excelsior Editions is an imprint of State University of New York Press.

For information, contact State University of New York Press, Albany, NY
www.sunypress.edu

Library of Congress Cataloging-in-Publication Data

Name: Rosenblatt, Albert M., author.
Title: The eight : The Lemmon Slave Case and the fight for freedom /
    Albert M. Rosenblatt.
Description: Albany : State University of New York Press, [2023] | Includes
    bibliographical references and index. | Series: Excelsior Editions.
Identifiers: ISBN 9781438492650 (hardcover : alk. paper) | ISBN 9781438492667
    (ebook) | ISBN 9781438492643 (pbk. : alk. paper)
Further information is available at the Library of Congress.

10 9 8 7 6 5 4 3 2 1

Contents

Illustrations

Foreword

JUDGE RAYMOND J. LOHIER JR., UNITED STATES
COURT OF APPEALS FOR THE SECOND CIRCUIT

Important stories about the struggle against American slavery in the critical decade prior to the Civil War are too often neglected by legal historians and the general public. These stories are both personal and national in their scope and effect, and the Fugitive Slave Act of 1850, later fortified by the infamous 1857 Supreme Court *Dred Scott* decision, is at their legal center. The act accelerated the mass seizure of fugitive enslaved people and threatened to nationalize slavery. The conditions compelled New York and other free states to grapple with fundamental moral, political, and legal questions arising from slavery.

At the heart of these questions was the dangerous quest of Black people, aided by the efforts of abolitionists and others, to secure their voyage from bondage to freedom. By the mid-1850s, New York, which had abolished slavery on July 4, 1827, became a focal point of efforts to help runaway slaves, as well as an important stop on the Underground Railroad. All told, in the decades before the Civil War, New Yorkers helped over 3,000 runaway enslaved people escape slavery to upstate New York and Canada.

The *Lemmon* slave case, which unfolded from 1852 to 1860, exemplifies New York's legal stand against slavery in the run up to the Civil War. *The Eight* recounts the critical role that New York courts played in freeing eight enslaved women and children who sailed into New York harbor with their white owners, the Lemmons from Virginia. As Judge Rosenblatt observes, the question in the *Lemmon* case "came down to whether someone entering New York could carry with them not only their shoes and overcoats but also their *laws*." Put differently: if slaves were property, could New York prohibit slave owners from traveling through its territory with their slaves, as they had the right to do with the rest of their property?

Weaving together the conflicting social, cultural, legal, and commercial currents and interests at stake in the case, both in New York and nationwide, Judge Rosenblatt's book powerfully details how the New York courts struggled to answer this question. It recounts the Eight's arduous legal journey from the 1852 decision of Judge Paine, the New York trial judge who initially freed them, to their resounding victory eight years later before the New York Court of Appeals. Along the way, it introduces us to a cast of courageous Americans: the two mothers, Emeline Thompson and Nancy Johnson, who demanded freedom for themselves and their children; Black abolitionist Louis Napoleon, who oversaw New York's Underground Railroad and secured legal representation for the Eight; John Jay II, grandson of the first Chief Justice of the United States, who represented the Eight during their habeas corpus proceeding; and William Evarts, a future United States Attorney General and Senator, who successfully represented the Eight on appeal.

No one who reads Judge Rosenblatt's careful history and analysis of the *Lemmon* case and the regional and national questions about freedom and equality that it raised will be able to ignore its echoes to the present day. The role of state courts in shaping and determining constitutional law remains vital, and vexing questions about federalism, state's rights, and state conflicts endure.

Preface

This book tells the story of *Lemmon v. New York*—or, as it's more popularly known, the Lemmon Slave Case. All but forgotten today, it was one of the most momentous civil-rights cases in American history. There had been cases in which the enslaved had won their freedom after having resided in free states, but the Lemmon case was unique, posing the question of whether an enslaved person can win freedom by merely setting foot on New York soil—when brought there in the keep of an "owner."

The case concerned the fates of eight enslaved people from Virginia, brought through New York in 1852 by their owners, Juliet and Jonathan Lemmon, along with the seven Lemmon children. The group, 17 in all, had been heading for Texas, to take up residence there, but a quirk in travel plans brought them to New York harbor.

Learning of their arrival in New York, local abolitionists joined in a fight to liberate the Eight on the strength of a New York state law, passed in 1841, that granted liberty to any enslaved person brought into the state. The case was litigated for eight years in the New York courts, ultimately reaching New York State's highest court, the Court of Appeals, a few months before shots rang out at Fort Sumter, signaling the start of the Civil War.

For several years, I served as a judge on that court. During my tenure, I heard occasional talk of the Lemmon case as having emanated from "our court," although I hasten to say I arrived there 140 or so years after the ink on the decision had dried, and decades after people had any detailed recollection of it.

One day, as a legal exercise, I sat down and actually read the decision. Here is how it begins:

On the 6th day of November, 1852, Louis Napoleon, a colored citizen of this State, made application upon a sufficient petition and affidavit to Mr. Justice [Elijah] Paine of the Superior Court of the city of New York, for a writ of habeas corpus to be directed to one Jonathan Lemmon and the keeper of house No. 3 Carlisle street, New York, requiring them to bring before said justice the bodies of eight colored persons, one man, two women and five children, who on the day preceding were confined and restrained of their liberty on board the steamer City of Richmond, in the harbor of New York and were taken therefrom on the night of that day to No. 3 Carlisle street, and there detained under the presence that they were slaves.[1]

I was intrigued. Who was Louis Napoleon? What was he doing bringing a petition on behalf of "eight colored persons?" More to the point, the case involved not eight legal entities but eight real people, whose freedom hung in the balance.

Of the Eight, Emeline and Nancy were mothers, and they spoke for the group. They could not know how Judge Paine would rule, but they took their chances, appreciating that the wrong ruling would not only keep them enslaved but would paint them in the eyes of their owners as rebellious, making their lives, and the lives of their children, even worse.

And who was Judge Elijah Paine? Not one lawyer in a thousand today knows anything of him, and yet he was asked to make an important, unprecedented ruling at that hour: Can the enslaved claim freedom when brought to a free state by their owners? (The law was clear on fugitive slaves, who had to be returned to bondage even when captured in free states, but the Eight were *brought* to New York by Juliet and Jonathan Lemmon—a situation the courts had yet to rule on.)

The case presented a profoundly moving human drama in which eight people fought for their freedom. Any lawsuit between A and B might well become more interesting when we pull back the curtain and learn something about the people involved, but the Lemmon case was not like most lawsuits. In this case, the Eight were in court seeking, legally, to *become* people—to change their status under law from objects into human beings. Under the law in Virginia and other slave states, the enslaved were property—chattel—to be treated however their owners saw fit: to be sold, traded, inherited, separated from their spouses, parents, and children, sexually abused, or whipped for trying to read a book.

Their story of the Eight reveals, at a powerful personal level, what it was like to try to get out from under a system like that. It includes a remarkable cast of characters. Louis Napoleon, for example, the son of a slave, was an abolitionist activist and a "conductor" of the Underground Railroad, who took enormous risks to help others. We count him as part of an anti-slavery movement in which African Americans played an integral role in the fight for freedom, working actively in the realms of politics, economics, law, and culture. They sometimes collaborated with white abolitionists but often did their work independently.

Slavery in the Americas began in Virginia and New York in the early 1600s and ended with the Civil War, more than two centuries later. I found it impossible to write this volume without trying to understand, and to present, what I learned about how the American system of slavery was justified for so long, socially, morally, and legally. How were slavery's cheerleaders able to convince people that enslavement was benevolent, part of the natural order of things, and, as they so often proclaimed, endorsed by God?

The case was part of the broader judicial landscape at the time: If a law was morally repugnant but enshrined in the Constitution, what was the duty of the judge? Should there be, as some people advocated, a "higher law?" A "natural law" that transcends the written law? Issues of law and morality abounded.

These questions were at the heart of the Lemmon case and of the jurisprudence of the era. They were difficult and important ones in the 1850s—and, more than a century and a half later, we must still grapple with them today.

Dramatis Personae

The Eight: The eight people enslaved by Juliet and Jonathan Lemmon. In 1852, the Eight began their legal battle for freedom in a New York court. They were kinfolk, in two family groups, one headed by Emeline Thompson and her children and her siblings, the other by Nancy Johnson and her children. See entries for Emeline Thompson and Nancy Johnson below.

Juliet Douglas Lemmon: Owner, with her husband, Jonathan Lemmon, of the Eight. She acquired some or all of them by inheritance from her father, William ("Billy") Douglas.

William ("Billy") Douglas: Father of Juliet and owner of over 30 slaves, whom he devised to his children on his death, in 1836.

Jonathan Lemmon: Owner, with his wife, Juliet, of the Eight.

Emeline Thompson: At age 23, the oldest of the Eight. Sister of Lewis (about 16) and Edward (about 13). Mother of Lewis Wright and Robert Wright (twins, either 7 or 5 years old) and Amanda (2).

Nancy Johnson: At age 20, the second oldest of the Eight. Mother of two-year-old Ann. Sister of Richard Johnson.

Lemmon children: Nancy (9), Joseph (8), James (7), Caroline (6), Juliet (4), Sarah (2). Also, Douglas (16), son of Juliet and her first husband, Adam Stewart (sometimes Stuart).

Richard Johnson: Nancy Johnson's brother. Learned of the Lemmon case while in Cleveland, realized his sister was one of the Eight, and came to New York to help get the Eight to Canada.

Nathan Lobam: Steward on the steamer *City of Richmond*, which brought the Lemmons and the Eight to New York. Aiding the Eight in their quest for freedom, he sent messages to Louis Napoleon and Erastus Culver, telling them that the Eight were aboard the steamer in New York Harbor.

Louis Napoleon: Conductor on New York's Underground Railroad and collaborator with the anti-slavery editor Sydney Howard Gay. He initiated the Lemmon case in 1852 by petitioning for a writ of habeas corpus before Judge Elijah Paine.

Erastus Culver: Attorney for the Eight at the habeas corpus proceeding before Judge Elijah Paine. Chester A. Arthur, later to become president of the United States, was a young attorney in his office.

John Jay II: Son of Judge William Jay and grandson of the founding father John Jay, he joined Erastus Culver in representing the Eight at the habeas corpus proceeding before Judge Elijah Paine in 1852.

Elijah Paine Jr.: Judge of the Superior Court of New York City, before whom the Lemmon case was brought, by way of habeas corpus, in 1852.

William M. Evarts: Attorney for the Eight at the first level of appeal in New York, in 1857, and before the New York Court of Appeals, in 1860.

Joseph Blunt: Joined William M. Evarts as attorney for the Eight, on behalf of the State of New York at the first level of appeal in New York, in 1857, and before the New York Court of Appeals, in 1860.

Charles O'Conor: Attorney who argued against the liberation of the Eight, representing the State of Virginia, which had substituted for Juliet and Jonathan Lemmon.

Chapter 1

Life in Bath County, Virginia

Juliet and Jonathan Lemmon's eight slaves began their fight for freedom in a New York courtroom in 1852, several years before the Civil War. The lawyers for both sides argued the heart of the case, which represented the heart of the national divide: Can there be property in human beings?

The historical setting gives the case its importance, and it is easy to consider it in abstract terms, as a page or two in a book about slavery or legal history. For the Eight, however, the case was not an abstraction. Enslaved, they were in a battle to change their condition from owned objects into human beings.

Emeline Thompson, the oldest of the Eight, made her first official appearance in 1830, as one of the 469,757 enslaved people recorded by that year's census as living in Virginia. She was one year old. Nameless, she was subsumed within a category of "slaves under the age of 10," belonging to William ("Billy") Douglas of Bath County, Virginia.[1]

Emeline first appears by name in 1836, when she was seven years old, in Billy Douglas's last will and testament. There, Douglas listed her as an item of "personal property," along with "twelve head of sheep, the stock of hogs, provisions of every kind, waggon, gears, farming utensils of every kind, all the grain as well as that which may have been gathered as well as that which may be in the ground and also my salt petre kettles."

Bequeathing 2000 acres of land and 34 slaves, Douglas gave Emeline to his 19-year-old daughter Juliet, who later married Jonathan Lemmon (see figures 1.1 and 1.2). Under Virginia law, Juliet's property, including Emeline, belonged to her husband.[2]

Figure 1.1. Portrait of Juliet Lemmon (1817–1909). Courtesy of Shirley Craft/
Find a Grave.

Figure 1.2. Portrait of Jonathan Lemmon (1808–1890). Courtesy of Shirley Craft/
Find a Grave.

Douglas had 13 children, borne by three women, none of whom he married, one of whom was Juliet's mother.[3] With a few exceptions, such as Emeline, Billy Douglas did not direct which slave should go to whom, leaving it to his children to sort them out. Five of the 34 enslaved were born after Douglas died. Executors could treat enslaved children born after the testator's death "no otherwise than Horses or Cattle," as a Virginia court put it.[4] In his will, Douglas emancipated Ben, one of his slaves, "because of his great fidelity and service to me which on one occasion resulted in the loss of one of his eyes." He continued, "I further bequeath unto the said Ben a young brown mare and one hundred dollars."

In addition to Emeline, Juliet also gained title to Emeline's two younger brothers, Lewis and Edward, and to Nancy, a four-year-old girl. Douglas also left Juliet a sizable homestead with large acreage.

Sixteen years later, in 1852, the "Lemmon slaves" had increased from four to eight. Emeline, now 23, was the mother of five-year-old twins, Robert and Lewis, and a younger girl, Amanda. Nancy, now 20, had a daughter, Ann, about two years of age. Emeline's brothers, Lewis and Edward, were about 16 and 13.[5] They all had grown up in Bath County, Virginia, which—at least until West Virginia came into existence, in 1863—lay near the center of the state, covering over a half million acres of beautiful vistas, and locales with colorful names like Paddy Knob, Bull-pasture Mountain, Windy Cove, Muddy Run, Sister Knobs, Red Holes, Dry Run, Panther Gap, Falling Spring Run, and Sideling Hill. In the late 1840s, as the Eight were growing up, nearby resorts like Warm Springs and Hot Springs began to attract thousands of people in the summer.

Billy Douglas and the Lemmons farmed land intersected by the Cowpasture River and the James River, producing corn, oats, hay, wool, and butter. The market for enslavement says something about the size of Billy Douglas's slave holdings. In 1840, not long after he wrote his will, Bath County had a population of 4,300 people, including 1,045 enslaved—of whom Douglas had owned 34.[6]

Within a decade, by 1850, Bath County had nine sawmills, eight grist mills, four wool-carding mills, two agricultural manufactories, two tanneries, and six churches.[7]

∽

By 1852, the Lemmon family farm was teeming with children—15 in all. Juliet and Jonathan had seven, including 16-year-old Douglas (from her previous marriage), followed by Nancy, 9; Joseph, 8; James, 7; Caroline, 6; Juliet, 4; and Sarah, 2. The seven lived in the main house. Those they enslaved, the Eight, lived in cabins nearby (see figure 1.3).

It was not like summer camp. In slave-owning settings, enslaved children did not sit around the table together with the owners' children or play hide-and-seek with them in the family parlour. Emeline and Nancy, the oldest of the enslaved children, were expected to look after the younger Lemmon children, to cook and clean, to work in the fields, and to do whatever chores it took to help keep the household and the farm going.

When Juliet acquired Emeline's brothers, Lewis and Edward, they were infants. As they grew up, their chores increased, and by 1852, as teenagers, they were old enough to do work on the farm. Unlike large plantations that enslaved dozens, the Lemmon operation did not have an overseer. The boys took their orders from the Lemmons and, probably, from their oldest son, Douglas, then 16.

In slave societies, it was not uncommon for enslaved young women to wet-nurse white babies. When Juliet Lemmon inherited them, Emeline

Figure 1.3. A cabin built on the Douglas property before 1837. Courtesy of Jean Nooe Miller and Katie Shepard, originally published in *Wiggum Stories*.

was seven and Nancy three, but in the world of enslavement, they grew into "productive assets." After about nine years, at age 16, Emeline could work in the fields and in the house. She had also given birth to twin boys and a girl. This "increase" meant not only three more slaves, but also a young mother who could wet-nurse the owners' children (see figure 1.4).

Nancy, about three years younger than Emeline, followed a similar path, and could be called on for the same duties as Emeline.

It is inconceivable that some sort of rapport did not develop among these 15 young people, eight white and seven Black. The relationships between the enslaved and the family children were complicated. A Black female slave wet-nursing her white master's infant was bound to create an intimate bond. Surely, affection ran both ways. Films like *Gone With the Wind* would romanticize that side of things.

But that was in the movies. In day-to-day life, the rules of enslavement controlled. One commentator recorded accounts of how slave children were subjected to the "tyranny" of the master's children. We do not know, for

Figure 1.4. Photo of Mary Allen Watson, an enslaved African American girl carrying a white infant, 1866. Library of Congress, Prints and Photographs Division, LC-DIG-ppmsca-11038.

example, how eight-year-old James Lemmon might have treated Emeline's twin boys. It would have depended on Juliet and Jonathan's supervision and sense of decency. We do know, however, that under slavery law, a master had the right to inflict brutal physical punishment—short of murder—on the enslaved.

After all, the victims were "owned property," which meant that owners could do with them pretty much as they pleased. But, as with any other "property," they had an incentive to treat the human beings they owned at least well enough to maintain their "value."

From the time Emeline and Nancy were old enough to get the idea, they understood that they were not members of the Lemmon family but were more like appendages, living in fear of being sold, or enduring the sale of their mothers or their fathers—and later, their partners or their children.

This fear was real. In paragraph 10 of his will, Douglas had directed that if there was not enough money to pay his debts and expenses, "the negroes" were to constitute a "fund," and his children were to have "the privilege of designating such of the said slaves as they would prefer being sold." Testamentary provisions of that kind were common.

We do not know how many of Douglas's slaves were given over to the auction block. If any had been sold, the calculus would have taken into account the subject's age, strength, and congeniality, along with the capacity for hard work and robust breeding.

Nancy, we know, was not sold off but wound up in the Lemmon household, where she would have been expected to "increase" the inventory. Appalachian slave mothers lost one of every three offspring to sales. This grim prospect was epitomized by the plaintive cry, "Buy us too" (see figure 1.5).

What of running away? From the earliest age, any such thought would be met with tales of what happens to anyone daring enough to try it. Yes, they knew, some did make it, but most were hunted down and whipped—if they were not killed in the pursuit or capture, that is. This was long engrained in establishing the rules of ownership. There were countless advertisements offering rewards for runaway slaves, but none made the point more clearly than one that offered 10 pounds either for the runaway alive, or "for his Head, if separated from his Body."

$$\backsim$$

THE PÀRTING "Buy us too".

Figure 1.5. "Buy us too." Library of Congress, Prints and Photographs Division, LC-USZC4-2525.

The relationships between owners' children and slaves varied from plantation to plantation, but the basic idea was not only spelled out in custom but backed up by law. An influential court decision came down in 1829, the year Emeline was born. The case, *State v. Mann*, came from the Supreme Court of North Carolina, but it spoke for the entire South.

John Mann, a widowed sea captain, hired a slave, Lydia, for one year. He chastised her for some small offense, and as she was running away, he shot and wounded her, for which he was tried. The judge instructed the jurors that if they believed the shooting cruel and disproportionate, it would constitute an assault and battery. The jury found Mann guilty, and he was fined five dollars.

On his appeal, the court overturned his conviction and wrote a landmark decision, answering a question basic to American slavery: Short of willful murder, does the law impose *any* limits on slaveowners or renters in their treatment of slaves? The decision's author, Chief Justice Thomas C. Ruffin (1787–1870), was one of America's most eminent jurists. The prosecution had argued that Mann's crime should be treated like that of a parent charged with shooting a child. The court said no, noting that in a free family, "the end in view is the happiness of the youth, born to equal rights with that governor, on whom the duty devolves of training the young to usefulness, in a station which he is afterwards to assume among freemen." Enslavement, the court declared, was different. For slavery to work, domination had to be total and unconditional. "The end is the profit of the master, his security and the public safety; the subject, one doomed in his own person, and his posterity, to live without knowledge, and without the capacity to make any thing his own, and to toil that another may reap the fruits."[8]

There was another reason that slave power insisted on total and unconditional domination: a legitimate fear of insurrection. Imagine a plantation with, say, four family members at home, and dozens or even hundreds of slaves at hand. News of rebellions, like Denmark Vesey's in South Carolina in 1822, and Nat Turner's in Virginia in 1831, kept slaveowners vigilant. Insurrection was punishable by death, but the Virginia legislature also tried to prevent uprisings by forbidding slaves even from attending gatherings, where they might foment discontent and rebellion. Not only were slaves prohibited from congregating, but Juliet and Jonathan Lemmon knew that even they could get into trouble for allowing a slave on their property for more than four hours without the owner's consent. Worse yet, if the Lemmons allowed more than five other slaves to remain, for even a moment, all stood to be punished.[9]

By and large, these statutes were grounded on skin color, but religion also played a part, insofar as Africans were looked down on as "heathen." An early statute read, "If any Negro lift up his hand against any Christian he shall receive thirty lashes."[10]

Laws like that raised concerns about baptism. If slaves became Christian, would that serve to unchain them? This posed a dilemma, because many slaveowners were not about to liberate their slaves, but could find some moral comfort in seeing them Christianized. The Virginia legislature came to the rescue, assuring slaveowners that baptism would not undo the slave's status, at least in this world. The Lemmons were free to have the Eight baptized with no fear of losing their "property."[11] We do not know whether any of the Eight were baptized. (Lest anyone think that these concerns existed only in the South, New York had passed similar legislation before the state abolished slavery.[12])

Nor do we know how often, if at all, the Lemmon family or the Eight attended religious services. Under Virginia law, the Lemmons were allowed to take the Eight to church with them, as long as the Eight sat in a separate section. But slave power was grudging, ever mindful of allowing the enslaved to get any ideas about freedom, and so they were forbidden by law from attending any service conducted by a non-white minister.[13]

Nor could any of the Eight, or any other slave, own property. They would have understood that their clothing was "theirs," but owned by the Lemmons—just as they themselves were.

Slave power enacted harsh laws dealing with slaves stealing. An early Virginia statute warned: "[The penalty] for the first offense of hog stealing by a Negro or a slave is set at thirty lashes on the bare back, well laid on; for the second offense, two hours in the pillory with both ears nailed thereto, at the expiration of the two hours the ears are to be cut off close by the nails. For the third, death."[14]

～

As for the family lives of the enslaved, the respective names of the Eight tell us something. Emeline went by the last name of Thompson, Nancy's last name was Johnson, and Emeline's twin boys were Lewis Wright and Robert Wright.

Many of the enslaved simply took the names of their owners. The names Thompson, Johnson, and Wright leave us guessing. Neither Emeline nor Nancy, nor any of the Eight, could legally enter into any form of contract, and marriage was a contract, so it was barred.[15] Emeline probably took the name Thompson from a partner, possibly a slave named after his owner, on a nearby plantation. The same for Nancy Johnson.

Slaveowners like the Lemmons not only allowed but encouraged young women like Emeline and Nancy to have "abroad spouses," meaning mates owned by neighboring slaveowners. But there was a limit: Lasting unions between slave husbands and wives created divided loyalties and worked against the structure of slavery.

At their discretion, or at their whim, the slaveowner would allow for visitation at the slave quarters.[16] That Emeline Thompson called her twin boys Lewis and Robert Wright suggests that their father was named Wright, possibly a slave from a nearby plantation. Interestingly, at the sale of Billy Douglas's estate after his death, one of the buyers was named Thompson Wright.

Nancy and Emeline also understood, from an early age, that as females they were available for the taking, to satisfy the sexual appetites of their owners or other white assailants. Rape laws did not apply.[17] As one researcher tells it, slaveowners would select women and bring them to the "big house" as cook or nursemaid, within easy access.[18] Emeline's twin boys were Mulatto, which speaks to her having been "taken" by a white man. Nancy was also Mulatto.

With impunity, a white man could rape a slave, but marrying a Negro (free or enslaved) was against the law. As early as 1691, Virginia enacted a law prohibiting racial intermarriage, to prevent the "abominable mixture and spurious issue which hereafter may encrease, in this dominion, as well as by negroes, mulattoes, and Indians intermarrying with English, or other white women, as by their unlawfull accompanying with one another."[19]

And yet, slaveowners commonly fathered Mulatto children. We do not know how many of his slaves—or the slaves of others—Billy Douglas had fathered. But there is a clue.

In his will, Douglas made a point of giving his daughter, Theresa, four slaves as *separate* property, going out of his way to direct that after her death, the slaves should descend to her children. Douglas expressly prohibited Theresa's husband from selling the four—a form of "family retainer." Why did he go to such lengths, including a provision of questionable enforceability?

The provision suggests that Douglas may have been their father, and, while he was not prepared to say so in writing, he gave the four slaves possible protection from being sold into a harsher life. The protection was only a possibility, because it is not clear that the Virginia courts would honor a provision interfering with a husband's ownership of his wife's assets and his right to sell them. But Douglas gave it a sporting try.[20]

As for literacy, teaching slaves to read and write was a dangerous business both for whites and for the enslaved. Slaveowners understood that a literate slave would likely be less content than one open to recitals about the "blessed state of bondage." Even under the most tranquil circumstances, most slaveowners were not disposed to teach their slaves to read or write. The thought of literacy among slaves became even more fearsome with the growing flood of abolitionist literature flowing South in the 1840s.[21]

∽

By 1848, when Emeline and Nancy were about 19 and 16, the Supreme Court of Virginia handed down a decision that summed up the legal status of the enslaved in the state.

The case, *Peter v. Hargrave*, concerned James Hargrave, of Dinwiddie County, Virginia, who in his last will and testament had emancipated his 12 slaves and their children. He also left them some money to leave Virginia, considering that emancipated slaves were not permitted to remain in the state, under pain of re-enslavement. Slave power saw free Blacks as a threat to public order, capable of inciting slave discontent and revolt. At the top of his will, Hargrave had quoted the words of Alexander Pope: "Teach me to feel another's woe, / To hide the fault I see; / That mercy I to others show, / That mercy show to me."[22] After Hargrave's death, his "emancipated" slaves had to sue for their liberty. They won, but in the interim they had been improperly kept in bondage—and sued for compensation. Virginia's high court rejected their claim, citing the fundamentals of enslavement. "Persons in the status of slavery," the court held, "are not entitled to any of the remedies of freemen: they are slaves whatever may be their right to freedom, and have no civil privileges or immunities."

The enslaved, the court explained, "from colour, and other physical traits, carry with them indefinitely the marks of inferiority and degradation; and even when relieved from bondage can never aspire to association and citizenship with the white population." And what of freedom itself? Freedom to them, the court said, "is a benefit rather in name than in fact; and in truth, upon the whole, their condition is not thereby improved in respectability, comfort, or happiness."

The court then proclaimed that slavery was beneficial to the enslaved, in that they are exempt from the "wretchedness of actual want," the cares and anxieties of a precarious subsistence, and are provided for in infancy, old age, and infirmity. Allowing them compensation "would not promote those habits of industry, temperance and humility, without which their recently acquired liberty must prove a curse instead of a blessing."

The judges were able to compartmentalize things. The law was the law; slavery was slavery. They explained that it was not their job to introduce concerns about humanity into the jurisprudence of enslavement. "In deciding upon questions of liberty and slavery, such as that presented in this case," the opinion read, "it is the duty of the Court, uninfluenced by considerations of humanity on the one hand, or of policy (except so far as the policy of the law appears to extend) on the other, to ascertain and pronounce what the law is; leaving it to the Legislature, as the only competent and fit authority, to deal as they may think expedient, with a subject involving so many and such important moral and political considerations."[23]

Emeline and Nancy were not familiar with these writings, of course, but they knew all too well the lessons taught in them, to which they had been exposed throughout their young lives. And they were still governed by them in October, 1852, when the Lemmon family decided to leave Bath County, Virginia, taking the Eight with them to start a new life in Texas, another slave state.

Chapter 2

From Virginia to New York

At some point in 1852, Jonathan and Juliet Lemmon decided to move to Texas.

Why would a couple with seven children and long-established roots in Bath County, Virginia—not to mention the eight people they enslaved—pick up stakes and move a thousand miles away to an uncertain life in an unfamiliar part of the country?

We have no record of the reasons, but we might conjecture: The couple had inherited part of Juliet's father's vast farm, which had been a thriving enterprise, but the people they enslaved were not suited for rigorous farm work. Emeline and Nancy were young mothers with small children to care for, and even the oldest boys were only about 16 and 13.

Texas beckoned. The Lemmons lived near the Bath County resorts, which were frequented by sophisticated travelers, and the couple had likely been hearing a good deal of talk about opportunity and cheap land in Texas, advertising itself as hospitable to slavery. "We want more slaves," one newspaper editor said, "we need them."[1]

And they were getting them. By around 1850, there were 58,000 slaves in Texas, compared with 397 free Blacks. In the decade that followed, the Texas legislature had passed laws particularly favorable to the growth of slavery and the importation of slaves, guaranteeing the right to own slaves and protecting property rights of slaveowners.[2] The laws had worked so well that by 1860, the number of slaves in the state had risen to 182,000 (see figure 2.1).

On October 13, 1852, the 17-member Lemmon group left the Bath County farm, traveling by horse-drawn coach and wagon, heading for what

13

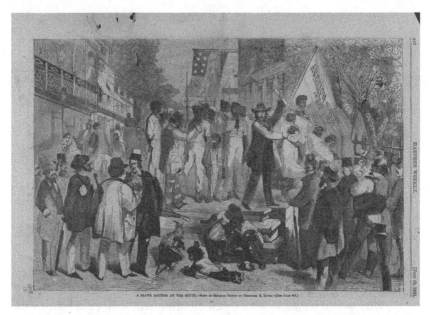

Figure 2.1. Auction of enslaved people in Austin, Texas, c. 1850–1860. Library of Congress, Prints and Photographs Division, LC-DIG-ds-10813.

they hoped would be a new life in Texas. The first leg of their journey would take them to Richmond, and from there they planned to go by sea to New Orleans, and then on to Texas.

This was not an easy journey, even by 19th-century standards. Seventeen people, mostly children, with even a minimum of their worldly possessions, could not fit into a single stagecoach or even two, so they would have been distributed among several wagons. We have no diary as to the details, but we know that the trip to Richmond alone—which today can be comfortably managed in an afternoon—took them 17 days. This tells us a lot about the challenges and the pitfalls.

The journey called for proceeding first to nearby Cloverdale, and from there to Staunton, a major metropolis and the largest town in the upper Shenandoah Valley, with a population of almost 4,000, served by banks and businesses of all kinds. Staunton offered stagecoach lines and drivers, who might have been white or Black. It also had grist and saw mills, and factories that made boots, shoes, woolen clothing, and blankets.[3]

At Staunton, the group would have picked up the Three Notch'd Road, the main route to Richmond, so-called because trees alongside it at periodic intervals bore three ax-cut notches to show travelers the way (see figure 2.2). Sometimes referred to in early accounts simply as an Indian trail, the road had existed since colonial times, linking Richmond with the Valley and western Virginia. It was also the only thoroughfare for mail delivery and commercial wares in those regions of the state. Part of it had been surveyed by Peter Jefferson, Thomas Jefferson's father.

A hardy letter carrier with a horse and a pouch, and even a wagon-load, could have easily managed the trip from one post office to another along the Three Notch'd Road. So could the wealthy, who used the road to visit the Bath County resorts and had the money to travel in style, stopping at choice inns and hotels along the way.

For the Lemmons and the Eight, however, travel along the Three Notch'd Road—with nine children under the age of nine, wedged in among boxes of clothing and food—would not have been easy or comfortable. That it took 17 days meant that the group needed to stop in some locations for two or three days to recuperate, to retrench, and perhaps to dry out by a warm fire.

Figure 2.2. A tree on what had been the Three Notch'd Road. Originally published in *The Route of the Three Notch'd Road: A Preliminary Report* by Nathaniel Mason Pawlett and Howard H. Newlon Jr. Used with permission from the Virginia Transportation Research Council.

Contemporary accounts of travel along the Three Notch'd Road survive, one by a diarist who told of having met someone who displayed a "brake" that would lock the hind wheels and take the weight off the horses. Eager to install one, the diarist told of the blacksmith who said he could do it in half a day, but was unable to finish the job until the next morning.[4] We can imagine that the Lemmons experienced similarly time-consuming adventures during their journey.

Mud, in places very deep, slowed the journey. Figure 2.3, which shows a portion of the Three Notch'd Road near Short Pump, gives an idea of what the Lemmons might have encountered along the way.

Any time the Lemmon wagons got stuck, Jonathan and Juliet and the driver would have had to manage the extrication effort, with the teenagers from among both the Eight and the Lemmon children pitching in.

There were also water crossings. With effort, a swollen stream might be forded, but larger bodies of water they encountered, of around four feet or so, called for some sort of rafting, with the wheels removed and laid flat. Perhaps, as in other parts of the country at that time, some creeks had rough bridges built by entrepreneurs who, for a price, would help travelers cross.[5]

Figure 2.3. Three Notch'd Road, near Short Pump. Originally published in *The Route of the Three Notch'd Road: A Preliminary Report* by Nathaniel Mason Pawlett and Howard H. Newlon Jr. Used with permission from the Virginia Transportation Research Council.

After Staunton, the group probably stopped at Waynesboro (sometimes referred to in local records as Waynesborough) for food, provisions, and lodging. Smaller than Staunton, but with a population of several hundred, the town offered a blacksmith and a wheelwright—essential occupations, given the stream of travelers likely to have needed repairs to their wagons and coaches.[6]

The next hurdle for the Lemmons was an especially difficult one: the Blue Ridge Mountains. From Waynesboro, they would have traveled through the mountains, possibly via the Jarman Gap or the Rockfish Gap, which featured the Rockfish Inn (later, Mountain Top Inn) and a separate building.

After that would have come Waylands Crossing (today Crozet), and the D. S. Tavern (formerly owned by Chief Justice John Marshall, of Charlottesville). From there, the party would have proceeded to Charlottesville, a most eagerly awaited stop for supplies, repairs, and lodging.[7] With a population of around 12,000 whites and 14,000 slaves, the town would have offered the Lemmons separate lodging for their family and for the Eight.[8]

Leaving Charlottesville, the party would somehow have had to cross the Rivanna River.[9] The next village along the Road was Palmyra, which by 1835 had stores, taverns, and churches, and the means to repair any broken wagon parts. The town had a wool factory and a shoe factory, where the Lemmons could have found dry clothing. They might have lodged at Walker Timberlake's Hotel and Tavern. Census records reveal that many of the farmers in the region had slaves, which meant that there would have been quarters for the Eight. Timberlake enslaved over 30 people and could readily have found room, in their quarters, for the Eight.[10]

Passing next through Goochland, the party might have stopped at Leake's Tavern or Gun Spring Tavern, readying themselves for the final lap of their trip to Richmond. Mrs. Leake leased the premises to John M. Trevelian, who operated it as a tavern.[11] We cannot be sure that the party stayed there, but it seems apt, in that Trevelian is listed in the 1850 census as having 27 slaves, with quarters that could have accommodated the Eight.[12]

Exactly how long the party spent at each of these stops along the way we can't know, but we do know that on Saturday, October 30, 1852, they finally reached Richmond. There they found a thriving and sophisticated city—but one with an underside that showed how different life in the region was for well-to-do whites and for the people they enslaved.

By an interesting coincidence, when the Lemmons arrived in Richmond, Charles Dickens had recently written about slavery in Richmond—in a September 1852 article, a sequel to what he had written about the city

10 years earlier, in *American Notes*.[13] Who better than Dickens to describe Richmond at the time the Lemmons encountered it?

During his original visit to Richmond, Dickens had been showered with praise and with every imaginable comfort by the city's dignitaries, and in *American Notes* he thanked them for the royal reception they gave him. But he also described the Richmond region as a place "where slavery sits brooding." What he saw of slavery sickened him, and he developed powerful feelings of shame and self-reproach for having been waited on by slaves. He wrote of "the curses of this horrible institution," and of the squalor he saw in slave quarters—"crazy wretched cabins near to which groups of half-naked children basked in the sun or wallowed on dusty ground."

The contrast between wealthy whites and the wretched conditions of the enslaved—along with the slave auctions in their midst—would have been jarring even to the Eight. It could have only confirmed, in their own minds, what it meant to be on the wrong side of the color line (see figure 2.4).[14]

∾

Figure 2.4. *Slaves Waiting for Sale* by Eyre Crowe, an English painter who arrived in Richmond in March 1853 and witnessed several auctions of enslaved people. Heinz Collection, Washington, DC, provided by *Slavery Images: A Visual Record of the African Slave Trade and Slave Life in the Early African Diaspora.*

Not long after their arrival in Richmond, the Lemmons received frustrating news: A ship for New Orleans had sailed just the day before, and it would be three weeks before the next passenger vessel would go there. They did learn of an alternative, however: They could travel another 140 grueling miles to Norfolk, where they could book passage to New Orleans. The hitch was that this would take them via New York—an oddly circuitous route, but one that would more reliably get them to New Orleans. Norfolk was 300 miles from New York by sea. So they opted for it, which meant they had to stay in Richmond until Tuesday. They might have looked at a copy of the local newspaper to see what was going on in town, or perhaps where to find suitable lodgings to divide their group in two, one at a hotel or rooming house, the other at segregated quarters.

Had they consulted the *Richmond Dispatch* on the day of their arrival, they would have seen a front page article about a speech given by a certain Louis Napoleon, at the Bordeaux Chamber of Commerce. It's a delightful moment of random foreshadowing: Just days later, the Eight would have their lives changed forever by a *different* Louis Napoleon.

Their chief concern, however, was to get to Norfolk, and, just below an advertisement by an executor selling 16 slaves, they would have seen an ad picturing the *City of Richmond*, the steamer that they would board on Tuesday in Norfolk (see figure 2.5).

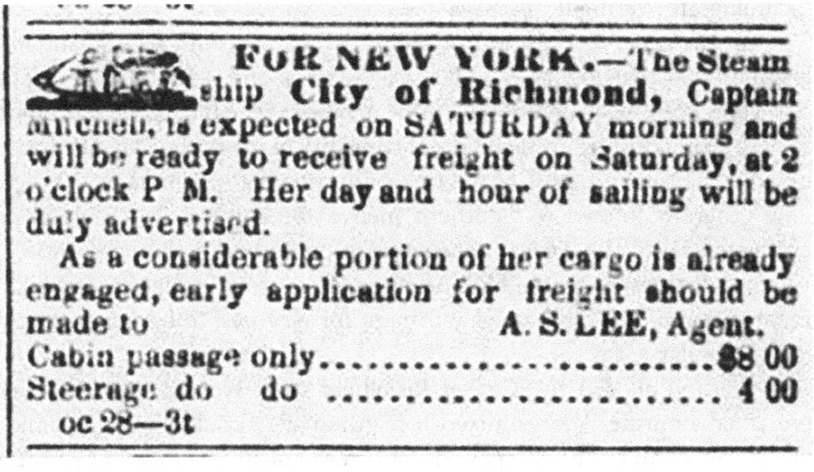

FOR NEW YORK.—The Steamship City of Richmond, Captain Mitchell, is expected on SATURDAY morning and will be ready to receive freight on Saturday, at 2 o'clock P M. Her day and hour of sailing will be duly advertised.

As a considerable portion of her cargo is already engaged, early application for freight should be made to   A. S. LEE, Agent.
Cabin passage only..........................$8 00
Steerage do   do 4 00
oc 28—3t

Figure 2.5. Steamship advertisement. From the *Richmond Dispatch*, Virginia, October 30, 1852.

The Lemmons knew that bringing the Eight to New York, a free state, could be risky. Tensions about slavery between the North and South were running high. But they planned to stay in New York harbor only long enough to move from one steamer to another, and soon be off to New Orleans, and so it all seemed worth the risk.[15]

Immediately after learning that he and everybody in his charge would be sailing from Norfolk to New York harbor, Jonathan Lemmon took an interesting precaution. On Monday, November 1, 1852, the day before leaving Richmond, he presented himself before a justice of the peace to swear out a document attesting to his ownership of the Eight. The document is the most accurate description we have of the Eight. It provides more information and is more reliable than incomplete census records in which we can identify the Eight only by inference, deduction, and other devices worthy of Sherlock Holmes.

In the document, Jonathan Lemmon tells us that the Eight consist of "a negro woman named Emeiline [sic] and her three children, Bob, Lewis and Amanda—a negro Girl named Nancy & her child Ann—a negro man named Lewis and a negro Boy named Ned."[16]

~

The following day, the group left Richmond for Norfolk, likely by steamer. An advertisement in the *Richmond Dispatch* of November 1, 1852, tells us of a steamer from Richmond to Norfolk, taking about a day and a half, including an overnight.

At the time, Norfolk was a prominent seaport, with a population of about 14,000 that included 1,000 free Negroes and 4,200 enslaved. The city supported seven churches, three newspapers, and a philharmonic society. Commenting on racial proportionality in town, the City Directory noted, "The slow progress of the free negro population confirms the view now generally known by Southern men to be correct, that freedom is not beneficial to the African when it is in contact with the white race."[17]

The Lemmons would have been reassured to know that if any of the Eight got sick, Norfolk had an infirmary for Negroes, to be taken care of for one dollar a day.

Getting aboard the *City of Richmond* from Norfolk to New York presented a hurdle. A large mixed-race group of 17 could hardly go unnoticed, least of all by the skipper and the crew. Luckily, we have an account of what happened, as witnessed by Nathan Lobam, a 21-year-old-Black steward on the steamer.[18]

Born free in Poughkeepsie in 1831, Lobam got his first job at age 13 on a steamer in Long Island Sound. Aboard one vessel or another, he traveled from Maine to Mexico, to America's west coast, and as far as Hong Kong. He had been around and likely had seen the horrors of slavery.

Lobam recalled that the skipper of the *City of Richmond* was wary about transporting the group from Norfolk to New York—but that he agreed to do so surreptitiously. The slaves would have to be held hidden in close confinement down below.

The steamer *City of Richmond* was the jewel of the line, newly built and designed to carry 70 first- and second-class passengers.[19] One hundred fifty feet in length, with three masts, the vessel was a model of comfort with spacious cabins and staterooms. It had a deck for the cabin passengers to take in the morning air after a single night at sea en route to New York harbor. Not so for the Eight, of course, who would be in steerage.

Steerage meant sleeping, cooking, eating, and performing other bodily functions in the tightest of spaces, in unsanitary conditions, with little possibility of privacy. Emeline and Nancy, the two adults, had to manage the other six—boys, girls, infants, and breast-feeding babies all crowded below decks for the duration of the trip.

Although Jonathan Lemmon had some lingering discomfort about whether transporting slaves would sit well under New York law, the clerk of the *City of Richmond*, a man named Ashmead, assured him that he need not worry about the Eight being emancipated by New York authorities. The law in New York, Lemmon recalled Ashmead telling him, was "in my favor."

Ashmead also told Lemmon that when the group reached New York, he would immediately book passage to New Orleans on the steamer *Memphis*.

It was Nathan Lobam who altered the course of the lives of the Eight. Once the steamer *City of Richmond* was at sea, with the Eight safely below, Lobam sought them out.

"Do you want to be free?" he asked them.

Imagine the boldness of such a question. Since birth, the Eight had known nothing but bondage. It would have been hard for the younger ones even to conceptualize the meaning of liberty. They had read no abolitionist tracts, but they understood what it meant to be subservient and they knew all too well that they were different from the Lemmon children.

They also knew that as slaves, they had a home where they would be "taken care of." From other slaves, they likely had heard talk of freedom—of its rewards but also of its perils. Slaveowners had long promoted the idea that for the enslaved, a life of bondage in the sunny climes of the South was better than being cast adrift, or running away, only to freeze and starve, they were told, in the callous North (see figure 2.6).

The teenage boys, Lewis and Edward, were timid about being cut loose from their masters, but the mothers held sway. As the mother of three and older sister of two, Emeline was the dean of the group. She opted for freedom, as did Nancy. As women, and as mothers, they understood that slavery was not the blissful state described by slaveowners. It meant living with sexual abuse and the prospect of their family members being sold out from under them.

Lobam told the group they must tell no one, and when reaching New York they must "stick to it." All were at risk, including Lobam.

∾

THE NEGRO IN THE NORTH—AND IN THE SOUTH

Figure 2.6. The Negro in the North—and in the South. Sarin Images/Granger.

The *City of Richmond* entered New York harbor late in the afternoon on Friday, November 5, 1852. An announcement in the *New-York Tribune* records its arrival.

The area around the docks was a rough and noisy place, a throbbing mix of commerce, smokestacks, pushcarts, passengers, ships' cargo, horses, and wagons all brushing up against one another.

Lobam immediately sent three companions ashore with messages. One went to that *other* Louis Napoleon, a free Mulatto who was an active conductor of the Underground Railroad, which had dispatched hundreds of runaway slaves to upstate New York and Canada. A second went to Erastus Culver, and a third to David Curry. There could not have been a better way to get word out about the Eight's arrival. Culver was one of New York's most energetic abolitionist lawyers. Curry operated what Lobam described in his account as "a large restaurant for colored people."

As it turned out, Ashmead was unable to book passage for the second leg of the journey, so Jonathan Lemmon had to go ashore to do it himself, paying $161 in advance.[20] The office agent told him that his group's baggage would be transported from the *City of Richmond* to the *Memphis*. Everything seemed perfectly in order.

Soon afterward, however, two hack drivers appeared alongside the *City of Richmond*, supposedly to take the group to the *Memphis* for the next leg of their journey. Instead—if Jonathan Lemmon is to be believed—the drivers unexpectedly deposited the group and their belongings not on the *Memphis* but on dry land near the docks, at a lodging house on Carlisle Street, at the southern tip of Manhattan, near Trinity Place, close to today's World Trade Center.

The cabs then drove off. The party would now have to spend the night, in separate quarters, on Carlisle Street.[21]

Chapter 3

Rescue

Nathan Lobam knew what he was doing in sending messages to Erastus Culver and Louis Napoleon. He could not have chosen better.

Erastus Culver (figure 3.1) had brains and grit. Born Erastus Dean Culver, in 1803, at the family's parsonage-farm in Whitehall, Washington County, New York, on the Vermont border, he was a committed enemy of slavery. His uncle, Nathaniel Colver (1794–1870), was well known and a Baptist minister and abolitionist.

A graduate of the University of Vermont, Culver by 1852 had already distinguished himself as a private lawyer, a New York assemblyman, and a Whig member of Congress. Starting in 1841, he had made his reputation as a spirited anti-slavery advocate in the state assembly, lacing his speeches with wit and anecdote. In Congress, where he served a term from 1845 to 1847, he continued his assaults on enslavement, calling for its abolition in the District of Columbia and opposing its extension into the territories.[1] His anti-slavery stance cost him reelection as the Free Soil candidate for Congress in the November, 1848, election, losing to his Whig opponent. He then moved to Brooklyn, where he started a law practice and picked up the abolitionist cause. By 1852, he was known to activists—among them Lobam and the people at Curry's restaurant—as a trusted warrior.

Representing the enslaved in the 1840s and 1850s was not an easy line of work. The moneyed and commercial interests lined up on the other side. Worse yet, the United States Congress piled on a heavy layer of adversity, enacting federal laws favoring slaveowners, and created a cadre of "commissioners" who had full judicial powers and saw it as their job

Figure 3.1. Portrait of Erastus D. Culver (1803–1889). Courtesy of the owner, Henry D. Ryder, Culver's great-great-grandson.

to send alleged fugitive slaves into bondage. In the courtroom, they were the Goliaths. Culver was a David.

Louis Napoleon had a very different story. A 52-year-old woodworker, janitor, and messenger in the anti-slavery building headquarters, he moonlighted as a conductor of the Underground Railroad. No records survive of the work he was doing for the Underground Railroad in the early 1850s, but we do know that he worked in that capacity between 1855 and 1857 with Sydney Howard Gay (figure 3.2), the editor of the *National Anti-Slavery Standard* in New York. During their partnership, they shepherded hundreds of runaway slaves northward to freedom. Napoleon came to meet and collaborate with people on the front lines in the battle against enslavement, from Black runaways and former slaves to prominent white abolitionists and lawyers.

Napoleon knew his way around the docks, and when fugitive slaves reached New York, he helped harbor them, feed them, and send them to the next "stop" along the way. The stops often belonged to Quakers, who were very good at concealing runaway slaves in barns, attics, and hidden rooms. The runaways often went through the Hudson Valley, across central New York, to the western part of the state, and on to Canada. Some settled in

Figure 3.2. Portrait of Sydney Howard Gay (1814–1888). Collection of the Massachusetts Historical Society.

upstate cities like Syracuse; others went to a terminus like Buxton, Ontario, in Canada, north of the Lake Erie shore, about 50 miles east of the border at Detroit and about 200 miles west-southwest of the border at Niagara Falls.

We know almost nothing of Napoleon's origins. He was the child of an enslaved mother, whose name we do not know. According to obituaries of Napoleon that ran in 1881, his father, also unknown to us, was said to be a free man of Jewish extraction.[2]

After getting word from Lobam of the Eight's arrival, Napoleon and Culver recognized that every minute counted. The *Memphis* was soon to depart for New Orleans, and if the Eight were moved aboard they would be enslaved indefinitely. The alternatives were limited. Ushering them on to the Underground Railroad was out of the question for two main reasons: separating them from their owners could result in a commotion that could bring on unfriendly police; and anyone traveling the Underground Railroad had to be strong and resourceful enough to navigate long distances over terrain fraught with danger. The Eight were mostly children and infants. In the South, the enemy of a runaway slave was a slave catcher, armed with a gun. There were also slave catchers in the North, but a most dangerous foe was a federal commissioner armed with a gavel.

Culver and Napoleon quickly put their heads together and decided that the only path to freedom for the Eight was by way of a New York court of law. Using his legal toolbox, Culver drew up a petition for writ of habeas corpus, the get-out-of-jail card that had been employed for centuries to challenge a claimed illegal confinement.

Getting the slaves and their owners into court would be difficult. Convincing a judge to liberate them would be even harder. And unprecedented.

Because Culver had not even met the Eight, he could not rightfully call them clients. Instead, he drew the petition in the name of Louis Napoleon, who could at least provide some sketchy facts and swear that "according to the best knowledge and belief . . . your petitioner is informed and believes" that the Eight were in bondage. It would be enough to get a foot in the courthouse door.

Napoleon also stated, accurately, that the Eight were at a location on Carlisle Street and were about to be taken to Texas. Which raises the question: How and why did the group go ashore? Although Jonathan Lemmon denied it, he may have actually needed a place for the group to stay the night. It's not unreasonable to assume that the skipper of the *Memphis* might have been unwilling to accommodate a party of 17 the night before his vessel was to head south. As we have all heard at one time or another: "Sorry, the rooms are not yet made up." He may also simply have been opposed to providing lodging for eight slaves. But it is equally possible that Napoleon or others acting with him—even the hack drivers—somehow contrived to get the group ashore for the night, where it would be easier to apprehend the Eight and serve the writ. The *New York Journal of Commerce* and the *Boston Pilot* asserted that by an "infamous fraud" the group was diverted to Carlisle Street rather than to the *Memphis*. There was speculation that Ashmead, the clerk on the *City of Richmond*, was in on it.

The booking agent for the *Memphis* said that he had warned the "purser" of the ship *City of Richmond* that it was unwise to leave the slaves in New York City and that the Lemmons would do well to take them to some secure location until safely aboard the *Memphis*. Given the abolitionist elements in New York, he cautioned, the slaves could be seized or "kidnapped." If the booking agent was speaking of Ashmead, did Ashmead keep this from Lemmon? Jonathan Lemmon said that he did not think Ashmead was part of any diversionary scheme.

On November 6, 1852, a Saturday, Culver and Napoleon entered the courthouse of the Superior Court of the City of New York, a tribunal having jurisdiction to issue writs of habeas corpus.

It had been a momentous week. Just a few days earlier, Franklin Pierce had defeated Winfield Scott to become the country's 14th president, succeeding Millard Fillmore (see figure 3.3).

Figure 3.3. The election of Franklin Pierce. From the *Pittsburgh Daily Post*, Pennsylvania, November 3, 1852.

At that time, the Superior Court was a trial court, with seven judges on its roster. It appears to have been a matter of chance as to which judge was present and free that Saturday morning to entertain Culver and Napoleon's application.

The court had been created in 1828 as part of a judicial realignment. Its judges were elected. Culver knew that some had been friendlier than others to New York's mercantile interest in Southern products—and less considerate than others when it came to fugitive slaves. In *Jack v. Martin*, for example, a case involving an alleged fugitive slave named Jack Lockley, Judge Josiah Hoffman had ruled that the federal Fugitive Slave Act of 1793 called for Lockley's summary rendition. Hoffman saw no room in the statute for any extended hearing or trial, let alone a trial by jury, which in the context of this case he considered a "dilatory and expensive proceeding."[3] He was cheered on by the *New York American*, which asserted, "New York's judges and politicians had as little right to meddle with any property at the South, as a South Carolinian has to set himself up as the judge and jury in the validity of our remote deeds from the Indians." Opposition to slavery, the newspaper continued, was "a delerious fanaticism."[4]

Figure 3.4. New York City Hall. Courtesy of Municipal Archives, City of New York.

But Judge Hoffman was no longer on the New York City Superior Court. Instead, that morning Culver and Napoleon found themselves in the presence of Judge Elijah Paine (see figure 3.5). They couldn't have known what to expect. At age 56, Elijah Paine was fairly new to the bench, with three years of experience, having been elected in 1849. He had co-edited two legal treatises, one on civil practice in New York, the other on United States Supreme Court cases. He had handled a variety of cases, but none of the scope or importance of this one.[5] He would have made arrangements for someone to look after his young son, Horatio, at the family house, on 13th Street, east of Second Avenue. His wife, Louisa, had died seven years earlier, at age 29. The couple had known tragedy; their firstborn, Elijah, died in infancy, eight months old, in 1837.[6]

Culver would have known of Judge Paine's exemplary reputation, but that said nothing about his attitude regarding enslavement. It had been only 25 years since New York abolished slavery, in 1827. Some lawyers and judges may even have lived in slave-owning households, or themselves owned slaves.

Figure 3.5. Portrait of Judge Elijah Paine. Photographed by Mark Hemhauser, 2017, and courtesy of Margaret Paine Hasselman, Albany, CA.

On the plus side, Judge Paine had been born and raised in Vermont, the first state to separate itself from slavery by constitutional decree. Born in the town of Williamstown in 1796, Paine grew up as part of a prominent New England family.[7] His father, Elijah Paine Sr. (1757–1842), was a founder of Northfield, Vermont, a member of the Vermont House of Representatives, a justice of the Vermont Supreme Court, a United States senator, and a federal judge.[8]

The younger Elijah was the second of four children, each of whom would lead a life of distinction. His brother Martyn (1794–1877) would become a distinguished physician and professor at the University of the City of New York; his brother Charles (1799–1853) would become the governor of Vermont in 1841;[9] and his sister Caroline (1801–1887) would become a writer.[10]

Young Elijah grew up privileged, but his personal writings show a lot of humility and some hilarious self-effacing humor. As his father had before him, he attended Harvard College, graduating in 1814. From there, he went to Litchfield Law School, in Connecticut.

Culver and Napoleon knew that Judge Paine had been elected to the bench as the Whig candidate. But that didn't tell them much about how he would approach their case, as the party concentrated less on slavery than on taxation, trade, and banking.

In 1841, however, Judge Paine's brother Charles, as Vermont's governor, had made a proclamation asking that the "Heavenly Father . . . inspire the American people with the noble resolution speedily to number the institution of Slavery among the forsaken iniquities of the world."[11]

Judge Paine, nevertheless, had no track record dealing with slavery cases, let alone one that presented an issue so novel as to give pause even to judges who had no stomach for slavery. Culver's real challenge, as the Eight's attorney, lay at the most fundamental level: the law.

Culver appreciated that judges routinely have to apply laws that they themselves might not have enacted had they been legislators. He was familiar with a recent case in which the Massachusetts Supreme Court ordered an alleged fugitive slave returned to bondage, based on what it saw as a constitutional imperative. The decision was authored by an eminent judge: Lemuel Shaw of Massachusetts, known to be antipathetic to slavery. Decisions of that kind were not uncommon.[12]

At the courthouse, Robert G. Campbell, Clerk of the Court, put Louis Napoleon under oath, as a petitioner, swearing that his allegations were true. Napoleon then signed the petition with his mark, an "X."

Judge Paine issued the writ. It took the form of a command on behalf of the People of the State of New York, requiring the "Lemmings" [*sic*] to "have the bodies of eight colored persons, brought before the court" the following Monday, to show the cause of their detention.[13] Such is the power of the writ of habeas corpus. To guarantee that it was obeyed, a police officer accompanied Culver and Napoleon. The group traveled directly to Carlisle Street. Culver would later describe the scene:

> As we opened the door, we saw two colored women and three or four children. They were badly frightened. My officer was a brute . . . and he went up and said to them, "D—n you, get up! What are you doing here?" I saw they were terrified, and I told him, if he spoke another word to one of those women, I would send him off and get another officer. I went round to one of the women and said, "Nancy, don't you be afraid; we are your friends; we are going to take you to the City Hall, and give you your freedom."

Culver was acting as a lawyer, but his most lasting memory of the event was about the humanity of it all. "I shall never forget," he said, "the look of that woman while I live on this earth. She got up, and took her youngest child in her arms, and the others followed. She straightened up straight as a Connecticut rolling-pin and walked right up to the City Hall."[14]

Chapter 4

At the Courthouse

By the time the Eight arrived in the courtroom, word of the case had spread rapidly around the country, and press interest was high. From newspaper accounts, we know a good deal about who was in court that day, and how events unfolded.

Jonathan and Juliet Lemmon were there, of course. As was Erastus Culver, joined by an eminent co-counsel: John Jay II (1817–1894).

At 35, Jay was already a well-established lawyer, committed to abolition—and he had the pedigree to go with it. His paternal grandfather was the founder John Jay (1745–1829), New York's first chief judge and the first chief justice of the United States Supreme Court. He had also served as the governor of New York. Under his administration, in 1799, the state had begun the gradual abolition of slavery. His son, John Jay II's father, Judge William Jay (1789–1858), was also an ardent anti-slavery advocate in his own right. In 1839, 13 years before the Lemmon case, he had written *A View of the Action of the Federal Government, in Behalf of Slavery,* deriding the outsized role of Southern slaveholder interests in the federal government (see figure 4.1).[1]

Jay and Culver had just recently worked together in a slavery case before the federal commissioner George W. Morton—and the experience left them with a sobering understanding of the forces they were up against. A Maryland slaveowner had claimed a Brooklyn laborer named Horace Preston as his runaway slave. Jay and Culver had defended Preston, but he never had a chance: Morton summarily sided with the slaveowner and had cynically dispatched Preston back to him. The commissioner held all

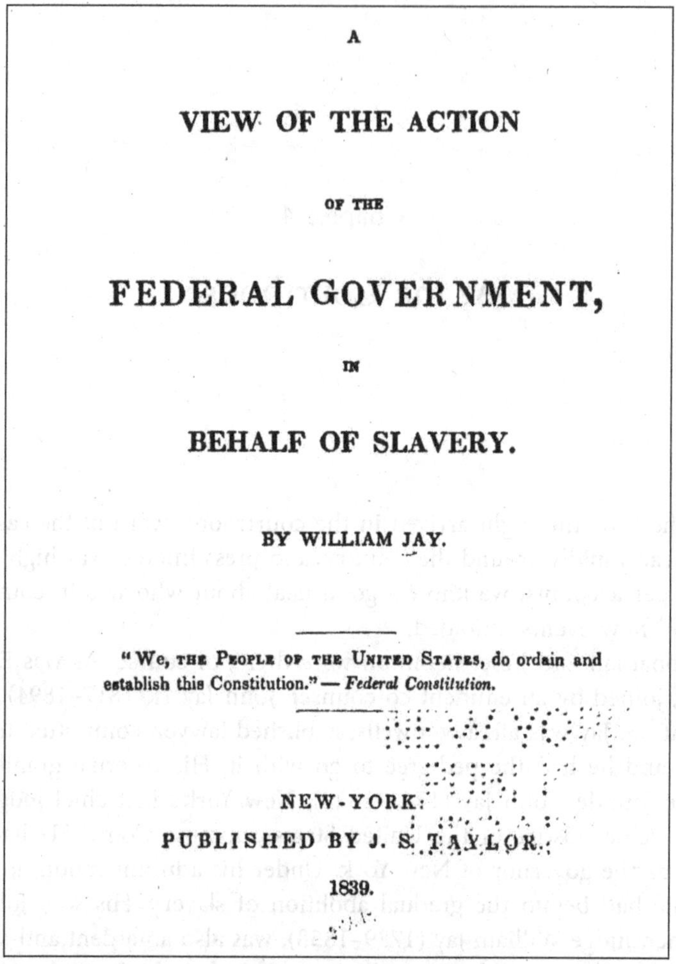
A

VIEW OF THE ACTION

OF THE

FEDERAL GOVERNMENT,

IN

BEHALF OF SLAVERY.

BY WILLIAM JAY.

"We, the People of the United States, do ordain and establish this Constitution." — *Federal Constitution.*

NEW-YORK:

PUBLISHED BY J. S. TAYLOR.

1839.

Figure 4.1. *A View of the Action of the Federal Government, in Behalf of Slavery* by Judge William Jay, father of John Jay II, who represented the enslaved people, 1839.

the cards; under federal law, there could be no appeal from his ruling.[2] They tried to get a writ of habeas corpus from federal Judge Andrew T. Judson, but he refused, saying that he was "engaged in another case." All Culver and Jay could do in the end was to write a public letter scorching the commissioner's decision, saying that his conduct should be submitted "to the judgment of the community."[3]

Louis Napoleon, the other critical member of the Lemmon team, was in court that day too. The Lemmon case was not the first time Napoleon had asked a court to come to the rescue of a slave, nor was it the first time that he had worked with John Jay. The two, in fact, were a resourceful pair. In 1846, six years before the Lemmon case, they had gone to court on behalf of the 22-year-old George Kirk, a runaway who had secreted himself on a brig out of Savannah. When the brig had docked in New York, Kirk was discovered by the crew, who put him in chains and began beating him. Abolitionists heard Kirk's cries and quickly got word to Napoleon, who, working with Jay, got a writ of habeas corpus ordering Kirk and the brig's captain before Judge John Edmonds.

Once in court, Jay asserted, in a prelude to the Lemmon case, that under the common law of New York a person is no longer a slave when in New York, notwithstanding the law of Georgia. It was a heavy-duty argument that no New York Court had ever bought. Judge Edmonds dutifully took it in, but chose not to stretch that far. Instead, he simply held that there was no proof that the brig's captain was authorized to act on behalf of Kirk's owner, and he set Kirk free.[4]

A superb technicality.

Things then took a bizarre turn for Kirk. At the captain's behest, New York's Mayor Andrew Mickle, drawing on a large police contingent, ordered Kirk rearrested. Mickle invoked a New York statute, under which New York had obligated itself to give stowaway fugitive slaves back to their owners—a concession to the South, as New York was abolishing slavery.

Kirk, however, was gone. After Judge Edmonds had freed him, Napoleon and his other protectors, sensing danger, had immediately taken Kirk out of sight and into the Anti-Slavery office at Nassau Street, where he was hiding. The building was the headquarters of the *National Anti-Slavery Standard*, edited by Sydney Howard Gay, and where Napoleon worked as a porter. The case brought Napoleon and Gay into close collaboration, culminating in their successful efforts to help hundreds, if not thousands, of runaway slaves onto the Underground Railroad.[5]

Inside the Anti-Slavery building, Kirk's protectors placed him in a large box bearing the address of Rev. Ira Manley, in Essex, New York, near the Canadian border. But when a cartman left the building with the box, police officers on the lookout for Kirk seized and opened it, and found Kirk inside. Reporting on the incident, the *New York Tribune* thundered against the idea that New York's police had been conscripted as "bloodhounds" to find and return Kirk to bondage (see figure 4.2).[6]

Figure 4.2. Arrest of the Slave George Kirk, lithograph by H. R. Robinson, 1846. Courtesy of American Antiquarian Society.

Jay again swung into action, urging Judge Edmonds to release Kirk from the clutches of Mayor Mickle. This created a jurisdictional dispute between the judge and the mayor, as to who had the power to do what, and to whom. Jay's argument was as resourceful, legally, as was the plan of Napoleon and his affiliates to box up Kirk and send him to Vermont: Jay invoked a shamefully pro-slavery Supreme Court case, *Prigg v. Pennsylvania*, which had held that only Congress, and not the states, could pass laws dealing with fugitive slaves—and their return. He cleverly used the case to argue that any state legislation concerning fugitive slaves was prohibited, even legislation that *aided* recapture.

Judge Edmonds agreed. One can imagine the judge applying this precedent with a smile.[7]

Jay had appeared before Judge Edmonds in another case.

In December 1848, in broad daylight, on Duane Street in New York, two slave catchers seized Joseph Belt, allegedly a fugitive who had escaped from bondage in Maryland. On the pretense that he had stolen a coat, the slave catchers transported him to Long Island intending to return him to slavery. Rescuers learned of the scheme and, led by Jay, managed to get before Judge Edmonds, who signed a writ of habeas corpus ordering the police to bring Belt and his captors to court.[8]

At the hearing before Judge Edmonds, Belt's owner argued that he had every right, personally or with the help of his slave catchers, to seize Belt in New York for recaption South. He claimed he needed no warrant, adding that those who stood in the way of recaption were "agitating a subject that puts the union in jeopardy."

That was as good an argument as anyone could make at the time. Many people disposed against slavery felt that the union was paramount, and they were willing to abide some compromises.

In response, Jay argued that under the Fugitive Slave Act of 1793, a fugitive slave could be held in captivity in New York only long enough to be brought before a tribunal for a certificate of removal. Here, however, the captors had concealed and held Belt captive for two days—not to bring him before a court but to spirit him off to bondage in Maryland.

Judge Edmonds agreed, ruling that the slaveowner could get no help from the Fugitive Slave Act. If the master or the master's agent, he said, "can do this for two days, he can for two years or twenty." Justifying this, he continued, "would warrant every slaveholder in the nation to hold his slaves in this state as long as he pleases, notwithstanding that slavery was unknown to our laws." This, the judge added, perhaps with a dash of seasoning, was not in conformity with the laws of Congress.

The slaveowner then asked Judge Edmonds for an order transferring Belt to the custody of a federal court, so he could get a certificate of removal authorized by federal law. Most federal commissioners at the time could be counted on to sign certificates authorizing the return of slaves to Southern bondage, routinely and perfunctorily.

Judge Edmond responded with a memorable line: "I must decline your application. My official duty does not require it, and if it is asked on other grounds, it would not be a proceeding to my taste." Belt was free.[9]

Judge Edmonds's decision was brilliant. By hewing *within* the language of the Fugitive Slave Act and the Prigg case—both formidable pro-slavery writings—he was able to blunt their impact and give a measure of protection to alleged fugitive slaves. One wishes to have met him.

Important as it was, the Belt case dealt with alleged *fugitive* slaves. An open question remained concerning slaves who were not fugitives but traveled with their owners: Could they be declared free when their owners' journeys brought them, in transit, through a free state, such as New York?

That was left for Judge Paine to decide.

∾

When they arrived that morning to argue the Lemmon case, Culver and Jay were well aware that no judge had ever ruled that slaves in the keep of the owners become free when setting foot in New York. But they knew enough about Judge Paine to expect that at least he would consider their argument with an open mind.

Just before the proceedings began, an extraordinary exchange took place in the courtroom

As Nancy and Emeline were nursing their infants, Juliet Lemmon walked over to where they were sitting. She urged them not to "rob" her of their labor. Juliet's tone and manner, according to an account of the

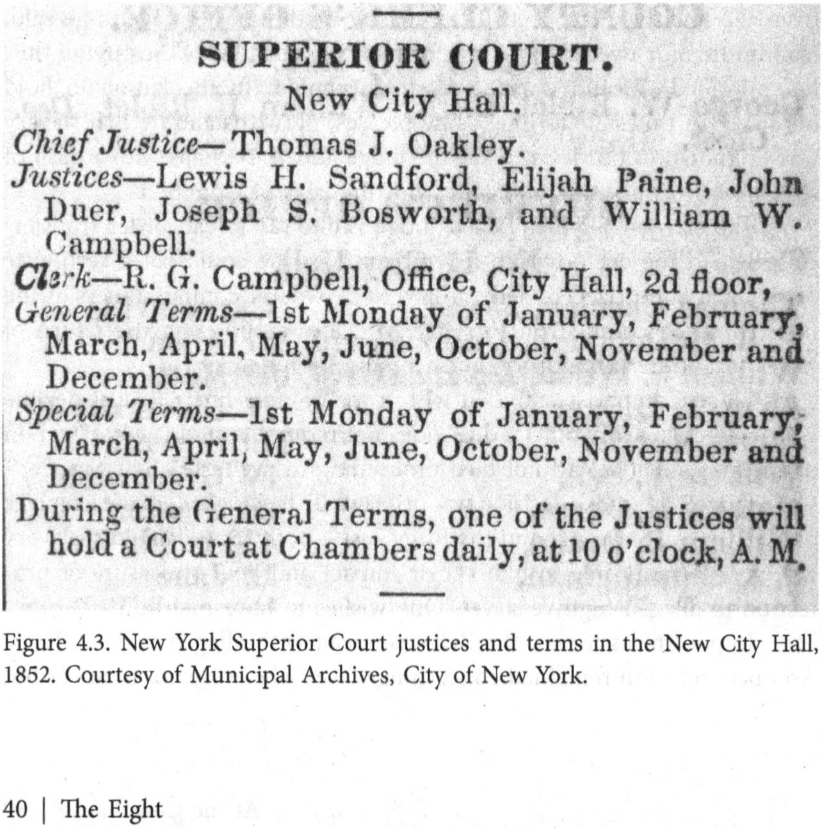

SUPERIOR COURT.
New City Hall.

Chief Justice—Thomas J. Oakley.

Justices—Lewis H. Sandford, Elijah Paine, John Duer, Joseph S. Bosworth, and William W. Campbell.

Clerk—R. G. Campbell, Office, City Hall, 2d floor,

General Terms—1st Monday of January, February, March, April, May, June, October, November and December.

Special Terms—1st Monday of January, February, March, April, May, June, October, November and December.

During the General Terms, one of the Justices will hold a Court at Chambers daily, at 10 o'clock, A. M.

Figure 4.3. New York Superior Court justices and terms in the New City Hall, 1852. Courtesy of Municipal Archives, City of New York.

exchange that appeared in the *New York Journal of Commerce*, a pro-slavery newspaper, was "highly excited, but more indicative of a mother to her children than a mistress to her slaves."[10]

"Have I ever ill-treated you?" Juliet asked Nancy and Emeline imploringly. "Have you not drank from the same cup, and eat [sic] from the same bowl with myself? Have I not taken the same care of your children as if they were my own? Did I not give up all I possessed in my native land, in order that you and I might go to another, where we could be more comfortable and happy? Did you ever refuse to come along with me, until you were prompted to do so?"

That Juliet could speak these words in apparent earnestness to women she had enslaved says a lot about the country in 1852. As if to emphasize that New York was ambivalent on the subject, a local newspaper asserted that the Eight were perfectly content to go to Texas as slaves of their kindly owners until the "tender mercies of the abolitionists [were] aroused on their behalf."

Emeline and Nancy now had to make a life-altering decision. They had to weigh the imploring words of Juliet—someone whose orders they had had to obey for their whole lives. Disobedience for them had always been fraught with peril, never more so than now. Runaway slaves, they knew, were generally greeted with the whip when returned to their owners. Technically, the Eight had not run away—but by taking their case to court and refusing Juliet's pleas, Nancy and Emeline knew they would be doing much the same thing.

It must have been a breathtaking moment. Juliet Lemmon begged Nancy and Emeline not just to consider the law, which she felt was on her side, but also to "look to their consciences" and to the past kindness of the Lemmon family.

Emeline and Nancy could only guess how severely the Lemmons would punish them if Judge Paine were to rule against the Eight and keep them enslaved. A favorable ruling, setting them free, was far from a sure thing.

As the exchange transpired, everyone, including Emeline and Nancy, could see Judge Paine. What did they see in his countenance? Perhaps something that gave them hope—or courage?

Weeping, and drawing on every ounce of fortitude she could summon, Emeline responded to Juliet. "No," she said. "You sold my husband away from me three years ago, and I have never been able to hear from him since. I don't call that good treatment."[11] (See figure 4.4.)

UNITED STATES SLAVE TRADE.
1850.

Figure 4.4. With the US Capitol in the background, the scene suggests the breakup of a family, with the father being sold while the mother and children look on, bereft. Emeline's husband was sold at about the same time as this illustration was created. Library of Congress, Prints and Photographs Division, LC-DIG-ds-13992.

In that one instant, Emeline threw off an entire lifetime of abject subservience. She must have felt a dizzying mixture of liberation and fear. She would take her chances with the judge.

∞

To represent them, the Lemmons had engaged two prominent New York attorneys—Henry Dampier Lapaugh (1826?–?) and Henry Lauren Clinton (1820–1899).

Their argument was predictable and straightforward: Because slave ownership was valid under the laws of Virginia and Texas, and because the Lemmons had not intended to bring the Eight to New York except in transit, New York had no right to emancipate them. "The slaves in question, being property," they argued, could readily be brought by their owners from one state to another and pass through New York with no risk of losing ownership. This right, they claimed, was supported not only by the Constitution but by the "law of nations."

Culver and Jay countered, asserting that because New York had no law allowing slavery—and, indeed, had passed a law abolishing it—the common law of liberty must prevail, and the Eight must be freed.

They also pointed out that in 1817, during its gradual abolition of slavery, New York, by statute, allowed owners to keep their slaves in New York for up to nine months—but that the state legislature had repealed even that exception in 1841. The implication of that repeal was that any slave brought to New York, even for just a moment, should be considered free.

Describing that repeal, Culver told the court, "As we got rid of the last dregs and abominations of slavery, the legislature, in both houses, by a large majority, swept away [the nine-month exemption] and no longer made it allowable for a man to come to Saratoga Springs or to the city of New York, and sojourn with his slaves."[12]

Lapaugh and Clinton countered, arguing that New York had no right to do away with the nine-month exemption. No statute, they said, could deprive an owner of lawfully held "property" merely because the owner had briefly stopped in New York, whether compelled by "necessity or accident." They laid heavy emphasis on the United States Constitution, claiming that it prohibits New York from liberating any slave lawfully owned under the laws of a slave state.

When lawyers make constitutional arguments, judges take special note, as the document is transcendent. Lapaugh and Clinton invoked the Constitution in six separate contexts.

First, and most compellingly, they argued that because the Constitution implicitly recognizes slavery, no state had the power to deprive the owner of slave property.

Second, they argued that under the Constitution's "Commerce Clause" (Article I, sec. 8, cl. 3), Congress alone has the power to regulate commerce. By prohibiting the Lemmons from bringing their slaves to New York under pain of forfeiture, New York, they argued, not only interfered with commerce but usurped the Congress's power to regulate it.

Third, they invoked the Fugitive Slave Clause of the United States Constitution (Article IV, sec. 1, 2), which obligates states to "deliver up" runaway slaves. In particular, they directed Judge Paine to the stern ruling laid down on this subject by the Supreme Court just a decade earlier, in 1842, in *Prigg v. Pennsylvania*. "The [fugitive slave] clause," the Court had declared, "manifestly contemplates the existence of a positive, unqualified right on the part of the owner of the slave, which no state law or regulation can in any way qualify, regulate, control, or restrain. The slave is not to be discharged from service or labour, in consequence of any state law or regulation."[13]

Lapaugh and Clinton based their fourth argument on the Constitution's "Full Faith and Credit" clause (Article IV, sec. 1), which states, "Full Faith and Credit shall be given in each State to the public Acts, Records, and judicial Proceedings of every other State." This provision, they argued, obligates New York to recognize the laws of Virginia. New York could not, they argued, pick and choose which of Virginia's laws it will or will not honor. Nor could anybody have expected that the Constitution's drafters could have foreseen and spelled out every imaginable situation in which the clause would kick in.

Judge Paine would have understood the use of the clause, for example, to enforce judgments of other states. He knew that if a creditor in Connecticut won a money judgment against a debtor in Connecticut, the judgment would follow the debtor and be enforceable in New York. The United States Supreme Court had said as much, in 1813.

But that was a relatively easy application. Money judgments are one thing, but what about laws—particularly those obnoxious to the state's own public policy?

In their fifth argument, Lapaugh and Clinton asserted that under the Privileges and Immunities Clause of the Constitution (Article IV, sec. 2), a citizen of one state is entitled to the privileges and immunities in the several states. They maintained that New York, in denying them the right of transit with their property, was subordinating the rights of Virginians, denying them the "privileges and immunities" to which they were constitutionally entitled.

Finally, Lapaugh and Clinton argued that under our national compact, the concept of interstate "comity"—a sense of deference and reciprocity—requires that New York recognize the property and laws of Virginians. Seizing slave property, they contended, flies in the face of comity.

Judge Paine appreciated that these constitutional arguments were not empty assertions from uninformed windbags. The claims, advanced by eminent lawyers, were worth debating.

The lawyers on both sides also discussed the importance of England's *Somerset* case, a landmark—perhaps *the* landmark—slavery case under the common law, in 1772. The case concerned James Somerset, an enslaved African, whom Charles Stewart had purchased in Boston. Stewart brought Somerset to England, where he escaped two years later. In Somerset's suit for freedom, the English high court had to decide whether Somerset became free simply by having been brought to the free soil of England.

The court freed Somerset, ruling that abolition in England necessarily meant that the country would not recognize a master–slave relationship, even on a transitory basis. The case is associated with the majestic phrase, "the air of England was too pure to be breathed by a slave."

Lemmon's lawyers argued, in substance, that the Somerset case was not binding on the United States, and that our Constitution calls for a different result.[14]

Judge Paine allowed the lawyers to go on at length, asking a brief question every now and then. When the slaveowners' lawyers contended that "this court cannot go behind the *status* of these people in the state from whence they escaped," Judge Paine posed a three-word question "Were they escaping?" How astute. He was probing the decisive difference between fugitive slaves apprehended in New York and those brought to New York by their owners.

Looking on, as the arguments unfolded that day, Juliet and Jonathan Lemmon were not alone in seeing themselves as victims. The *New York Journal of Commerce* took their side, noting that they had no other assets and calling the case one of "extreme hardship to the owners of the slaves." The *New York Day Book* hoped that Judge Paine would put down this "vile scheme of the abolitionists."[15]

In turn, the *New-York Tribune* referred to the *New York Journal of Commerce* as an "exemplar of cotton piety and humanity." *The Liberator* joined in: "The pathos of this canting villain, whose sympathies are so strongly excited for the slave claimants, is absolutely overpowering. 'You that have tears!' "

The Southern press was indignant. Slaves do not lose their status as "property" merely because they happen to be passing through a free state with their owners, they asserted. Clearly, the owners have no intention of staying or of "practising slavery" in that state in anything but the most fleeting sense. Wresting slaves from the very arms of their rightful owners, Southern papers fumed, was at least as bad as refusing to give back runaways.[16]

To any observer, the exchanges between the attorneys and Judge Paine were legalistic and on occasion highly technical, delivered in the suitable language of the lawyers' brief. But there was something else going on, only slightly beneath the surface, lodging somewhere around the heart and the stomach: Is it right for people to own one another? Is that a natural state of affairs? Should it be?

Only one side—Culver and Jay—touched on this, as if to say: We are citing case law and statutory interpretation but do not want to leave out something at the bottom of it all. They had a term for it: "natural law."

Jay spoke of "the inflexible principles of the common law touching the natural rights of personal liberty." Culver cited Chief Justice John Marshall's writing, in the 1825 *Antelope* case, that slavery is contrary to the law of nature, in that people have a natural right to the fruits of their own labor.[17]

Judge Paine surely knew of that case, and that Justice Marshall had also gone on to say that even though slavery was contrary to the law of nature and had its origin in force, "the world has agreed that it is a legitimate result of force, the state of things which is thus produced by general consent, cannot be pronounced unlawful."

Judge Paine did what judges do in these situations: After hearing both sides out, he told the parties that he planned to deliberate for a time and would hand down his decision the following Saturday, November 13th, 1852. Pending his decision, he kept the Eight at the Carlisle Street location, in the charge of a police officer, and ordered that Jonathan Lemmon pay for their provision. This did not work out smoothly. Lapaugh would later tell the judge that when Jonathan Lemmon tried to give the money to the police officer, he "was met at the door by a hundred colored people, who said he had no business there." Hearing that, Culver and Jay resolved the issue, saying that Culver would give the money to the policeman, sparing Jonathan Lemmon the expense.[18]

In preparing his decision, however, Judge Paine had a lot to think about.[19]

Chapter 5

We Wish to Plead Our Own Cause

When Judge Paine said he would take a few days to deliberate before deciding the fate of the Lemmon Eight, he was not about to write on a clean slate and simply decide the case based on how he felt about enslavement. He had to deal with the constitutional issues surrounding the case, and New York's own slavery jurisprudence.

New York had a checkered history when it came to slavery. The state had sponsored a system of slavery for most of its existence, and had finally declared itself a free state only 25 years before the Lemmon case reached the New York courts in 1852.

Slavery in New York began in the early 1600s after the arrival of European settlers in New Netherland, a Dutch colony (see figure 5.1).[1]

Dutch New York had no slave code. The practice was informal, based on custom, usage, and an ordinance passed here and there.

Slavery had existed for centuries, but a distinctive form of bondage soon arose—one justified by and based on race. After New York became an English Colony, the New York Legislature, in 1702, created a slave code, institutionalizing the practice of slavery. It was not long before courts presumed Negroes enslaved, unless they could prove otherwise. That explains a lot about racism.[2]

The 1702 law gave slaveowners free rein in punishing their slaves, short of taking their "life or Member." The law also provided for a "common whipper" on the public payroll. Special punishment awaited a slave who would "presume to assault or strike any freeman or Woman professing Christianity."[3] Building on that foundation, in 1708, New York also passed

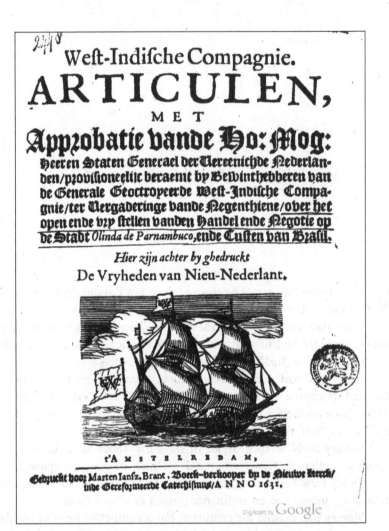

Figure 5.1. The Dutch West India Company beckoning settlers to New Netherland. Originally published in *West Indian Company Articles* printed for Marten Jansz, 1631.

the "Act for Suppressing of Immorality," which required that a slave be publicly whipped for talking "impudently" to a Christian.[4]

The legislature also reassured its constituents that they could baptize their slaves without fear of inadvertently freeing them by making them Christian. Such fears, the lawmakers wrote, were "groundless."[5]

Not surprisingly, as the numbers of enslaved people in New York grew, so did the likelihood—and the fear—of rebellion. The city's first significant uprising took place on April 6, 1712. It was harshly and successfully put down by the authorities, who tried, convicted, and executed those involved. Instead of prompting the legislature to question the practice of slavery regime, the uprising led only to more repressive laws. The clenched fist remained the state's response of choice,[6] leading to another uprising in 1741 (see figures 5.2 and 5.3).[7]

∾

When the Lemmon case arose, in 1852, it had been only 75 years since New York, in its first Constitution (1777), declared itself a child of the English common law.[8] Writings from the Mother Country played a key role in the

The Negroes Sentenced.

Figure 5.2. The Negroes Sentenced. Three enslaved people sentenced by Chief Justice Daniel Horsmanden to be hanged for complicity in a robbery in New York City, 1741. The New York Public Library, The Miriam and Ira D. Wallach Division of Art, Prints and Photographs: Picture Collection, 812585.

The Mob demanding that Quack be burnt.

evident absurdity, and nobody remem-
bering that on that morning a plumber

Figure 5.3. A mob demanding that an enslaved person be burned at the stake following the uprising of 1741. The New York Public Library, The Miriam and Ira D. Wallach Division of Art, Prints, and Photographs: Picture Collection, 812586.

evolving American ideas about slavery. Decisions of English judges were a staple of American jurisprudence. New York judges like Elijah Paine grew up in that common-law tradition. In 1765, William Blackstone, England's preeminent legal commentator, used words that would plant the seeds for Culver and Jay's argument in the Lemmon case: "This spirit of liberty is so deeply implanted in our constitution, and rooted even in our very soil, that a slave or a negro, the moment he lands in England, falls under the protection of the laws, and with regard to all natural rights becomes *eo instanti* a freeman."[9] (See figure 5.4.)

The 1780s marked one of the early points at which the North and South parted company over the issue of slavery. A landmark moment came in 1785, when the founder John Jay (the grandfather of John Jay II of the Lemmon case), Alexander Hamilton, Melancton Smith, and others

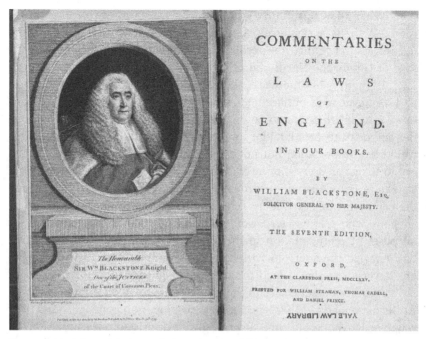

Figure 5.4. William Blackstone's *Commentaries on the Laws of England*, 1765. Rare Book Library, Lillian Goldman Law Library, Yale Law School.

formed the New York Manumission Society, which promoted abolitionist ideals and the education of the enslaved.[10]

At around the same time, an aged Benjamin Franklin became the president of the Pennsylvania Society for Promoting the Abolition of Slavery. He had denounced slavery on moral grounds and also played an active educational role, establishing three Negro schools in the American colonies.[11]

These ideas were in the air. The Manumission Society was formed only two years before the framers of the United States Constitution met in Philadelphia in 1787. The country had recently won independence from England, beginning with its Declaration of Independence, in 1776, which spoke of inalienable rights, among them life, liberty, and the pursuit of happiness, and proclaimed that all men are created equal. The words, and the lofty ideals behind them, however, did not apply to the hundreds of thousands of enslaved people who formed an appreciable part of the American population.

When the Constitution was written, slavery was the elephant in the room. With its agricultural economy resting on slave labor, the South needed assurance that its "peculiar institution" would be secure. For the sake of Union, the North obliged.

Without using the word *slave* or *slavery*, the constitutional drafters in 1787 dealt with enslavement in a number of clauses. And everyone knew exactly what was going on. The delegates agreed to give Congress the authority to prohibit the importation of slaves after 20 years. That would halt importation but not slavery. Slaveowners fully expected slavery to thrive as domestic slaves "increase."[12] Two of the most important clauses in the Constitution proved lasting and contentious—up through the Lemmon case era. The most notorious was the compromise by which anybody who was enslaved would count as three-fifths of a person, for purposes of representation in the House of Representatives. The provision enabled the South to wield political power enough to write federal pro-slavery laws that helped the institution flourish until the Civil War.

Another potent clause in the Constitution related to runaway slaves. As the national divide hardened, slaves escaping from bondage found their way North. The South, not surprisingly, had insisted on a provision for their return. As the price of Union, the North agreed and found room in the Constitution for the Fugitive Slave Clause (Article IV, Sec. 2): "No Person held to Service or Labour in one State, under the Laws thereof, escaping into another, shall, in Consequence of any Law or Regulation therein, be discharged from such Service or Labour, but shall be delivered up on Claim of the Party to whom such Service or Labour may be due." We will never know how things might have turned out had the North refused to go along with this clause. Charles Pinckney of South Carolina, its chief proponent, thought he did well to get it into the Constitution, considering that the Articles of Confederation—under which the states had been operating—had no such written guarantee. He told his constituents back home that they had now "gained a right we had not before."

Emerson called the Fugitive Slave Clause poison at the fountain; the clause generated arrests, rancor, resistance, litigation, and, following its enforcement, heartbreak. John Quincy Adams said that the bargain between freedom and slavery in the Constitution was "morally and politically vicious, cruel, and oppressive."[13]

Adams's description was apt. In 1842, the Supreme Court seized on the Fugitive Slave Clause to proclaim that a slaveowner had an "unqualified right" that no state could take away. No state law, the nation's high court said, could serve to liberate a slave.[14] The Lemmon attorneys would thrust that language upon Judge Paine, as an argument against his liberating the Eight.

After the Constitution was drafted, in 1787, the slavery question reached a critical hour when each of the fledgling states held conventions to decide whether they wanted to ratify the Constitution and join the Union. The delegates knew that adoption would bind the state to slavery compromises that some found hard to swallow—and that would haunt the courts for years to come. The delegates at New York's convention in 1788 could not have predicted the precise facts of the Lemmon case, still some 64 years away, but they knew that pro-slavery aspects of the Constitution would beset future judges and lawyers, with lives and freedom in the balance, for many people.

The delegates initially resisted ratification out of their fear that a new political creature—an unknown entity to be called the "federal government"—could dilute New York's economic power, and they expressed concern that the Constitution lacked a Bill of Rights to check the proposed new, central government.[15] In its reluctance, New York was also more outspoken than the Constitution's framers about the evils of slavery.

Melancton Smith, a leading delegate at New York's Constitutional Ratification Convention, which was held in Poughkeepsie in 1788, summed up the three-fifths clause with a characterization that has stood the test of time. "What adds to the evil," he wrote, "is, that . . . for every cargo of these unhappy people which unfeeling, unprincipled, barbarous and avaricious wretches may tear from their country, friends and tender connections, and bring into those States, they are to be rewarded by having an increase of members in the General Assembly."[16] De Witt Clinton of New York also spoke up, criticizing the enabling provisions in the Constitution. "It does not seem to be justice," he said, "that one man should take another from his own country, and make a slave of him; and yet we are told by this new constitution, that one of its great ends, is to establish justice; alas!"[17] New York ratified the United States Constitution on July 26, 1788, by a vote of 30–27, becoming the 11th state to join the Union. In its lengthy ratification message, New York proposed numerous items in a Bill of Rights and various amendments to the Constitution.

Many colonists believed that the Constitution could do without a Bill of Rights, as Americans were no longer subject to a monarch. Others, though, had a different reason for declining it. South Carolina's Pinkney, for example, worried that a rights declaration would have to begin with high talk of freedom and equality. "We should make that declaration with a very bad grace," he said, "when a large part of our property consists of men who are actually born slaves."[18] The Bill of Rights, however, amending the Constitution in 1791, did not address slavery. It would take a civil war.

∽

After gaining a constitutional provision in 1787 for the return of runaway slaves, the South needed a statute to provide a process, so as to get it up and running. In response, Congress passed the first Fugitive Slave Act, in 1793. President George Washington signed it into law.[19] Given the political and economic power of the South—power recently enhanced by the invention of the cotton gin and the importance of sugar driving the slavery market—the Act was heavily weighted toward slaveowners with scant regard for the rights of people seized in the name of ownership (see figure 5.5).[20]

Under the 1793 Act, slaveowners could capture alleged runaway slaves and take them before a judicial official authorized to issue a certificate allowing the slaveowners to capture alleged fugitive slaves and send them south to bondage. This process lacked even the most meager elements of fairness.

Figure 5.5. *Effects of the Fugitive-Slave-Law* by Theodor Kaufman, 1850. Library of Congress, Prints and Photographs Division, LC-DIG-ds-14484.

Instead of having an official authorize the initial capture, the slaveowner (often with the help of a "slave catcher") would find and forcibly seize the alleged fugitive. Only then would the slaveowner bring the alleged fugitive before an official—simply for a summary hearing, not a meaningful trial, let alone a jury trial. The procedure typically called for nothing more than a written statement from the slaveowner, claiming title to the alleged fugitive. Defenders of the Act pointed out that the alleged fugitive, after being captured and transported to the slave state, could get a trial back home.[21]

Given the tilt of the playing field in the slave states, the odds of an alleged fugitive getting a fair trial after being returned were almost nonexistent. The Supreme Court of Virginia, for example, made the rules of the game very clear: "In the case of a person visibly appearing to be a negro, the presumption is, in this country, that he is a slave, and it is incumbent on him to make out his right to freedom: but in the case of a person visibly appearing to be a white man, or an Indian, the presumption is that he is free, and it is necessary for his adversary to shew that he is a slave."[22] Further, in some suits for freedom in Southern courts, if the judge or jury decided against the alleged runaway and in favor of the slaveowner, the court was "empowered to inflict such corporal punishment, not extending to life or limb, on the [runaway], as they in their discretion shall think fit."[23] The 1793 Act, in short, all but invited violence, perjury, and pro-forma rubber stamping of removal certificates, not to mention the kidnapping and enslavement of free citizens with dark skin.

In the years after the passage of the Fugitive Slave Act, judges in the North, troubled by such practices, started to consider their moral dimensions. By 1799, New York's Supreme Court of Judicature ruled that "All presumptions ought to be made in favor of personal liberty."[24] Nevertheless, up to the early 1800s slavery in New York was still common—as advertisements in New York newspapers make clear (see figure 5.6).

Figure 5.6. An enslaved woman for sale in New York State. From the *Albany Register*, New York, February 22, 1790, 8.

Even after New York was well on the way to becoming a free state, the question of what to do with runaways from slave states persisted. Under federal law, the state was still obliged to return them to their owners—a legal obligation the Lemmon attorneys would later cite in support of their position.

In 1818, the New York City Common Council made clear that it was not about to go out of its way to help catch and return runaway slaves. The council decreed that any alleged fugitive ordered housed at a city jail could not be held for more than 60 days, and the claiming owner would have to pay for the cost of incarceration.[25]

New York's mayor, Cadwallader D. Colden (1769–1834), posed this gem of a question:

> The Mayor begs leave to call the attention of the Board particu-
> larly to this case, and to submit whether it be agreeable . . . that
> the public prison should be rendered subservient to the
> authority of slave holders. Our laws permit a master under
> certain circumstances to hold a fellow creature in slavery, but
> it is believed that they do not [authorize] the commitment of
> a slave to a public prison to be held there during the pleasure
> of the master.[26]

In the following year, 1819, Colden, as head of New York's Manumission Society, resolved to block expansion of slavery into the Territories, and praised James Tallmadge for his role in what turned out to be gradual emancipation in Missouri.[27] Expressions of this kind nudged New York's political climate toward meaningful abolition, but even at the time of the Lemmon case, a quarter century after New York had finally become a free state, pro-slavery sentiment was still very much alive.

New York faced a test at its state constitutional convention in 1821. By statute, abolition was almost final, having begun in 1799, aided by an 1817 statute, proclaiming an absolute end to slavery on July 4, 1827.[28] But would New York go beyond its statute and, as a symbolic gesture, engrave abolition into its constitution? An even more difficult question was whether New York would allow free Blacks an equal right to vote. Some New Yorkers, even those in favor of abolition, felt that newly emancipated Black people would not be sufficiently informed to cast their ballots intelligently.

Once again, the Jay family was on the scene, fighting the good fight. Just as John Jay, the founder, had introduced statutory abolition as New York's Governor, 22 years earlier, in 1799, this time it was his eldest son, Peter Augustus Jay (1776–1843), who spoke forcefully for equality.

His efforts failed. Abolition would continue by statute in New York but not by state constitutional decree. Worse yet, the 1821 convention imposed a $250 property qualification for Black people only. As a result, in 1825, only 298 of New York's nearly 6,000 free Black men met the property requirement.[29]

Nonetheless, New York's decision in 1799 to gradually abolish slavery did produce results. In 1800, the size of the enslaved population was about 20,000; by 1810, it was about 15,000; and by 1820 it was about 10,000. In 1840—twelve years before the Lemmon case—the census reported no slaves in the state.[30]

Some anti-slavery advocates, however, still considered New York to be just a "prolongation of the South," given that Southern slaveholder commerce was linked with New York banks, insurance, real estate, and other business entities. New York certainly was doing plenty of business with the South, which in 1849 purchased more than $76 million of merchandise from New York.[31] These interests would later line up on the side of the Lemmons, as slaveholders.

∾

In 1827, not long after New York had finally become a free state, the city's first African American newspaper, *Freedom's Journal*, came into being (see figure 5.7).[32]

The opening editorial movingly described the growing voice in the affairs of African Americans. "We wish to plead our own cause," the editors wrote. "Too long have others spoken for us." Increasingly, and integral to the movement, Blacks were becoming activists on their own behalf. They formed the New York Committee of Vigilance in 1835 and the United Anti-Slavery Society of the City of New York in 1836. In all, they played a critical abolitionist role that cannot be underestimated, standing up for their rights both with white associates and, more importantly, independently, and in every realm, be it political, economic, legal, and social.

But along with all abolitionists, they had their work cut out for them, especially when it came to the question of fugitive slaves. New York's jurisprudence on the matter was bound up with the federal Fugitive Slave Act of 1793.

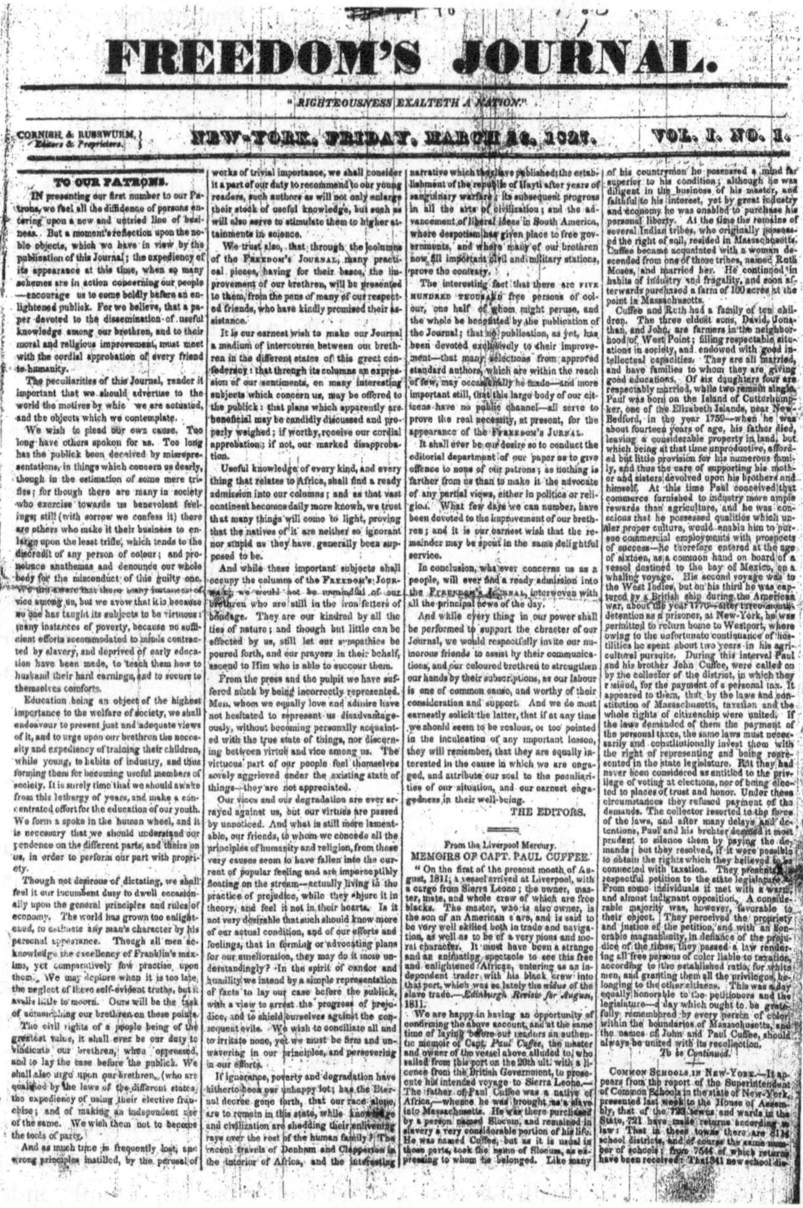

FREEDOM'S JOURNAL.

"RIGHTEOUSNESS EXALTETH A NATION."

CORNISH & RUSSWURM, Editors & Proprietors. | NEW-YORK, FRIDAY, MARCH 16, 1827. | VOL. I. NO. 1.

TO OUR PATRONS.

IN presenting our first number to our Patrons, we feel all the diffidence of persons entering upon a new and untried line of business. But a moment's reflection upon the noble objects, which we have in view by the publication of this Journal; the expediency of its appearance at this time, when so many schemes are in action concerning our people—encourage us to come boldly before an enlightened publick. For we believe, that a paper devoted to the dissemination of useful knowledge among our brethren, and to their moral and religious improvement, must meet with the cordial approbation of every friend to humanity.

The peculiarities of this Journal, render it important that we should advertise to the world the motives by whic we are actuated, and the objects which we contemplate.

We wish to plead our own cause. Too long have others spoken for us. Too long has the publick been deceived by misrepresentations, in things which concern us dearly, though in the estimation of some mere trifles; for though there are many in society who exercise towards us benevolent feelings; still (with sorrow we confess it) there are others who make it their business to enlarge upon the least trifle, which tends to the discredit of any person of colour; and pronounce anathemas and denounce our whole body for the misconduct of this guilty one. We are aware that there are many instances of vice among us, but we avow that it is because no one has taught its subjects to be virtuous: many instances of poverty, because no sufficient efforts accommodated to minds contracted by slavery, and deprived of early education have been made, to teach them how to husband their hard earnings, and to secure to themselves comforts.

Education being an object of the highest importance to the welfare of society, we shall endeavour to present just and adequate views of it, and to urge upon our brethren the necessity and expediency of training their children, while young, to habits of industry, and thus forming them for becoming useful members of society. It is surely time that we should awake from this lethargy of years, and make a concentrated effort for the education of our youth. We form a spoke in the human wheel, and it is necessary that we should understand our pendence on the different parts, and theirs on us, in order to perform our part with propriety.

Though not desirous of dictating, we shall feel it our incumbent duty to dwell occasionally upon the general principles and rules of economy. The world has grown too enlightened, to estimate any man's character by his personal appearance. Though all men acknowledge the excellency of Franklin's maxims, yet comparatively few practise upon them. We may deplore when it is too late, the neglect of these self-evident truths, but it avails little to mourn. Ours will be the task of admonishing our brethren on these points.

The civil rights of a people being of the greatest value, it shall ever be our duty to vindicate our brethren, when oppressed, and to lay the case before the publick. We shall also urge upon our brethren, (who are qualified by the laws of the different states,) the expediency of using their elective franchise; and of making an independent use of the same. We wish them not to become the tools of party.

And as much time is frequently lost, and wrong principles instilled, by the perusal of works of trivial importance, we shall consider it a part of our duty to recommend to our young readers, such authors as will not only enlarge their stock of useful knowledge, but such as will also serve to stimulate them to higher attainments in science.

We trust also, that through the columns of the FREEDOM'S JOURNAL, many practical pieces, having for their bases, the improvement of our brethren, will be presented to them, from the pens of many of our respected friends, who have kindly promised their assistance.

It is our earnest wish to make our Journal a medium of intercourse between our brethren in the different states of this great confederacy: that through its columns an expression of our sentiments, on many interesting subjects which concern us, may be offered to the publick: that plans which apparently are beneficial may be candidly discussed and properly weighed; if worthy, receive our cordial approbation; if not, our marked disapprobation.

Useful knowledge of every kind, and every thing that relates to Africa, shall find a ready admission into our columns; and as that vast continent becomes daily more known, we trust that many things will come to light, proving that the natives of it are neither so ignorant nor stupid as they have generally been supposed to be.

And while these important subjects shall occupy the columns of the FREEDOM'S JOURNAL, we would not be unmindful of our brethren who are still in the iron fetters of bondage. They are our kindred by all the ties of nature; and though but little can be effected by us, still let our sympathies be poured forth, and our prayers in their behalf, ascend to Him who is able to succour them.

From the press and the pulpit we have suffered much by being incorrectly represented. Men, whom we equally love and admire have not hesitated to represent us disadvantageously, without becoming personally acquainted with the true state of things, nor discerning between virtue and vice among us. The virtuous part of our people feel themselves sorely aggrieved under the existing state of things—they are not appreciated.

Our vices and our degradation are ever arrayed against us, but our virtues are passed by unnoticed. And what is still more lamentable, our friends, to whom we concede all the principles of humanity and religion, from these very causes seem to have fallen into the current of popular feeling and are imperceptibly floating on the stream—actually living in the practice of prejudice, while they abjure it in theory, and feel it not in their hearts. Is it not very desirable that such should know more of our actual condition, and of our efforts and feelings, that in forming or advocating plans for our amelioration, they may do it more understandingly? In the spirit of candor and humility we intend by a simple representation of facts to lay our case before the publick, with a view to arrest the progress of prejudice, and to shield ourselves against the consequent evils. We wish to conciliate all and to irritate none, yet we must be firm and unwavering in our principles, and persevering in our efforts.

If ignorance, poverty and degradation have hitherto been our unhappy lot; has the Eternal decree gone forth, that our race alone, are to remain in this state, while knowledge and civilization are shedding their enlivening rays over the rest of the human family? The recent travels of Denham and Clapperton in the interior of Africa, and the interesting narrative which they have published; the establishment of the republic of Hayti after years of sanguinary warfare; its subsequent progress in all the arts of civilization; and the advancement of liberal ideas in South America, where despotism has given place to free governments, and where many of our brethren now fill important civil and military stations, prove the contrary.

The interesting fact that there are FIVE HUNDRED THOUSAND free persons of colour, one half of whom might peruse, and the whole be benefitted by the publication of the Journal; that no publication, as yet, has been devoted exclusively to their improvement—that many selections from approved standard authors, which are within the reach of few, may occasionally be made—and more important still, that this large body of our citizens have no public channel—all serve to prove the real necessity, at present, for the appearance of the FREEDOM'S JOURNAL.

It shall ever be our desire so to conduct the editorial department of our paper as to give offence to none of our patrons; as nothing is farther from us than to make it the advocate of any partial views, either in politics or religion. What few days we can number, have been devoted to the improvement of our brethren; and it is our earnest wish that the remainder may be spent in the same delightful service.

In conclusion, whatever concerns us as a people, will ever find a ready admission into the FREEDOM'S JOURNAL, interwoven with all the principal news of the day.

And while every thing in our power shall be performed to support the chracter of our Journal, we would respectfully invite our numerous friends to assist by their communications, and our coloured brethren to strengthen our hands by their subscriptions, as our labour is one of common cause, and worthy of their consideration and support. And we do most earnestly solicit the latter, that if at any time we should seem to be zealous, or too pointed in the inculcation of any important lesson, they will remember, that they are equally interested in the cause in which we are engaged, and attribute our zeal to the peculiarities of our situation, and our earnest engagedness in their well-being.

THE EDITORS.

From the Liverpool Mercury.

MEMOIRS OF CAPT. PAUL CUFFEE.

"On the first of the present month of August, 1811, a vessel arrived at Liverpool, with a cargo from Sierra Leone; the owner, master, mate, and whole crew of which are free blacks. The master, who is also owner, is the son of an American slave, and is said to be very well skilled both in trade and navigation, as well as to be of a very pious and moral character. It must have been a strange and an animating spectacle to see this free and enlightened African, entering as an independent trader with his black crew into that port, which was so lately the nidus of the slave trade.—*Edinburgh Review for August*, 1811.

We are happy in having an opportunity of confirming the above account, and at the same time of laying before our readers an authentic memoir of Capt. *Paul Cuffee*, the master and owner of the vessel above alluded to, who sailed from this port on the 20th ult. with a licence from the British Government, to prosecute his intended voyage to Sierra Leone.—The father of Paul Cuffee was a native of Africa,—whence he was brought as a slave into Massachusetts. He was there purchased by a person named Slocum, and remained in slavery a very considerable portion of his life. He was named Cuffee, but as it is usual in those parts, took the name of Slocum, as expressing to whom he belonged. Like many of his countrymen he possessed a mind far superior to his condition; although he was diligent in the business of his master, and faithful to his interest, yet by great industry and economy he was enabled to purchase his personal liberty. At the time the remains of several Indian tribes, who originally possessed the right of soil, resided in Massachusetts, Cuffee became acquainted with a woman descended from one of those tribes, named Ruth Moses, and married her. He continued in habits of industry and frugality, and soon afterwards purchased a farm of 100 acres at the point in Massachusetts.

Cuffee and Ruth had a family of ten children. The three eldest sons, David, Jonathan, and John, are farmers in the neighborhood of West Point; filling respectable situations in society, and endowed with good intellectual capacities. They are all married, and have families to whom they are giving good educations. Of six daughters four are respectably married, while two remain single. Paul was born on the Island of Cutterhunker, one of the Elizabeth Islands, near New-Bedford, in the year 1759—when he was about fourteen years of age, his father died, leaving a considerable property in land, but which being at that time unproductive, afforded but little provision for his numerous family, and thus the care of supporting his mother and sisters devolved upon his brothers and himself. At this time Paul conceived that commerce furnished to industry more ample rewards than agriculture, and he was conscious that he possessed qualities which under proper culture, would enable him to pursue commercial employments with prospects of success—he therefore entered at the age of sixteen, as a common hand on board of a vessel destined to the bay of Mexico, on a whaling voyage. His second voyage was to the West Indies, but on his third he was captured by a British ship during the American war, about the year 1776—after three months detention as a prisoner, at New-York, he was permitted to return home to Westport, where owing to the unfortunate continuance of hostilities he spent about two years in his agricultural pursuits. During this interval Paul and his brother John Cuffee, were called on by the collector of the district, in which they resided, for the payment of a personal tax. It appeared to them, that by the laws and constitution of Massachusetts, taxation and the whole rights of citizenship were united. If the laws demanded of them the payment of the personal taxes, the same laws must necessarily and constitutionally invest them with the right of representing and being represented in the state legislature. But they had never been considered as entitled to the privilege of voting at elections, nor of being elected to places of trust and honor. Under these circumstances they refused payment of the demands. The collector resorted to the force of the laws, and after many delays and detentions, Paul and his brehter deemed it most prudent to silence them by paying the demands; but they resolved, if it were possible to obtain the rights which they believed to be connected with taxation. They presented a respectful petition to the state legislature. From some individuals it met with a warm, and almost indignant opposition. A considerable majority was, however, favorable to their object. They perceived the propriety and justice of the petition, and with an honorable magnanimity, in defiance of the prejudice of the times, they passed a law rendering all free persons of color liable to taxation, according to the established ratio for white men, and granting them all the privileges belonging to the other citizens. This was a day equally honorable to the petitioners and the legislature—a day which ought to be gratefully remembered by every person of color within the boundaries of Massachusetts, and the names of John and Paul Cuffee, should always be united with its recollection.

To be Continued.

COMMON SCHOOLS IN NEW-YORK.—It appears from the report of the Superintendent of Common Schools in the state of New-York, presented last week to the House of Assembly, that of the 723 towns and wards in the State, 721 have made returns according to law: That in these towns there are 8114 school districts, and of course the same number of schools; from 7544 of which returns have been received: That 341 new school di-

Figure 5.7. The first issue of *Freedom's Journal*, March 16, 1827, published by Samuel Cornish and John Brown Russwurm.

In the early 1800s, the kidnapping, transportation, and enslavement of dark-skinned people under a claim of ownership posed real threats, with no protection under federal law from false claims of "ownership" (see figure 5.8).[33]

After 1827, resistance to these practices—and to the federal Fugitive Slave Act of 1793—grew in New York. In 1828, as part of a reaction against them, New York passed a habeas corpus act, as part of a Northern effort to pass "personal liberty laws."[34] Like other Northern states, New York could not simply flout its obligation to return fugitives. Instead, it tried to build in some procedural protections for alleged fugitives, so that they would not be swept up and summarily dispatched south into bondage.

New York had always had a writ of habeas corpus, but in 1828 its legislature enlarged it to deal with these abuses. The writ could be used

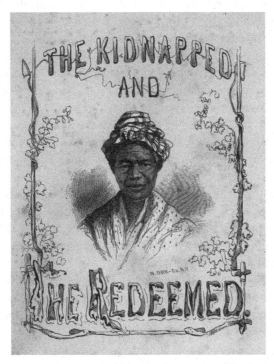

Figure 5.8. The cover image of *The Kidnapped and the Redeemed: Being the Personal Recollections of Peter Still and His Wife "Vina," after Forty Years of Slavery*, by Kate E. R. Pickard, 1856.

by someone seeking freedom—as it would in the Lemmon case—but, significantly, it could also be used *against* someone asserting title to a claimed runaway.[35]

Under the 1828 act, slaveowners in New York could not begin by seizing an alleged fugitive and only then going to court, as they could under federal law. Instead, they would have to start in court. If satisfied as to proof of title, the judge would then issue a writ directing the sheriff to arrest and bring the alleged fugitive before the court. There was nothing pro forma about it. To bring about the arrest, proof of ownership had to be by affidavit, "setting forth *minutely and particularly* [emphasis mine] the ground for such claim to the services of such fugitive, the time of the escape of such fugitive, and where he then is." The words "*minutely and particularly*" seem redundant but in fact are a signal from New York that it would not casually deliver Blacks into bondage based on flimsy claims. The alleged fugitive was now also allowed to testify, unlike in Southern states, where slaves, and even alleged slaves, were only allowed to testify against one another.[36]

Seven years later, in 1835, the New York State Supreme Court took a major step in the judiciary's anti-slavery stance, when it decisively rejected the claim of a slaveowner who had challenged New York's emancipation law as unconstitutional, claiming that the state had confiscated his property without payment.[37]

Of course, by 1852 no one involved in the Lemmon case questioned New York's right to abolish slavery. The issue was how far should New York continue to go in recognizing Virginia's slavery laws. On that front, some cases were notorious.

On April 4, 1837, for example, William Dixon was seized by two New York policemen, Tobias Boudinot and Daniel Nash, both slavery profiteers (see figure 5.9 for a previous case involving the pair). Dr. Walter Allender of Baltimore claimed that Dixon was actually Jake Ennis, a slave of his who had escaped in 1832.

The newly formed New York Committee of Vigilance, along with the New York Manumission Society, came to Dixon's defense, engaging the attorney Horace Dresser to represent him at a proceeding before New York City Recorder Richard Riker in City Hall.[38]

Many anti-slavery people considered Riker unfriendly to their cause. After testimony had begun, and while Dixon was in custody, a crowd of hundreds of people surged forward, freeing Dixon. He was recaptured almost immediately, but his case was never resolved.[39]

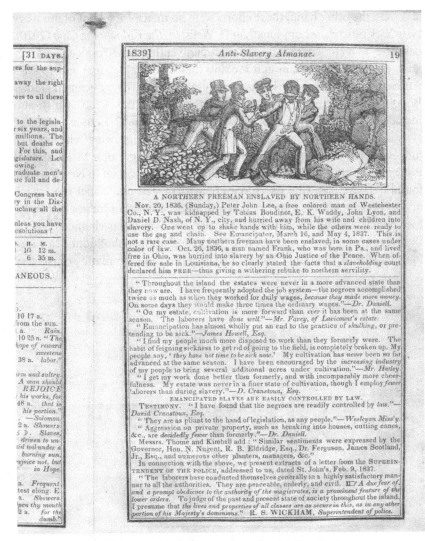

Figure 5.9. "A Northern freeman enslaved by Northern hands," Boston, 1839. The New York Public Library, Schomburg Center for Research in Black Culture, Manuscripts, Archives, and Rare Books Division, NYPG94-S11885.

The Dixon case says something about New York's mixed attitude toward slavery. On the one hand, we see a crowd of hundreds overcoming police, to rescue an alleged fugitive slave. That would have been unimaginable years earlier, and it shows a trajectory.

On the other hand, those efforts were no match for a knot of unsavory New York officials, whom Jonathan D. Wells, in *The Kidnapping Club* (2020), describes as a confederation bent on circumventing New York's anti-slavery laws, encouraging racism, and looking the other way as free and fugitive African Americans were kidnapped into slavery. The policemen Tobias Boudinot and Daniel D. Nash stood at the apex of the "Club," which also included Richard Riker and Federal Court Judge Samuel R. Betts as members.

Another case from that same year reveals the growing reluctance of judges in New York to entertain recaption proceedings. John McPherson of Frederick County, Maryland, claimed that on Clinton Street in New York, he found his slave Nat, who had run away in 1833. The newspaper reports tell of McPherson and his attorney going through a series of judges before the case finally reached Judge Betts, who gave Nat over to his claimed owner.[40]

Communities in upstate New York revealed their abolitionist side (see figure 5.10). In 1836 the City of Utica experienced a dramatic anti-slavery

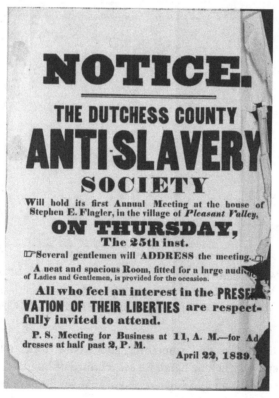

Figure 5.10. Announcement for a meeting of the Dutchess County, New York, Anti-Slavery Society, 1839. Courtesy of the Dutchess County Historical Society.

event following the arrest of two men, at the behest of their alleged owner, John Geyer, of Shenandoah County, Virginia. Brought before Oneida County Judge Chester Hayden, the two alleged fugitives, "Harry Bird and George," were in the judge's office, represented by attorney Alvan Stewart, when a crowd assembled, overcame the captors, and rescued the two, who were never heard from again.[41]

In 1840, the New York Legislature added another layer of difficulty for slaveowners, granting a jury trial and appointing the district attorney as counsel for the alleged fugitive. It also authorized the governor to appoint agents to help restore liberty to persons kidnapped and to help return them to New York State (see figure 5.11).[42]

Southern slaveowners, of course, were not happy having their claims adjudicated by Northern jurors, many of whom had no stomach for returning someone who had escaped from slavery.[43] But how far could Northern states like New York go in resisting the easy recaption procedures of the Fugitive Slave Act of 1793?

The United States Supreme Court provided the answer just two years later, in 1842, in *Prigg* v. *Pennsylvania*. It was a case that would have been on Judge Paine's mind a decade later, when he began to consider the Lemmon case.

RESCUE OF A FUGITIVE SLAVE.

Figure 5.11. "Rescue of a Fugitive Slave," 1888. The New York Public Library, The Miriam and Ira D. Wallach Division of Art, Prints and Photographs: Picture Collection, 807845.

Chapter 6

Self-Help for the Slave Owner

The facts in the Prigg case were plain enough. In April 1837, Edward Prigg and three collaborators captured a Negro woman, Margaret Morgan, and her children in York County, Pennsylvania, claiming them to be runaway slaves from Maryland. Unable to acquire a certificate of removal from a local Pennsylvania magistrate, Prigg and his cohorts forcibly took the Morgans to Maryland, to be put into bondage. In response, Pennsylvania convicted the slave catchers of kidnapping, under a statute it had enacted in 1826 to prevent the abduction of alleged fugitive slaves.

Pennsylvania's statute was among the most prominent of the Northern states' "personal liberty laws"—testing the extent to which states could resist federal pro-slavery laws. Prigg's appeal reached the United States Supreme Court as a test case of whether a state—in this instance, Pennsylvania—had the right to punish slave catchers as kidnappers, as against the slaveowners' claim that they had a right to retrieve their "property."[1]

Ignominiously, the Court ruled 6–1 in favor of the slave catcher, Prigg. In doing so, it shot down all Northern state-court procedures designed to allow fairness in dealing with alleged fugitive slaves. In place of due process, the Court substituted self-help: It gave slave catchers the green light to seize and transport alleged slaves without any intervention by a court.

This was a landmark moment in American legal history. As one scholar has pointed out, in *Prigg* the Supreme Court for the first time explicitly recognized slavery as a constitutionally protected institution.[2]

Associate Justice Joseph Story, of Massachusetts, wrote the majority opinion (see figures 6.1 and 6.2). In it, he reached four conclusions that gave slave power a constitutional shield.

Figure 6.1. Justice Joseph Story, member of the US Supreme Court when it decided the *Prigg* case. Library of Congress, Prints and Photographs Division, Brady-Handy Photograph Collection, LC-DIG-cwpbh-02617.

First, that Congress had passed the Fugitive Slave Act of 1793 as a proper constitutional exercise of its power to regulate the rendition of fugitive slaves. That conclusion would open the way for Southern states to demand an even more aggressive enforcement of slaveowners' rights at the federal level.[3]

Second, that the Congress alone had the power to legislate on the subject of fugitive slaves. Prominent legal theorists, including Judge William Jay and New York Governor William H. Seward, had argued that the states had at least concurrent if not primary power to implement the Fugitive Slave Act, but *Prigg* settled the point, decreeing that Pennsylvania's anti-kidnapping law amounted to an unconstitutional interference with a slaveowner's rights.[4] This portion of the Prigg decision later came to be known as "federal preemption," a way of saying that valid federal law overrides state law when the two conflict.

Third, that slaveowners could seize and remove their alleged fugitive slaves without any legal process, as long they did not do so in a "riotous manner," in "breach of the peace," or by way of illegal violence. A slaveowner,

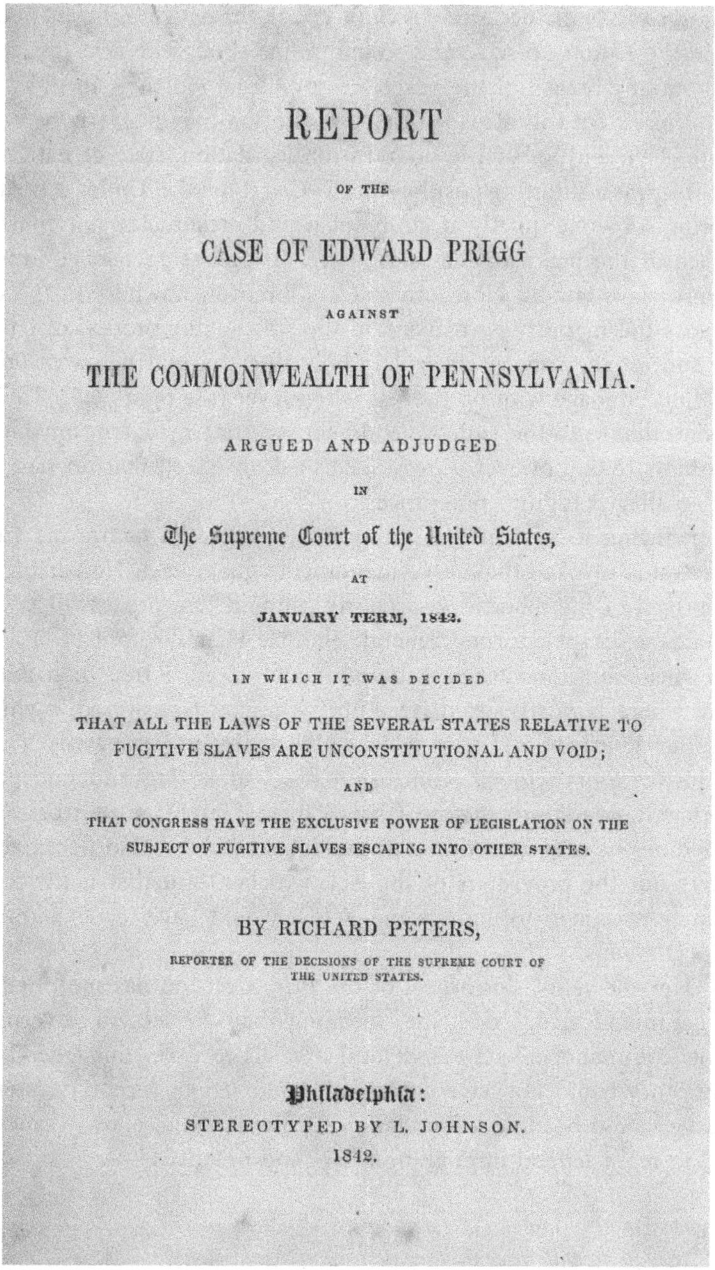

REPORT

OF THE

CASE OF EDWARD PRIGG

AGAINST

THE COMMONWEALTH OF PENNSYLVANIA.

ARGUED AND ADJUDGED

IN

The Supreme Court of the United States,

AT

JANUARY TERM, 1842.

IN WHICH IT WAS DECIDED

THAT ALL THE LAWS OF THE SEVERAL STATES RELATIVE TO
FUGITIVE SLAVES ARE UNCONSTITUTIONAL AND VOID;

AND

THAT CONGRESS HAVE THE EXCLUSIVE POWER OF LEGISLATION ON THE
SUBJECT OF FUGITIVE SLAVES ESCAPING INTO OTHER STATES.

BY RICHARD PETERS,

REPORTER OF THE DECISIONS OF THE SUPREME COURT OF
THE UNITED STATES.

Philadelphia:

STEREOTYPED BY L. JOHNSON.

1842.

Figure 6.2. *Report of the Case of Edward Prigg against the Commonwealth of Pennsylvania*, 1842.

the court confidently declared, "is clothed with the entire authority in every state in the Union, to seize and recapture his slave, whenever he can do it without any breach of the peace, or any illegal violence. In this sense, and to this extent this clause of the Constitution may properly be said to execute itself; and to require no aid from legislation, state or national."[5]

This was a stunning position for the Court to take. Under this ruling, capturing someone quietly at gunpoint would presumably not constitute a breach of the peace or illegal violence. In this respect *Prigg* imposed Southern slave law on Northern states. Moreover, nowhere in the decision does the majority even mention the words "due process of law," let alone address the concept or explain how a person may be swept up and taken into bondage with no process whatsoever (see figure 6.3). Think of it: Today, thanks to the 14th Amendment, no state may *deny* anyone due process. In 1842, however, *Prigg* established, in effect, that no state may *grant* an alleged fugitive due process.

In trying to sustain the statute in its argument before the Court, Pennsylvania invoked the Fifth Amendment's guarantee: "No person shall be deprived of life, liberty, or property, without due process of law." As the state's assistant attorney general, Thomas Hambley, put it, "If, then, under this most monstrous assumption of power, a free man may be seized, where is our boasted freedom?" The court answered, saying, in effect, that liberty would have to take a back seat to "property."

Justice Story's fourth conclusion has had lasting and unexpected importance. By way of dictum (that is to say, language unnecessary to the holding) he suggested that state and local officials could not be forced to carry out the provisions of the Act, which meant that if the federal government wanted to enforce the Act, it would have to do it through federal channels.[6]

Over the years, this aspect of the *Prigg* decision has morphed into "anti-commandeering" doctrine, meaning that the federal government cannot "commandeer" state and local officials to carry out federal law.[7] Justice Story could not have guessed that more than a century later, his language would become a foundation for the law that allows "sanctuary cities" to resist federal immigration laws and practices.[8]

∽

It did not take Northern states very long to figure out a way to seize on what little the decision gave them. They could not affirmatively obstruct

AMERICAN SLAVERY AS IT IS.

On the side of the Oppressors there was power.

The officer of Justice! arresting a helpless female fugitive in N. Y.
What has the North to do with Slavery?

Figure 6.3. Illustrations of slave recaption as a travesty of justice. The New York Public Library, Schomburg Center for Research in Black Culture, Manuscripts, Archives and Rare Books Division, 1150361.

federal fugitive law, but the best way of *not* helping, they realized, was to simply put their state and local apparatus off-limits to slaveowners.

They did so in varying degrees, enacting a new round of personal liberty laws, prohibiting state and local officials from participating in the rendition of alleged fugitives, barring the use of state and local jails to house any and closing state courts to slaveowners seeking to enforce seizure or removal of alleged fugitives.[9] These actions outraged many federal authorities whose interests aligned with the South, among them President James Buchanan, who called these forms of passive resistance "unconstitutional and obnoxious."[10] (See figure 6.4.)

In the *Prigg* case, Justice Story and the Supreme Court majority may have intended to give something to both sides (although it gave a good deal more to slaveowners). But in the short run, the decision succeeded only in disappointing everyone.

Chief Justice Roger Taney (figure 6.5) wrote a concurring opinion. He was perfectly happy with the portion of the decision that allowed kidnapping, but did not like the suggestion that the states need not help

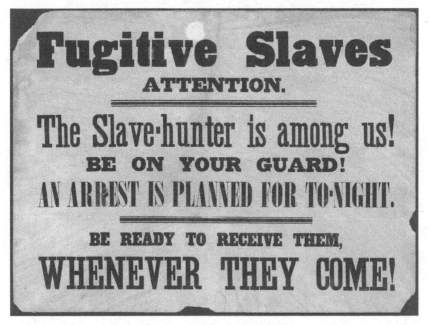

Figure 6.4. A warning to fugitive slaves about the arrival of slave hunters. Courtesy of Dartmouth College Library.

Figure 6.5. Chief Justice Roger B. Taney, member of the U.S. Supreme Court when it decided the *Prigg* case. Library of Congress, Prints and Photographs Division, LC-USZ62-107588.

catch runaways. John Quincy Adams declared that *Prigg* stood for "the transcendent omnipotence of slavery in these United States, riveted by a clause in the Constitution."[11] The *New-York Tribune*, for its part, called upon Congress to regulate the rendition of slaves, short of kidnapping.[12]

None of the criticism mattered much. At the end of the 1840s the chairmen of all the important congressional committees were Southern slaveowners. Slave states chose 30 of the 62 senators, and 90 of the 233 members of the House. Some members of Congress from non-slave states lined up with slavery interests, often in the name of union and the overriding authority of federal law—reasons that motivated Justice Story to rule as he did. Worse yet, the *Prigg* decision provided the mortar for the Fugitive Slave Act of 1850, which replaced the Act of 1793, swept away even the barest procedural safeguards in the seizure and enslavement of alleged fugitive slaves, and moved closer toward nationalizing slavery.

In 1852, the attorneys for Julia and Jonathan Lemmon would cite both that Act and the *Prigg* decision as reasons for keeping the Eight in bondage.

The Fugitive Slave Act of 1850 was at the center of the legal landscape in which the Lemmon case arose in 1852.

The Act formed part of the Compromise of 1850, introduced by Senator Henry Clay of Kentucky—one of the most important political events in American history. The provisions of the Compromise included admitting California into the Union as a free state, ending the slave trade (but not slavery) in Washington, DC, and creating the Utah and New Mexico territories, where the slavery issue was left to popular sovereignty. As part of the Compromise, the South came away with the new Fugitive Slave Act, which strengthened the 1793 version. Anti-slavery people such as William H. Seward and Salmon P. Chase opposed the compromise, rejecting the idea that the Union had to be built—or even could be built—on a foundation of human bondage. Having ardently defended Black rights, Seward declared the compromise "radically wrong and essentially vicious . . . involving the surrender of the exercise of judgment and conscience."

In 1851, in Elijah Paine's New York, not everybody had such firm convictions about the Act, or even about enslavement. Most New Yorkers had become used to abolition within the state's own borders and were, by and large, against enslavement as an institution. On the other hand, many also felt the tugs of Union, the Southern commercial dollar, and fidelity to federal law.

Nor were Northern judges monolithic in their thinking about slavery, or at least about the relevant laws.

Samuel Nelson (1792–1873), born and raised in upstate New York, was a justice of the United States Supreme Court in 1851. In April of that year, he appeared in New York City and instructed a federal grand jury on its obligations under the newly revised Fugitive Slave Act. In his discourse to the jurors, he criticized New York's legislature for interfering with the Act and for "paralyzing" its execution.

When instructing grand juries on the law, judges do not normally engage in political diatribe. Judge Nelson, however, took the opportunity to exaggerate what New York had done to resist the Fugitive Slave Act. Had he said—as did many others—that he was caught between competing pressures of humanity and constitutional fidelity, his words might have better withstood the judgment of history. We might ask why a justice of the United States Supreme Court went out of his way to give a federal grand jury a political lecture, and a misleading one at that, chastising the

New York Legislature for not cooperating in the capture and return of alleged fugitives under a reprehensible federal law.[13]

Judge Nelson's stance was shared by many others, who held that the Union was paramount, transcending all other considerations. He may have wrongly equated an unwillingness to help enforce the law with active interference, but in his view, both betrayed a lack of fidelity to the spirit of Union.[14]

Judge Nelson's discourse ran in dozens of newspapers across the country. No doubt, people in New York's judicial community read it and talked about it. Likely, the local judges found the commentary gratuitous and off-putting. Judge Paine, no doubt, read it in detail.[15]

Six years later, Justice Nelson would forecast the Lemmon case, when he concurred in the notorious *Dred Scott* decision. "A question has been alluded to, on the argument," he wrote, "namely: the right of the master with his slave of transit into or through a free State, on Business or commercial pursuits, or in the exercise of a Federal right, or the discharge of a Federal duty, being a citizen of the United States, which is not before us. . . . When that question arises, we shall be prepared to decide it."

Nelson gave his grand jury discourse in April of 1851. In the months that followed in New York, several slave cases arose that drew national attention—and raised questions about how the new Fugitive Slave Act would be enforced.

∽

In August, Daniel Davis was working as a cook aboard a steamer docked in Buffalo. Federal officials helped a slave catcher seize him, claiming he was a fugitive slave from Kentucky. Davis was injured in the violent arrest. His captors brought him before a federal commissioner, Henry K. Smith, who signed off on the paperwork and was prepared to dispatch him south. He even warned that anyone impeding his transfer could be shot. He added, however, that it might be possible to purchase Davis's freedom, even saying he would chip in 25 dollars.

Crowds assembled, and before Davis was whisked off, local abolitionists, along with attorney John L. Talcott, were able to get the case before Judge Alfred Conkling (1789–1874) of the United States District Court, on a writ of habeas corpus. Normally, antislavery lawyers would question the alleged slaveowner's title and the identity of the claimed fugitive. With Davis, they had an additional argument: If, as the owner claimed, Davis had run away in August 1850, a month before the Fugitive Slave Act was passed, who was to say that the Act should be applied retroactively?

Not Judge Conkling. He refused, and he freed Davis, who promptly set off for Canada.

Two weeks later, on September 1, the *Buffalo Daily Republic* wrote a sardonic article ridiculing commissioner Smith for his warning that anyone would be shot for interfering with his decision to send Davis back to Kentucky. Who interfered more than Judge Conkling? The piece spoke humorously of the "miraculous escape" of Judge Conkling, who was not ordered shot. Meanwhile, the *Fayetteville Observer*, a North Carolina newspaper, called Judge Conkling's ruling a threat to the Union.[16]

In October, it was Syracuse's turn. Several months earlier, in May, Daniel Webster, then the United States secretary of state, he had stood on a balcony facing Syracuse City Hall, promising that the Fugitive Slave Act would be executed *everywhere*, meaning that he particularly had it in for Syracuse, which he (rightly) considered an enemy of the Act.[17] Webster knew that the Liberty anti-slavery party convention would be held there in October, and he must have intended to cow the population. But he succeeded only in igniting it.

As if on cue, at around noon on October 1st, 1851, when the convention was in session, Deputy US Marshal Henry W. Allen arrested William "Jerry" Henry (sometimes Jerry McHenry) while at his job in Syracuse as a barrel-maker. Henry was about 40 years old, married and with children. He was said to have escaped from his owner, John McReynolds, of Marion County, Missouri.

Word of the arrest soon reached the Convention, in session at a nearby church. A crowd gathered at the office of federal commissioner Joseph F. Sabine, who was hearing the case to send Jerry back. Jerry was represented by the attorneys D. D. Hillis, Leroy Morgan, and Hervey Sheldon. In irons, Jerry escaped and, after a fierce struggle, was recaptured. He was in a rage. Officials asked Rev. Samuel J. May to calm him down, apparently not appreciating that Rev. May was bent on seeing Jerry not only calmed but freed. Rev. May whispered: "Jerry, we are going to rescue you; do be more quiet!"[18]

Using a battering ram, axes, and crowbars, a crowd of several hundred broke in, rescued Jerry, and took him to Brintnall's Hotel. From there he went to Oswego and on to Canada.[19]

The day after the rescue, abolitionist Gerrit Smith introduced a resolution adopted at the Liberty Party convention. It said in parliamentary prose what Whittier had said about Webster in poetry: "*Resolved,* That we rejoice that the City of Syracuse—the anti-slavery city of Syracuse—the city of anti-slavery conventions, our beloved and glorious city of Syracuse still remains undisgraced by the fulfillment of the satanic prediction of the satanic Daniel Webster."[20] Federal officials brought a score of indictments against the rescuers. The *New York Journal of Commerce,* slave power's dependable apologist, urged that the rescuers be indicted for treason. They were taken to Auburn for arraignment and were bailed out by, among others, William H. Seward, the US senator and former governor of New York. The proceedings dragged on for two years with nothing to show for it.[21]

In May 1852, several months before the Lemmon case, John Jay II fought another slavery case in New York. The case involved James Snowden, who in 1849 had escaped from his owner, Dr. Allen Thomas, of Anne Arundel County, Maryland. Fleeing north, Snowden found a job on a boat out of Providence, Rhode Island. After the vessel had arrived in New York harbor, Snowden took a skiff to get ashore, where he was arrested.

Jay, whose sense of practicality matched his legal acumen, convinced both his client—Snowden—and the sentencing judge that it would be better to send Snowden to New York's Sing-Sing prison for two years than to return him to indefinite enslavement in Maryland.[22]

Snowden served out his term at Sing-Sing, but when he was about to be discharged, Federal Commissioner George W. Morton directed that he be given over to the slaveowner.

That did not happen. Two days before Snowden was to be released to his owner, he was pardoned by New York Governor Washington Hunt (1811–1867), at the encouragement of the Rev. James Pennington, who took Snowden to Canada. Later that year, Pennington would also play a role in the Lemmon case. Explaining his action, Governor Hunt said he had pardoned Snowden only because he was innocent of the crime charged, and not to evade the Fugitive Slave Law, adding that he did not know Snowden was a fugitive.[23]

Southern editorialists blamed it all on the "monstrous machinations and mischievous fanaticism of the Seward influence," and of "playing into the hands of the fanatics who deprive southerners of their property."[24]

Syracuse was proud of the role it had played in resisting the new Fugitive Slave Act. In October, 1852, the city convened a celebration commemorating the first anniversary of the Jerry Rescue, with poetry and anti-slavery speeches from Lucretia Mott, Frederick Douglass, and William Lloyd Garrison.

At that very hour, the Lemmon family, and the Eight, were on their way from Virginia to New York.

∽

In 1852, Virginia and New York had become increasingly combative over the issue of slavery. When the Lemmon case reached Judge Paine that year, he would have known very well that it represented part of a larger political conflict over slavery that New York and Virginia had already been waging for years—one that for more than a decade had engaged the governors of both states.

The battle got started in 1839, when John G. Colley, of Norfolk, Virginia, ordered his slave, Isaac Colley, to do repair work on a schooner before it sailed for New York. Three African-American sailors, Edward Smith, Isaac Gancy (sometimes Gansey) and Peter Johnson, were among the crew. After speaking to one of them about freedom, Isaac Colley stowed away on the craft just before it left Virginia.

The slaveowner put out the alarm, and when the vessel arrived in New York harbor, his two agents forcibly went aboard, seized Colley, and sent him back to Norfolk in another vessel. That was not enough to satisfy the slaveowner, who aimed to teach the three sailors a lesson and have them imprisoned in Virginia. The sailors were apprehended and brought before Robert H. Morris, a New York judicial official, to determine whether there was reason to hold them or give them over to Virginia. One New York newspaper referred to the sailors as "black rascals" who, if guilty of helping the slave, should be jailed for life.[25]

Virginia then demanded that New York Governor William Seward give over the sailors.[26] Seward refused. New York would give over a fugitive, he said, only when the offenses charged are "recognized as crimes by the universal laws of all civilized countries." New York does not recognize slavery, he said—as if New York and Virginia were separate nations. Seward's letter did not read like a humdrum or stiff official communication; it cited political philosophers and international law, and read more like an essay.[27] New York had abolished slavery on its own soil, Seward said, but beyond that, New York would not be a willing partner in furthering the idea that someone could be owned. He had drawn a line in the sand.

The Virginia legislature responded with stern resolutions.[28] And then it did something almost unheard of. It asked the New York Legislature to put Seward in his place—believing, or at least hoping, that there were political and commercial interests in New York that would slap down its governor. Virginia characterized Seward's action as palpable and dangerous, of "monstrous and unconstitutional character." The New York Legislature, Virginia urged, should "control" a New York governor whom Virginia considered out of control.[29]

The New York Legislature responded, not with a rebuke of its governor, but with a potent anti-slavery statute. It was more than a poke in the eye. As Virginia would soon put it, in an 1840 report on its battle with New York, "A law more perfectly to obstruct and hinder the recovery of a fugitive slave could not be devised."

That was a very good description of the statute. It had two important components: First, it mandated a jury trial for anyone accused of being a runaway slave; and second, the district attorney was to represent the accused in recaption proceedings. Virginia, and the South, were infuriated. Slave power considered New York juries an impediment to the prompt and efficient return of runaway slaves. The other provision, appointing the district attorney to represent accused runaway slaves, was unmatched in symbolic importance. The district attorney, as representative of the people of the state, was to be pitted against the slaveholder in all fugitive slave cases. Enacting the right to jury trial for those charged as fugitive slaves, the legislation was no doubt prompted by the actions of officials who had cavalierly sent accused fugitives into slavery.

Retaliating, Virginia passed a law requiring that all New York ships leaving Virginia be inspected. Interestingly, Virginia made the law conditional, stating that it would not go into effect if New York reformed its ways.

Virginia spoke plainly as to how it saw things. Its report is worth quoting at some length, because it is a lesson in the economics of slavery:

> The slave property of Virginia, at a moderate calculation, is worth one hundred and thirty-four millions of dollars, which is two-thirds of the value of the entire real estate of the Commonwealth, and without which, that estate would be comparatively valueless! The people of the State have this immense mass of property staked upon this question, to say nothing about the moral, political, and social interests involved in it. New-York is the largest, the wealthiest, the most powerful, and most commercial State in the Union. . . . The position which she has taken, therefore, standing alone, places the property (to take no higher ground) of our people in the most imminent peril.[30]

Just six years before the Lemmon case, as the battle between New York and Virginia continued, New York had again displayed its racial ambivalence. Opposing slavery was one thing, but giving the unqualified vote to free Blacks was another. In New York's Constitutional referendum of 1846—just as in its Constitutional Convention of 1821—New York refused to repeal the property qualification for Black male voters.[31] Some delegates tried to remove the disability, but they succeeded only in having it written up as a separate question to voters on the election-day ballot.[32]

On election day, November 2, the Constitution of 1846 passed by a statewide vote of 221,528 to 92,436—but the special amendment, which would have repealed the property qualification for Blacks, lost by a lopsided vote of 223,834 to 85,306.[33]

Chapter 7

Fugitives

Arguing against the Eight, Henry Lapaugh had presented a hypothetical to Judge Paine. Suppose, he said, that a slave owner were to lawfully capture a fugitive, but then on the way back south had to pass through a free state. Should that spell freedom for the fugitive? Wouldn't that undo the recently enacted Fugitive Slave Act of 1850—and the clause in the Constitution requiring the return of runaway slaves?

Not a bad argument. And it nicely complemented the language of the Supreme Court, in *Prigg*, that the Constitution's Fugitive Slave Clause amounts to an unqualified right of slave ownership that no state can take away. Lapaugh's thrust was emphatic: New York had no constitutional authority to liberate the Eight by prying them out of the arms of their owners.

Judge Paine needed no schooling in these arguments. The new Fugitive Slave Act, after all, had been passed only two years earlier, after intense debate that had played out in every arena, from the newspapers to the barrooms to the pulpits. A lightning rod for sectional division, the Act made it easier and cheaper to retrieve claimed runaway slaves—and as such represents one of the most shameful Congressional enactments in American history.

On paper, the Fugitive Slave Act of 1850 had fulfilled slave power's every wish. It had created a novel branch of the judiciary—a cadre of federal "commissioners," who had the power to order the seizure and return of fugitive slaves. It was the job of these commissioners to conduct all legal proceedings relating to the Act. They were to function with no pretense of judicial independence, and they were to decide matters free from bothersome juries. Hearings were to be summary, arranged to return the accused runaway speedily and efficiently. Officials in free states were not to be trusted, and the proceedings were to be "conclusive," with no appeal.[1] Federal marshals were obliged to execute "all warrants and precepts issued under the provisions of this act, when to them directed," under penalty of a $1000 fine, payable to the claimant. No testimony was to be allowed from the alleged fugitive—the very person whose freedom hung in the balance. Slaveholders, on the other hand, did not even have to go to the trouble of appearing personally to testify. An affidavit was enough to win the day.

The authors of the Act had the foresight to expect that some federal marshals in Northern states might be unenthusiastic enforcers. The Act took care of this by requiring that marshals pay the full value of any fugitive who escaped from their custody. It also took aim at anyone who helped fugitives, by imposing on them either a $1,000 fine or a six-month jail sentence. So cynical was the Act that it paid commissioners double for ruling with the slaveholder.

Worst of all, federal officials could summon bystanders to form a "posse" to help capture claimed runaways. For many, that crossed the line.[2] We do not know how many times federal officials actually ordered Northern citizens into a posse, but the statutory command alone laid bare the government's alliance with slave power.[3]

～

On September 27, 1850, just nine days after it went into effect, the Fugitive Slave Act targeted one of its first victims: James Hamlet, a porter at Silas Wood's hotel in Brooklyn.

After tricking Hamlet into leaving his work, and then accusing him of having escaped from Mary Brown, of Baltimore, two years earlier, two US marshals brought him before Federal Commissioner Alexander Gardiner. Asa Childs, an attorney for Hamlet, appeared on the scene but was made to wait in the office of the deputy clerk—just long enough to give the commissioner time to rule against Hamlet and then say to the lawyer, "Sorry, too late."

Hamlet was then immediately dispatched south—so quickly that his employer didn't even have time to get to the commissioner's office, where he might have tried to buy his employee's freedom. Hamlet's wife and two children did not learn what had happened until after Hamlet was taken away. As an added twist, Gardiner ordered a force, at national expense, to protect the slave owner's agent, who feared molestation. This all met slave power's highest hopes.

Word of what had happened traveled fast. On October 3, reporting on the Hamlet case in his Rochester newspaper, Frederick Douglass wrote, "The atrocious work of slave-catching has already commenced. . . . We are all at the mercy of a band of blood-hound commissioners, who by the very act of taking upon themselves that office, prove that they are as ready to enslave the free, as to return the fugitive slave to bondage."[4]

Back in New York City, the Zion Church on Leonard Street hosted a community meeting that quickly raised $800, with which they brought Hamlet back from slave traders in Maryland.[5]

On October 5, after his return, thousands of people, white and Black, attended a celebration for him at a New York City park. A certain Robert Hamilton delivered a poignant welcome and then put into words what many in the audience were surely thinking. He was resolved, he said, "to strike dead the first man who dares to lay his hand upon a brother to throw him into bondage."[6]

When it was his turn to speak, New York City Mayor Caleb S. Woodhull declared that the city's police department would stand down and offer no help in the enforcement of the Fugitive Slave Act.[7]

Among the leaders of the event, according to the account in the *National Anti-Slavery Standard*, were three vice-presidents of the American and Foreign Anti-Slavery Society. One was already a leader in the city's Black community: Louis Napoleon, who two years later would initiate the writ of habeas corpus to liberate the Eight.[8]

~

The following month, in October, 1850, the nation saw the culmination of a case that began with one of the most imaginative escapes in the history of American slavery.

Ellen Craft and her husband, William, had escaped from Dr. Robert Collins and Ira Taylor, their owners, in Macon, Georgia, in 1848. The light-skinned Ellen dressed up as a young white male planter—top hat and all. She was "too ill to travel alone" and so was accompanied by her "slave"—in reality, William.

Illiterate, Ellen bound her right arm in a sling so as not to be asked to sign hotel registers and the like. The pair journeyed from Georgia to

Philadelphia in plain sight. Eventually, they settled in Boston where, within two years, they gained employment, literacy, and status. In the months that followed, the couple appeared before Boston audiences, telling what it was like to be slaves in Georgia, and how they had escaped.

After the passage of the Fugitive Slave Act of 1850, however, two slave catchers, Willis H. Hughes and John Knight, set about to capture the Crafts and return them to their owners, in Georgia. Hughes and Knight arrived in Boston in October of 1850.

They had no idea what they were in for. Boston abolitionists hid the couple, and their lawyers threw up an array of legal roadblocks and counter-measures. They had Hughes and Knight arrested for libel, attempted kidnapping, smoking in the streets, swearing in the streets, carrying a concealed weapon, and "driving fast through the streets," not to mention crossing the bridge over the Charles River without paying the toll (an omission Hughes stoutly denied). An anti-slavery newspaper wryly explained that Hughes and Knight had committed their "fast driving" offenses because they were being chased by a crowd. (It also gave Boston high marks for its traffic laws: "Truly the Bostonians are law-abiding people!")[9]

Worn down and feeling themselves in danger, Hughes and Knight left Boston with little to show for their efforts, and had to post $30,000 in bail for multiple charges against them.[10]

∽

A year after the 1850 Act, a number of New York cases tested the law's limits in ways that attracted national attention. Once again, Erastus Culver appeared in a case of national importance, one of the most notable that took place in the Hudson Valley.

It began when, on August 28, 1851, several armed men came to Poughkeepsie to capture 27-year-old John A. Bolding, who had escaped from slavery four years earlier. Bolding had settled into a quiet life in Poughkeepsie, where he opened a tailor shop and won the affection of the community. A visitor from South Carolina had spotted him in town and alerted his owner, setting into motion an episode that drew national attention.[11]

Bolding was captured by six armed men who would later turn out to be federal officials, led by Marshal H. F. Talmadge. In a tactic praised by the slaveholder press for its adroitness, the men stealthily approached Bolding's tailor shop and whisked him off in a carriage, choreographing the seizure with just enough time to catch the train to New York City, "leaving the sympathizers of the fugitive far distant behind."[12]

Marshal Talmadge and his men took Bolding to New York City, where they brought him before Federal Commissioner John Nelson. Erastus Culver, ever on call for slavery emergencies, appeared as Bolding's attorney, joined by New York County District Attorney Nathaniel Bowditch Blunt (1802–1854).[13]

By modern standards, the hearing was bizarre. One expert after another, physicians and phrenologists, gave testimony about Bolding's light-colored skin. The case turned on whether his complexion was too light for him to qualify as a slave. The rules were clear: If he had no African blood he could not be held, even with a stack of documents proving purchase and ownership. The commissioner concluded that Bolding, born of a slave mother, had enough African blood to be "susceptible" to enslavement.[14] The commissioner put the icing on his ruling by ordering an escort at United States expense, lest there be any rescue attempt.[15]

While this was going on, Culver was negotiating for Bolding's release, trying to raise some $2,000, a hefty amount set by the owner at twice what he had paid for Bolding. The Poughkeepsie community rallied and, with some help from New York and Albany, met the price, including a contribution from Commissioner Nelson.[16]

As an added twist, Bolding later explained his light skin, claiming that his father was a Virginia member of the United States Congress. This set off a newspaper duel, one side asserting (correctly) that there was never a Virginia member of Congress named Bolding, and the other claiming (also correctly) that there was a Congressman from Virginia named James Bouldin—who, for the record, would have been about 32 years old when Bolding was born. We will probably never know the truth.

One major event in the response to the Fugitive Slave Act was the case of the escaped slave Henry "Shadrach" Minkins. The case dominated national headlines in 1851.

Minkins (sometimes referred to as Frederick Wilkins) was born into slavery and owned by John De Bere in Norfolk, Virginia. In May of 1850, Minkins had escaped and reached Boston, where he got a job as a waiter at the upscale Cornhill Coffee House, at the corner of Court Street and Court Square.[17]

The trouble began in February of 1851, when Minkins was captured while serving customers. He was seized by United States Deputy Marshal Patrick Riley and a team of 11 police officers, who brought him to the courthouse for a pro-forma hearing before Federal Commissioner George T. Curtis. Riley expected this to be a brief stop on Minkins's way back to Norfolk. It was indeed brief, but it didn't go the way Riley had expected.

That's because five abolitionist lawyers—Robert Morris, Richard Henry Dana, Jr., Ellis Gray Loring, Charles G. Davis, and Samuel Eliot Sewall— rushed to the courthouse in Minkins's defense. Inside the courthouse, the abolitionists seized Minkins and took him first to Cambridge, then to Concord. From there, he soon found his way to freedom in Canada.[18]

Stung and embarrassed by the Minkins episode, federal officialdom would soon reassert itself, determined to demonstrate its zestful support for the Fugitive Slave Act. It got its chance in what came to be known as the *Sims* case.

In early 1851, the 23-year-old Thomas Sims had stowed away on a brig to escape his owner, James Potter, a Georgia rice planter. Sims reached Boston, but after several weeks, on April 3, his pursuers found and arrested him on a warrant signed by Federal Commissioner George T. Curtis (the same commissioner as in the Minkins case) and activated by Federal Marshal Charles R. Devens, Jr.

After Sims was arrested, officials put a chain around the courthouse in Boston, with hundreds of Boston police and special forces on hand. They were joined by 250 United States troops, who had two pieces of ordinance ready at the nearby Charlestown Navy Yard.[19]

The thought of a temple of justice in chains is chilling. Henry Wadsworth Longfellow found words to describe it: "O City without a soul! When and where will this end? Shame that great Republic, the 'refuge of the oppressed' should stoop so low as to become the hunter of slaves."[20]

After hastening to the courthouse, the attorneys for Sims, led by Samuel Eliot Sewall and Charles G. Loring, ducked under the chains and headed straight for the chambers of Lemuel Shaw, the Chief Justice of the Massachusetts Supreme Judicial Court.

What better place to challenge the Fugitive Slave Act than before the prestigious Massachusetts Supreme Court, whose chief justice, in his writings and beliefs, showed no sympathy to slavery as an institution? Had not a New Jersey court already observed, in 1845, that Justice Shaw was pointedly anti-slavery in his judicial opinions?[21] And did he not move in

New England intellectual and academic circles close to, or at least aware of, the likes of Ralph Waldo Emerson? Serving on the bench alongside Chief Justice Shaw were Justices Theron Metcalf, Richard Fletcher, and George T. Bigelow.[22]

The Massachusetts judges did not spend weeks struggling with the case. That very day, in a lengthy, unapologetic decision written by Chief Justice Shaw, the court denied the writ and upheld the constitutionality of the Fugitive Slave Act.

The court's decision to reject Sim's claims offends modern readers, who cannot be blamed for wishing that Sims's lawyers had argued, on constitutional grounds, against the idea of one person owning another. But that was not an argument that the lawyers could make. The Constitution and Fugitive Slave Act of 1850 had made the obligation to return fugitive slaves the law of the land. All the justices could do in their decision was take on the question of not *whether*, but *how*.

The lawyers did so by arguing—unsuccessfully—that because federal commissioners were not real judges, they should not decide matters dealing with fundamental liberty, and that Congress, as opposed to the states, had no power to promulgate the Act, which in any event lacked safeguards like jury trials and habeas corpus.

Eighteen months later, Shaw's decision, emanating from one of the country's most distinguished courts, would be on the table, staring at Judge Paine as he began deliberating about whether to return the Eight to Julia and Jonathan Lemmon.

Important as it was, the *Sims* decision involved a fugitive, and Justice Shaw went out of his way to point out the difference between a slave who had escaped and one brought to a free state by the slave owner.

In making this distinction, Shaw cited the Aves case, which he had authored on behalf of the Massachusetts high court 16 years earlier, liberating a slave who had *resided* in Massachusetts for a time, having been brought into the state by his owner.[23] In Aves, Shaw made a prophetic aside, noting that the court was not offering "any opinion upon the case, where an owner of a slave in one State is bona fide removing to another State where slavery is allowed, and in so doing necessarily passes through a free State, or where by accident or necessity he is compelled to touch or land therein, remaining no longer than necessary."

It would be hard to craft language that more clearly envisioned the Lemmon case—as Judge Paine must surely have recognized as he began his deliberations in early November. It is almost as if Paine had Justice Shaw sitting opposite him saying, "Elijah, I had little choice but to decide the *Sims* case in the way that I did. But here's a tougher case for you."

Chapter 8

The Court's Ruling

Just a week after having heard arguments in the Lemmon case, Judge Paine had his decision ready. It was a tour de force of judicial writing and reasoning, one that in other hands might have taken months to prepare.

Paine had let it be known that he would be announcing it in court late in the morning of Saturday, November 13, 1852.[1] Word soon got around. A crowd, mostly Black, began to form at City Hall very early in the morning. Among the first people admitted to Judge Paine's courtroom were Juliet and Jonathan Lemmon, along with their lawyer, Henry Lapaugh. Judge Paine arrived next, sometime between 11:00 and 12:00, after which members of the public were admitted. After that, at last, came the Eight, accompanied by Louis Napoleon, their lawyers Erastus Culver and John Jay, and a number of others. Soon the room was full, with overflowing crowds in the adjacent hallways. With everyone in attendance, Judge Paine brought the courtroom to order and, before a rapt audience, began reading his decision aloud.

He opened by straightforwardly summarizing the facts of the case. He then launched into the legal matter at hand, saying that he had to first examine three cases, decided by courts in Indiana, Illinois, and Massachusetts, cited as precedent by Jonathan Lemmon's lawyer. These cases, he said, had been offered to support the proposition that slaveowners from slave states may take their slaves with them from one slave state to another slave state and pass freely through a free state with the slaves with no risk of the slaves gaining freedom.

No one knew better than Judge Paine that the three decisions, being from out-of-state courts, were not binding on him. He appreciated, though,

87

that these cases were instructive, and he did not want to leave any gaps in his decision.

Judge Paine then discussed the three cases.[2]

He began with Indiana's Sewall case (1829). The slaves of William Sewall had run away from him in Indiana while he was taking them from Virginia, a slave state, to live in Illinois, a free state. A lower-court judge from Marion County, Indiana, Bethuel Morris, had liberated the slaves, ruling that the owner had voluntarily given up his Virginia citizenship (and whatever rights he had as a citizen of a slave state) when he made plans to reside in Illinois, a free state, and as he passed through Indiana, also a free state. Needlessly, however, and in language seized upon by Lapaugh, Judge Morris went on to say that the result *might* be different if Sewall had left one slave state to reside in another slave state—as the Lemmons would do 23 years later, in the case at hand.

Judge Paine found the argument unpersuasive. He noted that New York had a statute forbidding slaveowners to bring slaves within its borders, whereas Indiana did not—and that was that.

Judge Paine turned next to Illinois's Willard case (1843). Julius A. Willard had "secreted" a woman slave after she had escaped from her mistress in Illinois, a free state, while traveling from Louisiana to Kentucky, both slave states. Illinois at the time had a statute in place punishing anyone harboring a slave who owed service in a slave state, so Willard was indicted for harboring a runaway.

Judge Paine noted that the law in New York in 1852 was different from the law in Illinois a decade earlier. New York laws not only rejected slavery, he wrote, but they also made it impossible for any slave property to "exist within those limits, except in the single instance of fugitives from labor under the Constitution of the United States." If Illinois chose to enact a law punishing people for harboring slaves, Judge Paine suggested, that was its business. But New York had done the opposite, declaring by statute that with the exception of fugitives, anyone who sets foot on New York soil becomes free. Critically, the Eight were not fugitives, having been brought to New York by their owners.

Judge Paine found the Aves case (1836) to be the most pertinent of the three. In *Aves*, the Massachusetts high court had freed a slave who had *resided* for a time in Massachusetts. Paine noted that the Massachusetts court had gone out of its way to say that it was leaving open the question of freedom for slaves who merely passed through Massachusetts with their owners, in transit to another state—the very question that 16 years later would be laid at Paine's doorstep.[3]

Paine then turned to one of the slaveowners' postulates: namely, that the Eight, "being property," by "the law of nations" could be brought by their owners from one slave state to another slave state, free of any risk that they could be confiscated in New York.

By postulating that the slaves were property, and that owners could transport property under the law of nations, the lawyers for Jonathan Lemmon had inaptly put the cart before the horse. Paine set matters aright, meeting the lawyers on their own ground. "Writers of the highest authority on the law of nations," he said, referring to Vattel and Pufendorf, "agree that strangers have a right to pass with their property through the territories of a nation." But he then noted an important fact: "The property which the writers on the law of nations speak of is merchandise or inanimate things that by the law of nature belong to their owners." Nowhere, he wrote, did authorities on the law of nations—and, by extension, the law of nature—"speak of a right to pass through a foreign country with slaves as *property*."

This brought Judge Paine to an important conclusion. "It can scarcely, therefore, be said," he told the courtroom, "that when writers on the law of nations maintain that strangers have a right to pass through a country with their merchandise or property, they thereby maintain their right to pass with their slaves." This in fact was impossible, he continued, because the authorities had all agreed on one fundamental principle: "that by the law of nations alone, *no one can have property in slaves*."

As soon as Judge Paine uttered those words, many of the people of color in the courtroom shed tears.

∾

When Judge Paine declared that there could be no property in slaves, he was relying on solid legal precedent as well.

In 1835, not long after New York had abolished slavery, its highest court had written, "Property, strictly speaking, in the person of a human being cannot exist."[4] And less than a decade before that, Chancellor James Kent, of New York, had written in his *Commentaries on American Law* that under English common law, "one man could not have a property in another, for men were not the subject of property."[5] That was far short, however, of a ruling that a slaveowner may not even pass through New York with a slave, legally owned under another state's law.

Before abolition, New York judges, like those in the South, had considered slaves property.[6] There were many decisions from Southern courts proclaiming as much, but the Court of Appeals of Kentucky had articulated the point pithily in *Tyson v. Ewing*.[7] "Slaves," the Court wrote, "although protected in life and limb, by the humanity of our laws, are, nevertheless, regarded as property, in the strictest sense of the term. And so far as it respects the form of the action, we do not feel ourselves authorized to discriminate between them and any other kind of property."

The enslavement of people as property had been a subject of uncomfortable debate among the states since the inception of the republic. Writing in 1788, in *Federalist 54*, James Madison had put the matter on the table in the run-up to the ratification of the Constitution. "We must deny the fact," he declared, "that slaves are considered merely as property, and in no respect whatever as persons. The true state of the case is, that they partake of both these qualities: being considered by our laws, in some respects, as persons, and in other respects as property."

This dichotomy between people and property raised legal questions in slave states. How could a claim for freedom ever be raised in a court of law? For centuries, the traditional legal device to test confinement is to invoke the writ of habeas corpus and force someone to legally justify the cause for confinement. But when it came to enslavement, there was a catch. Only *persons* could bring on a writ of habeas corpus. A piece of property could not. In Southern courts, habeas corpus would work, for example, to test whether authorities could confine a free white person in jail on a criminal charge. But the writ could not be used by a slave contesting their owner's title.

Slavery jurisdictions considered it imperative that the enslaved be regarded only as property, to be sold, traded, inherited, mortgaged, and the like. Only a person, and not a slave, could bring a lawsuit, let alone a suit for freedom, in most such courts. As the Supreme Court of Georgia explained in 1831, "The writ of habeas corpus is intended for the protection of the personal liberty of freemen, and never was designed or used to try any right of property." A Virginia court put the disability more broadly: "Persons in the status of slavery are not entitled to any of the remedies of freemen: they are slaves whatever may be their right to freedom, and have no civil privileges or immunities. . . . While they remain in the status of slavery they have no personal rights, and of course no remedy by action for the redress of injuries."[8]

The Georgia case is particularly interesting because the judge was keenly aware that a justice system could not credibly close all courthouse doors to someone making a bid for freedom. It is one thing to deny a claim after a hearing, but quite another to say that there is no forum in which to even make the claim. And yet the judge seems to have felt boxed in by labels. Had he allowed an alleged slave to proceed by way of habeas corpus, he would have acknowledged her to be a person, as opposed to a piece of property. A ruling of that sort would undermine a pillar of the institution of slavery. He resolved the case by denying habeas corpus but he pointed out that there were other remedies available, such as a regular jury trial, as in any dispute over property. There were also exceptions to the slave's status as chattel, as when the slave committed a crime or was counted as three-fifths of a person for purposes of congressional representation.

Concerns of that kind did not affect Judge Paine, for whom the writ of habeas corpus was a proper way to make a claim for freedom.[9] Starting with the writ, he devoted considerable energy to it in his decision, dealing with how to think about slaves and property in the context of "the law of nature," or "natural law."

But what did he mean by that?

 ❧

Lawyers and judges today rarely speak of "natural law," but almost everybody would agree that some kind of higher principle should stand in the way of laws that are immoral or crazy.[10]

Today we might call such laws "unconstitutional," often on due process or equal-protection grounds. But that was not possible in the case of slavery. Given that it was contemplated in the Constitution, how could judges call slavery unconstitutional?

As Judge Paine knew when he was considering *Lemmon*, he could not. He supported his decision, in part, by turning to natural law.

The concept has had a place in culture and jurisprudence for a very long time. More than 2000 years ago, Aristotle described it as a timeless principle. "Not of to-day or yesterday it is," he wrote, "but lives eternal: none can date its birth."[11] People see this sense of timelessness in the Ten Commandments.

By the time Judge Paine set out to write his *Lemmon* decision, the concept of natural law had gone through several incarnations. In 2 Romans 14:15, St. Paul had described it to Christians as the law "written on their hearts." Cicero, for his part, had declared, "we are born for justice, and that right is founded not in opinion but in nature. . . . Nor is it one law at Rome and another at Athens; one law to-day and another hereafter; but the same law, everlasting and unchangeable."[12]

With the growth of Christianity, natural law took on an increasingly theological character, through the teachings of St. Augustine (354–430) and, later, St. Thomas Aquinas (1225–1274). Those teachings would influence legal and political thinkers for centuries. Edward Coke (1552–1634), the great jurist of the Elizabethan era, proclaimed that the eternal and unchanging nature of natural law superseded any earthly law created by a sovereign or parliament. By the 18th century, the concept was appearing in debates about slavery. In 1765, William Blackstone memorably used it to condemn slavery in humanistic terms, describing slavery as "repugnant to reason, and the principles of natural law."[13]

Judge Paine understood the many resonances of the term and used it or its equivalent more than 20 times in his *Lemmon* decision, in each instance making the same point: that freedom, not slavery, is our natural condition.

But that didn't mean that slavery couldn't exist. Judge Paine acknowledged, as had many jurists before him, that slavery could still be imposed and sustained through statutes that explicitly allow slavery—enactments that amounted to "positive law," rather than natural law. Liberty may be our natural condition, but a state or country was free to pass statutes (positive laws) authorizing slavery, as the Southern states had done, and as the Constitution had recognized. But in the absence of such positive laws, the condition of liberty subsisted, because it is our default condition.

This applied to the Lemmons, he reasoned. They had brought their slaves into the state of New York, a jurisdiction with no laws allowing slavery. When New York had abolished slavery in 1827, Judge Paine noted, slavery's platform in the state had collapsed, creating a void—and all that was left was natural law, which on its own does not support slavery. For good measure, he continued, emphasizing that New York had even gone a step further, filling the void with a positive prohibition *against* slavery.[14] Anybody—and everybody—in New York, therefore, had to be considered free, except fugitive slaves.

But what of the laws of Virginia? The Lemmons claimed they acquired good and legal title to the slaves, as recognized by Virginia. Paine acknowledged that under Virginia law, the Lemmons were lawfully free to own human property in Virginia. New York could do nothing about that. Nevertheless, he said, Virginia could not impose its concepts of human ownership on New York, a free state. Virginia residents could not bring Virginia laws with them wherever they went. To do so, Paine continued, would create "a perfect confusion of laws."

As for the universally accepted concept that people could pass through other sovereignties with their property, Paine agreed—provided that their property consisted of "merchandise or inanimate things." But neither of those terms, he wrote, could be applied to slaves, who were human beings (see figure 8.1).

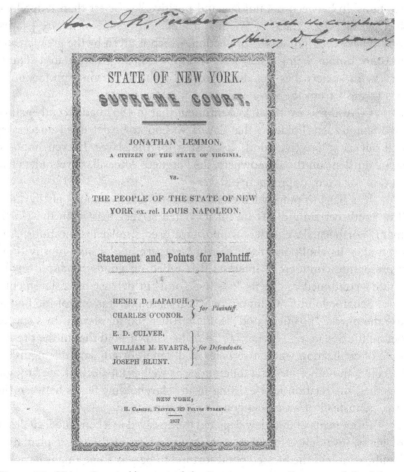

Figure 8.1. Henry Lapaugh's copy of the Lemmon case. Courtesy of the Library of Virginia (Accession 44648, Virginia Attorney General's Records Regarding the Lemmon Slave Case).

Not surprisingly, slave power chose to understand natural law very differently.

For the supporters of enslavement, natural law supported the institution, which they considered the natural order of things. On this point they, too, could cite Aristotle, who had famously declared slavery expedient and just—a natural condition in which some are simply born and destined to live.[15]

From the 19th-century slaveholder's perspective, no one expressed the relationship between natural law and positive law better than Judge John B. O'Neall (1793–1863) of South Carolina: "In a state of nature [slaves] would have the right of self-protection, which is given by the great creator to every human being. Their transfer from a state of nature to a state of slavery in society, has not destroyed the right of personal protection; it has taken it from the slave and given it to the master."[16]

O'Neall was expressing a sentiment that in 1852 had recently gained favor among slaveholders—that slavery was not to be defended a necessary evil but as a "positive good," a blessing for the slaves. It even imposed some burdens on the slaveowners, they argued: After all, slaveholders had to care for aged, unproductive slaves.

It is hard to pinpoint the onset of this "positive good" justification. The South certainly didn't invent it. When slavery existed in the North, many Northern slaveholders would have used similar justifications. And even after its abolition in the North, Northern apologists—mostly those representing commercial interests that relied on goods produced in the South—continued to cite its "positive good" in defense of enslavement.

Senator John C. Calhoun, of South Carolina, was one of the first to use the phrase "positive good" as the justification for slavery. In a speech before the Senate on February 6, 1837, he said, "I hold that in the present state of civilization where two races of different origin, and distinguished by color, and other physical differences, as well as intellectual, are brought together, the relation now existing in the slaveholding States between the two, is, instead of an evil, a good—a positive good."[17]

Proponents of this view depicted the enslaved as a contented, civilized, religious, loyal, cheerful, banjo-playing members of the larger plantation family, who had the blessed good fortune to be—as some might have put it—lifted out of barbarism, and to be guided, cared for, and protected by white superiors. In 1835, addressing his state legislature, George McDuffie, the governor of South Carolina, made the standard case, extolling the blessings of slavery: "Our slaves are cheerful, contented and happy, much beyond the general condition of the human race, except where those foreign intruders and fatal ministers of mischief, the emancipationists, like their arch-prototype in the Garden of Eden, and actuated by no less envy, have tempted them to aspire above the condition to which they have been assigned in the order of Providence."[18]

So it went—in sermons, editorials, and court decisions.

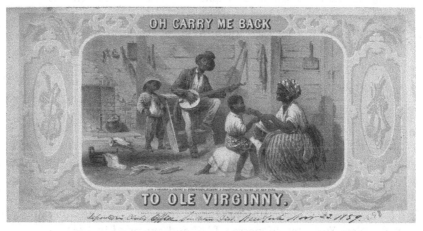

Figure 8.2. "Oh Carry Me Back to Ole Virginny," tobacco package label detail, 1859. Library of Congress, Prints and Photographs Division, LC-DIG-ppmsca-08346.

Figure 8.3. "The Breakdown," *Harper's Weekly*, April 13, 1861, 232.

Not surprisingly, the "positive good" paradigm was picked up by Southern judges. Prominent among them was Chancellor William Harper, of South Carolina, who in 1838 used it stridently to defend slavery:

> Slavery . . . has done more to elevate a degraded race in the scale of humanity; to tame the savage; to civilize the barbarous; to soften the ferocious; to enlighten the ignorant, and to spread the blessings of Christianity among the heathen, than all the missionaries that philanthropy and religion have ever sent forth. . . . Can there be a doubt of the immense benefit which has been conferred on the race, by transplanting them from their native, dark, and barbarous regions, to the American continent and islands?[19]

Wisely, Judge Paine did not base his decision entirely on the lofty grounds of natural law. A superb legal technician, he supported his ruling with a strong pillar, a New York statute. A critic might challenge his decision insofar as it rested on what they could call a philosophical abstraction like natural law. But there is nothing more mundane, and unimpeachable, than the New York statute, passed 1817 and amended in 1841.

When originally passed in 1817, New York's abolition law had included certain exemptions, one of which allowed out-of-state slaveowners to bring their slaves into New York for up to nine months. It was a concession that allowed Southerners to visit and vacation in the state—and bring their slaves with them. This exception, Judge Paine noted, would have applied to the Lemmons and the Eight, but it was no longer in force, because the exception had been repealed 11 years earlier, in 1841.

Any law repealing an exemption implies total, not partial, repeal. So in the aftermath of the repeal of the nine-month exemption, Judge Paine did not see how he could allow slaveowners to bring slaves into New York for *any* period of time—not even a two-day sojourn, a one-hour travel tour, or a five-minute stopover. Stripped of the exemption, he wrote, the law removed all ambiguity: The moment that people enslaved in other states set foot anywhere on New York soil, they were free.[20] "It is impossible," he declared, "to make this more clear."

And with that, it was time at last for Judge Paine to read out his verdict. "My judgment," he concluded, "is that the eight colored persons mentioned in the writ be discharged."

Exultation followed. "Scarcely had his Honor pronounced the concluding words, which decide the fate of the women and the children, than there arose a wild hubbub, and cries of 'good, good,' and other expressions of approbation. The crowd outside and inside the room, appeared to be intoxicated with joy, and it was some minutes before order could be restored."[21]

Lapaugh wanted the Eight to remain in custody until he could go to a higher court in New York. This was simply a way of trying to keep the Eight in New York rather than allowing them to leave for Canada, beyond the jurisdiction of the court. Lapaugh knew that Judge Paine would not order it, and so he asked that counsel (Jay and Culver) retain custody. Jay said even if he had the authority to do that, he would not. Culver agreed with Jay, adding, with a touch of feistiness, that he would be pleased nonetheless to meet Lapaugh in a higher court.[22]

One supporter of the Eight who was in the courtroom that day—Reverend James W. C. Pennington, a colleague of Louis Napoleon—later recorded his own recollections of that moment. He wrote, "One old coloured lady said, 'Well, if that judge don't get to heaven, no man will ever enter into that holy place.' Another said, 'God will surely bless the soul of that judge.' And another said, 'Well, that judge shall never pay another cent for cleaning his office again as long as I live.' "[23]

Despite their jubilation at the outcome of the case, everyone in the courtroom knew that the ultimate fate of the Eight, now free, remained uncertain. What lay in store for them now, with their connection to the Lemmons—and life as they had known it since birth—severed?

Judge Paine remarked that no one would be more desirous than he to see some means provided for the temporary maintenance for the Eight. "I must confess," he said, "that I feel much distress, in regard to the decision, that these persons may not be very happily situated thereafter."

Henry Lapaugh, the attorney for Julia and Jonathan Lemmon, seems to have hoped in this moment that the Eight, as they contemplated the upheaval their lives were about to go through, might have second thoughts. So he approached them one last time and asked if they would not prefer to return to the familiar life—of bondage!—they had always known with the Lemmons.

The Eight, predictably, declined. Instead, they soon made their way out of the courtroom and were placed in coaches by Louis Napoleon. As *The New York Times* described the scene:

[The Eight] were escorted to carriages, and rode off as free as if they had never known bondage. Before the colored people were fairly seated in their carriages, they were surrounded by a large crowd of men, women and children of their own color, who cheered them, waved their handkerchiefs, and tossed their caps, in the highest glee. The liberated bowed their acknowledgment to their friends and drove off, looking as happy as possible. A hundred or so of their African friends ran after the hacks, till they reached the Broadway gate of the Park, where they, of necessity, left them to pursue their way out into the free world.[24]

For the Eight, surviving in court was a triumph. But surviving out in the larger world, now that they were free, was a frightful challenge. Nancy and Emeline had no immediate way to support themselves and their charges.

Fortunately, some in the community offered help. On November 24, the *New York Tribune* addressed the plight of the Eight, whom it described as "poor, untaught, destitute women and helpless children" who were facing a hard winter "on the highway of responsible and independent life."[25] The *Tribune* then made an appeal to its readers. "Who will give $10, or $5, or even $1," the paper wrote, "for the relief and sustenance of these poor people? Do let us try to raise them $500 to-day, so that they may have it for a Thanksgiving present to-morrow."

A Lemmon Slave Fund was soon created, with John Jay as its treasurer, and as a result of the appeal and other fundraising efforts the Eight ultimately received $1,000 in donations. These came largely from what the abolitionist minister Samuel May, in his book *The Fugitive Slave Law and its Victims*, described as "the better disposed but less wealthy class." John Jay himself contributed $350 (see figure 8.4).[26]

The Eight desperately needed the money, not only for their daily needs but also to help fund their flight to points north. As their supporters surely explained to them, they could not possibly remain in New York, where they would be vulnerable to appellate-court reversals and more immediate physical dangers, as posed by slavecatchers.

Their obvious pathway was the Underground Railroad from New York to Canada, where they could enjoy their newly won freedom. That portion of the Railroad was a lot safer than further south. They also

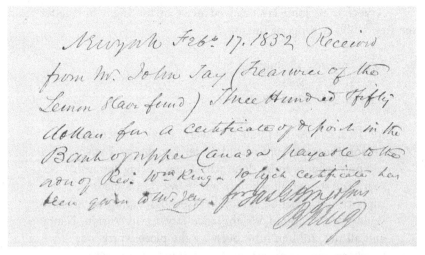

Figure 8.4. John Jay's $350 contribution to the Eight, reading "Received from Mr. John Jay (Treasure of the Lemon Slave fund) Three Hundred Fifty dollars for a certificate of deposit in the Bank of Upper Canada payable to the son of Rev. Wm. King. Which certificate has been given to Mr. Jay," February 17, 1852. Jay Family Papers, Rare Book & Manuscript Library, Columbia University in the City of New York.

soon got help from an unexpected source. Word of the Eight's victory in court had been reported nationally, and when a certain Richard Johnson (formerly "Levi"), who was working as a waiter in Cleveland, had heard people speaking of the case, he realized that one of the Eight was his sister, Nancy. He hastened to New York to help get the Eight to Canada.[27]

Very little information survives about how the Eight fared after that. What we know is this. At some point after being set free, the Eight were taken by Rev. James Pennington and his wife, Almira, to Hartford, Connecticut, where they were put in the care of Black families for a number of weeks. To help these families defray the cost of supporting the Eight, Pennington received financial help from Horace Greeley. In December, at a meeting that included Pennington, Richard Johnson, Louis Napoleon, and Charles Bennet Ray, of the New York Vigilance Society, it was agreed that the Eight would be taken from Connecticut to Buxton, Upper Canada, with Johnson accompanying them. Plans were also made at that time to purchase a plot for the Eight in an area in Buxton known as the Elgin settlement.[28]

A year later, John Jay received news of the Eight in a letter from the Rev. William King, of Buxton.[29]

John Jay Esq., 48 Bukman St.
New York, U. States
Buxton, Dec 22nd, 1853

My Dear Sir, As one year has nearly expired since the
Lemon Freemen were placed under my charge, I wish
to know what is to be done with them during the next
year; The sooner all who are able to work are made self-
supporting the better. Nancy Johnson has supported herself
since April, Edmund Wright since July. Lewis Wright, Nancy
and all the children have been on the place which was
purchased for them last winter, working in common. There
has not been much cleared, nor will there be a great deal
done by May of improvement till each person is placed on
his own proportion of the land; where the proceeds of his
labour will go to his own individual support; As the women
cannot support themselves and their children, and the men
do not seem inclined to support any but themselves. It
would be necessary to make some arrangements to keep
the children at school while the parents who are willing
to go out and support themselves; They are all willing
who are able to work to support themselves and save what
money is coming to them till they begin housekeeping
regularly; I have not provided for them any winter clothes
nor made any provision beyond the first of January, nor
will I do anything more till I hear from you; unless give
them provisions. I will send you their account on the first
of January. I have read this letter to the women who think
the best thing all of them can do is to work for themselves.
(Nancy is at home spending the Christmas Holidays) They
desire to be kindly remembered to you and the rest of the
committee. I remain, Yours truly, Wm. King

After that, the Eight largely disappear from the historical record.

✀

Life played out very differently for Juliet and Jonathan Lemmon.

After Judge Paine read his decision in the courtroom, the Lemmons "appeared to be much dejected."[30] But many people rallied behind them, in not only the South but also the North.

In New York, several newspapers loudly criticized Judge Paine's decision. The *New York Courier and Enquirer*, for example, wrote that it "would do more to separate the North and South than any other event which has happened since the birth of our confederation and will open at once the gaping breach which has but now with so much solicitude been closed."[31]

The *New York Day Book*, for its part, raged against the ruling, calling it "one of the most horrible pieces of cruelty ever perpetrated in a civilized community." The paper continued, "The case is no more nor less than robbing an American family, on their way from Virginia to Texas, of all their property. . . . All this is done under the pretence and in the name of 'philanthropy.' Horrible! Most horrible! A family robbed, mother and children destroyed—and honest, faithful men turned out of employment, out of doors, and out of LIVING! This is abolitionism."

Much more succinctly, and in a considerably more sober tone, the *New York Weekly Herald* denounced the decision as "coerced by law, not governed in justice."[32]

Some of the harshest criticism, however, appeared in the *New York Journal of Commerce*, the New York mercantile community's paper of record. Judge Paine, the newspaper said, had robbed the Lemmons of their property. What was worrisome about that, the paper declared, was that it would discourage slaveowners in the future from traveling through New York. In other words, it would have unfortunate consequences for commercial transportation in the state.

Worse yet, if New York persisted in what the *Journal* described as its "unneighborly and impolite" behavior toward the South, it might even prompt the creation of a transportation line from Baltimore to New Orleans, which would naturally be bad for business in New York.

Remarkably, the *Journal* then went on to claim, with no apparent irony, that such a line might even be created for not only for commercial interests but also for altruistic reasons. "Humanity would require us to be willing that the proposed Baltimore and New Orleans line should be established," the paper declared. "The transit of slaves, by convenient and rapid steamers to the distant South, is certainly more to their comfort than to march them across the country or to convey them in sailing vessels to the same destination."[33]

But the *Journal* did more than just publish criticism of Judge Paine's decision. Immediately after the Eight were freed, it launched a campaign to collect $5,000 to compensate Julia and Jonathan Lemmon for the loss of their property.

New York's merchants quickly opened their pocketbooks, wide. A Southern newspaper reported that the response was so heartening that by November 19, 1852—only six days after Judge Paine's decision—the subscription fund had reached $4,230. Judge Paine himself contributed $100.[34] Southern newspapers began publishing the names of the merchants who had contributed to the fund—and those who had declined.[35]

Four days later, on November 23, 1852, the *New York Tribune* reported with some dismay that the campaign had awarded the Lemmons the full $5,000, which, it claimed, exceeded by at least $2,000 the price that would have been paid for the Eight in any "slave mart in the world." Scornfully, the newspaper predicted that the New York merchants would end up making money out of their gift, because it would win them even more Southern business than they'd had before.

On November 24, 1852, after receiving the $5,000, Jonathan and Julia Lemmon signed an indemnification bond—in effect, a contract—acknowledging that they had been compensated "in full" for the value of the Eight. In exchange, they agreed to manumit them.[36]

Newspapers in the North and South editorialized on Judge Paine's decision in a strikingly polarized manner—one that says a lot about the national breach at the time.

A North Carolina newspaper attacked Judge Paine not only for taking property from the Lemmons but also because the Eight, the writer said, were the real victims. "These poor negroes are more unfortunate than Mr. and Mrs. Lemmon—the hardship is on their side." Satisfied that slavery is a far better state for the Eight than freedom, the writer predicted, in cartoon-trope style, that "the poor things will try, and try in vain, and a thousand times will they wish themselves 'back in old Virginny' but long before old age comes upon them, their bones will be mouldering in the grave." The writer continued, assailing Jay and Culver as well:

> [The] philanthropy of Mr. Jay, Mr. Culver and Judge Paine has robbed Mrs. Lemmon of all her property but it has ruined the negroes. Had they been let alone, they would have been useful, contented and happy, and probably lived to a good old age; now they will be of no earthly benefit to themselves, their race or

mankind. They will live miserably, be a curse to society, and die as soon as rum, debauchery, vice and crime, can kill them.

The following day the *National Anti-Slavery Standard*, taking a shot at the *New York Journal of Commerce*, presented a very different but similarly staunch take on the decision: "However pitiful, and sordid, and base, as is this whole business, we rejoice at such a conclusion of it. It is much to have the thin and sleazy veil of hypocrisy lifted from the effete, contemptible and sniveling pietism so well represented by the *Journal of Commerce*, and the real hearty love of its class for Slavery, for its own sake and for what it will bring, so completely exposed in its own naked deformity."[37]

By signing the indemnification bond after being fully compensated, the Lemmons had taken themselves out of the case. But probably not without some satisfaction. They had done well in the aftermath of Judge Paine's decision, after all—so well, in fact, that they decided not to move to Texas and instead returned home to Virginia.[38]

Chapter 9

Life, Liberty, or Property

Back in Virginia, having received compensation for the Eight, the Lemmons were probably quite happy to put their case behind them. But others in the state, and throughout the South, were not.

Judge Paine's decision was not behind them but in front of them, a thorn in the side of slave power. Owners no longer felt free to take their slaves, even if only in transit, through New York—or, for that matter, through any free state that decided to follow Judge Paine's ruling.

This restriction made the opponents of slavery happy, even on the other side of the Atlantic. Writing in Scotland, in the *Aberdeen Journal*, one anti-slavery editorialist commented with some satisfaction on the new restrictions. "This is something," he wrote, adding that it was "likely to prove an inconvenient something."[1]

The general reaction in the slaveholding South was outrage. Judge Paine's decision, critics complained, not only violated property rights but also threatened one of the purposes of the Union: free and safe travel across all state lines. Southerners bringing their slaves North, they said, would have to move about "skulking and hiding from the watchdogs of abolitionism."[2]

For Georgia's governor, Howell Cobb, the matter was existential. "If deliberately and wantonly persisted in," he declared, the enforcement of Judge' Paine's decision in the North would be "a just cause of war."[3]

The outcry against the decision was particularly loud in Virginia. "This is the most appalling decision that has ever been made by an American jurist, against the rights of property," the *Virginia Enquirer* declared on

November 20, commending to the Virginia legislature its views on the decision. Two days later, the *Richmond Dispatch* joined in. "There can be no more reason or justice in depriving Lemmon of his slaves," the paper wrote, "than there would be in depriving Judge Paine of his riding horse, should he happen to ride to this State."[4]

On December 17, 1852, just weeks after Judge Paine read his ruling in court, Virginia Governor Joseph Johnson stepped in, urging the Virginia legislature to sponsor an appeal to a higher court in New York, considering that Julia and Jonathan, having been fully compensated, were out of the case and that it was up to the State of Virginia to carry on the fight. Paine's decision, Johnson said, would hurt relations among the states, would seriously affect the value of slave property, and, above all, was unconstitutional.[5]

Three months later, on March 23, 1853, the Virginia legislature authorized Johnson to assign counsel for the appeal.[6]

In making its appeal, Virginia was required to post a bond as security for costs, and it put up $250. Erastus Culver, however, deemed the sum inadequate and returned it—with a lecture. "Instead of seeking to reverse decisions of New-York Courts," he wrote, "in which she has no legitimate concern, [Virginia] would be much better engaged in reversing her own decisions, especially those that imprisoned a woman for teaching Virginia children to read." A sardonic gem, that remark tells us something about Culver that we cannot otherwise appreciate from this distance: his feistiness.[7]

Virginia's appeal proceeded nonetheless. And the stakes were much higher now. The parties involved in the Lemmon case were no longer the Lemmons and the Eight. They were New York and Virginia—and, by extension, the North and the South.

It would take several years before the case would reach its first level of appeal. In the meantime, Rev. James Pennington (figure 9.1), the stalwart associate of Louis Napoleon in the Lemmon case, found himself in 1854 turning to John Jay and Erastus Culver for legal help in a slavery case involving his own family.

Pennington understood the institution of slavery well. Decades earlier, he had been enslaved himself, by a certain Col. Frisby Tilghman, of Hagerstown, Maryland. At the time, Pennington's last name was Pembroke, but he escaped in 1827 and subsequently changed his name.

Figure 9.1. Portrait of James W. C. Pennington (1807–1870) by John Robert Dicksee. © National Portrait Gallery, London.

In May of 1854, Pennington learned that his brother, Stephen Pembroke, and his two sons, Robert and Jacob, had been arrested in New York as fugitive slaves. Pennington had not seen his brother in 27 years and had never seen his nephews. The three had run away from enslavement in Maryland and, after having been pursued by slave catchers, had fallen into the grip of federal authorities determined to have them reinslaved.[8]

This time, the foe was Federal Commissioner George W. Morton. It was not the first time Jay and Culver had encountered him, having had a taste of his foul sense of justice in 1852, in the fugitive-slave proceeding against Horace Preston, several months before the Lemmon case (see chapter 4). Following Morton's contemptible conduct (and ruling) in that case, Jay and Culver had called him out in a letter to the public, shining the searchlights into the dark corners in which he operated.[9]

This time, Morton had teamed up with Federal Marshal Abraham Y. Hillyer. When it came to dealing with alleged fugitives, they had the power, and for the most part, the pair could act with impunity—one armed with a gavel, the other with a gun.

Learning that Pennington's brother and nephews were in the hands of slave catchers and federal officials, Culver and Jay sped to Marshal Hillyer's office, where the Pembrokes were being held. On the street, Jay met Commissioner Morton, who told him that he had made his ruling. That part was true. He went on to say that the Pembrokes had not wanted a lawyer, and that they had been removed from the building. That was untrue.

After speaking with Pennington's wife, Jay had good reason to distrust Morton's account. He then asked Hillyer's deputies where the Pembrokes were being held. They too told him, falsely, that the Pembrokes had been removed from the building.

Culver checked around and found the Pembrokes locked up inside the building. They told him they had not declined counsel; on the contrary, they were eager for a lawyer and for their freedom.

At that point, Culver rushed to the chambers of New York State Superior Court Judge Murray Hoffman, who signed a writ of habeas corpus ordering the captives produced. The federal officials—obviously aware that Jay and Culver were trying to keep the matter alive and before an unbiased tribunal—moved quickly enough to get the Pembrokes out of the building and on their way south before Jay could serve the writ.

Knowing that Hillyer and Morton held all the cards, and that under federal law Morton's ruling was final and could not be appealed, Culver was unwilling to simply sit still for it. He wrote a letter to the *Anti-Slavery Bugle*, exposing how he had been lied to by the officials.[10]

The community succeeded in buying Stephen from his owner but failed with respect to his sons.[11]

On Stephen's return, there was a celebratory gathering at Rev. Pennington's church. The group passed resolutions stating that "the fugitive slave law would no longer be executed except through the infamy of lies and subterfuges by United States officers." The meeting finally adjourned, pending a proposal to raise a committee to consider forming "an organization to resist the fugitive slave bill by force."

At the gathering, Culver spoke on behalf of the victims, stating that physical self-defense might well have a place in these circumstances.[12] A comment like that reveals the level of frustration with sham rendition proceedings conducted by federal commissioners.

The Pembroke proceedings drew a headline in the *New York Tribune*'s May 27, 1854, edition that read, "Three More Victims Hurried into Slavery." A headline of that kind spoke volumes. Decreasingly disposed toward slavery, many if not most New Yorkers thought it shameful that slaves could be captured and sent into slavery in a process marked above all by swiftness and cynicism.

Given the tilt of the legal playing field, Jay and Culver could not (nor could anyone) save a fugitive from recaption in a proceeding before the commissioner. Nonetheless, they did do something that in the long run would count for a lot: they exposed what was going on behind closed doors, where defenseless victims were pitted in shadowy proceedings against the full force of the federal government.

~

The Lemmon case was just one part of the larger national struggle over slavery that would play out in the 1850s. In this struggle, no case was more important than *Dred Scott v. Sandford*, which would reach the US Supreme Court in 1857 (see figure 9.2).[13]

The details of the case are well known. In the 1830s, Dred Scott, a slave from Missouri, was taken by his owner to Illinois, a free state, where they resided for several years. After being brought back to Missouri, in 1840, Scott sued for his freedom, claiming that his residence in Illinois had made him a free citizen.

The United States Supreme court rejected Scott's suit, in racist language that marks the case as a prime candidate for the most reprehensible in American law. At once perpetuating slavery and denying citizenship to both free and enslaved Negroes, Chief Justice Roger Taney declared that when the United States Constitution was written, the Negro was considered a subordinate and inferior class of being. Constitutionally speaking, he wrote, this meant that the Negro had "no rights which the white man was bound to respect," and that the Negro "might justly and lawfully be reduced to slavery for his benefit."

This language did not bode well for the survival of Judge Paine's decision. With good reason, anti-slavery interests feared that even if Virginia lost its appeal in the New York appellate courts, slave power could hasten to the Supreme Court, which could then overturn Judge Paine's decision and, worse yet, nationalize slavery.

But that's getting ahead of the story. When the Supreme Court decided *Dred Scott*, on March 5, 1857, the Lemmon case was still seven months away from reaching its first level of appeal in New York.

The interplay between the two cases is notable.

When the Missouri Supreme Court first ruled against Dred Scott, in April of 1846, six years before the Lemmon case arose, the justices used language that we today find astonishing:[14]

> As to the consequences of slavery, they are much more hurtful to the master than the slave. There is no comparison between the slave of the United States and the cruel, uncivilized negro in Africa. When the condition of our slaves is contrasted with the state of their miserable race in Africa; when their civilization, intelligence and instruction in religious truths are considered, and the means now employed to restore them to the country from which they have been torn, bearing with them the blessings of civilized life, we are almost persuaded that the introduction of slavery amongst us was, in the providences of God, who makes the evil passions of men subservient to his own glory, a means of placing that unhappy race within the pale of civilized nations.[15]

Scott, of course, didn't buy that reasoning, and in 1853 he sued for his freedom in the Circuit Court for the United States in the District of Missouri.[16] His purported owner raised a procedural argument: because Scott was a Negro slave of African descent, he was not and could not be a citizen of Missouri (or of any state), and therefore could not sue in federal court.

The federal district court did not accept that argument—but it ruled against Scott nonetheless. Judge Robert W. Wells wrote that Scott did have capacity to sue in federal court, but rejected his "once free, always free" argument.[17]

Scott then appealed to the United States Supreme Court, which heard the case in February 1856. By then, the Lemmon case had been awaiting its first level of appeal in New York for more than three years.

Shortly after the Supreme Court heard the argument in *Dred Scott*, Joseph Blunt, one of the lawyers for the Eight, asked the Supreme Court to postpone its decision. He was hoping that if the Lemmon case could be argued at its first appellate level in New York before the Supreme Court rendered its decision in *Dred Scott*, New York might provide some anti-slavery ammunition for any Supreme Court justices disposed that way. Ideally, New York would have presented its views in the *Dred Scott* case directly to the Supreme Court, but New York was not a participant in the case and had no standing to be heard. The next best course was to have the Supreme Court hold up its decision in *Dred Scott* until after New York presented its views in the Lemmon case itself at the first appellate level.

The Supreme Court did not grant Blunt's request. But in May of 1856 it did order reargument in *Dred Scott*, on a pivotal jurisdictional point: Whether Scott, as a Negro, was a "citizen," able to sue in a federal court.[18]

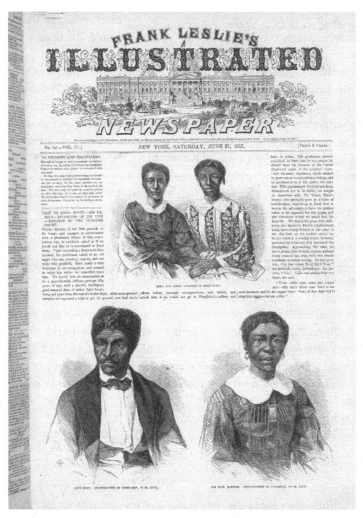

Figure 9.2. Dred Scott and his wife Harriet (bottom), and their children Eliza and Lizzie (top), originally published in *Frank Leslie's Illustrated Newspaper*, June 27, 1857. The New York Public Library, General Research Division, b16468401.

On March 5, 1857, the Supreme Court handed down its now-infamous *Dred Scott* decision. Taney, for the majority, agreed with the slaveowner that Scott lacked capacity to bring the suit. That would have been enough to decide the case—but with noteworthy aggressiveness, Taney felt motivated to go further and to nullify the Missouri Compromise, by which the Congress restricted slavery in some territories. Elevating the slaveowners' property rights over the life and liberty rights of slaves, Taney stated that prohibiting slavery in the territories violated slaveowners' Fifth Amendment property rights. Those rights, he contended, guarantee that no person—which was to say, no *slaveowner*—should "be deprived of life, liberty, or *property* without due process of law."

Northern editorial writers had expected nothing less from the Supreme Court, given its track record.[19] The *New-York Tribune* almost immediately put the case in historical perspective. "Scott and his family," the paper wrote, "must henceforth consider themselves as forever kicked out of all claims to 'be ever thought of or spoken of, except as property.' "[20]

Frederick Douglass minced no words. The decision, he said, considered enslaved Negro people as property "in the same sense that horses, sheep, and swine are property," with the result being "that slavery may go in safety anywhere under the star-spangled banner."[21]

What motivated Taney to go to these lengths? In *The Dred Scott Case: Its Significance in American Law and Politics*, Professor Don E. Fehrenbacher argues that Taney aimed to launch "a sweeping counterattack on the antislavery movement and to reinforce the bastions of slavery at every rampart and parapet."[22]

A final note: In his decision, Taney twice stated for the record that Dred Scott had no capacity to bring his suit.[23] Those remarks sharpen the legal question: If Scott lacked capacity to bring suit, shouldn't Taney have simply said so and stopped there? Weren't all of his other pronouncements gratuitous? Legally, such pronouncements are known as obiter dicta (Latin for "that which is said in passing"), or dicta for short—and as such are not considered binding as precedent.

∾

In the aftermath of the decision, the slavery interests supporting Virginia in the Lemmon appeal could now make a new argument that might go like this: "Under *Dred Scott*, slaves are property and do not lose their status as property even after residing in a free territory. How then could they possibly lose their status as property by merely being *in transit* through a free state? The Eight were in New York for the briefest time and under the dominion of their owners, who are non-residents of New York." The lawyers could also point to Taney's remarks that, constitutionally speaking, the Negro "had no rights which the white man was bound to respect," and that therefore the Negro "might justly and lawfully be reduced to slavery for his benefit."

The Northern press also quickly recognized the implications of the decision for the Lemmon case. The *Albany Evening Journal* promptly ran an editorial asserting that Congress and President James Buchanan were under the thumb of slaveholders, and that whenever the Lemmon case eventually made its way to the Supreme Court, the defenders of the Eight would find themselves dealing with a "corrupt fountain of law." The *Milwaukee Free Democrat* lamented that if the Lemmon case were to reach the Supreme Court, slaveowners would be able to call the roll of their slaves beneath the shadow of the Bunker Hill Monument.[24]

The *Chicago Tribune*, for its part, warned that it could now see nothing to prevent the Taney court from opening "a slave pen and auction block" in Chicago. "If there is any doubt on the subject," the paper continued, "the forthcoming decision in the Lemmon case will remove it." The *New York Tribune* made a similar lament, contending that in rendering their *Dred Scott* verdict, the justices on the Supreme Court had "announced beforehand what judgment they mean to give in the Lemmon case." Ominous, well-founded predictions.

The New York Legislature also reacted quickly, appointing a Joint Committee of the Senate and Assembly to consider how to protect the state's citizens "against the serious and alarming doctrines" set out in the Dred Scott decision. The committee set to work immediately, and in April of 1857, its head, Samuel Foot, a former judge of the New York Court of Appeals, delivered a scorching attack on the Dred Scott decision. It was, Foot wrote, the product of five politically motivated pro-slavery justices from Southern states, and its effect would be to "bring slavery within our borders, against our will, with all its unhallowed, demoralizing and blighting influences."

Foot then gave Taney a lesson in jurisprudence, taking him to task for including so much poisonous dicta in his writing. "No Judge of the Court," Foot wrote, "had a right, and far less was it his duty, to discuss, decide, or even express an opinion on any other question or subject." By choosing to do so, Taney entered into "forbidden territory," Foot declared.

The Report proposed three resolutions, which passed both New York houses: "[First, that] New York will not allow Slavery within her borders, in any form, or for any time. Second, that the Supreme Court has lost the confidence and respect of the people of New York, and, third, that the Governor transmit a copy of the report to the other Governors of the other States."

The South responded in kind. The *Baltimore Sun* assailed the Foot Report for trying to fortify the Lemmon ruling, and called the report a "malediction" that should be expunged once New York "recovered her reason." In an editorial titled "New York's Negrophilism" the *New Orleans Times-Picayune* made a similar claim, attacking the Foot report and its resolutions as New York's attempt to subvert the impact of *Dred Scott* on the Lemmon case.[25]

Even in the *Dred Scott* decision itself, at least one justice of the Supreme Court seemed to be anticipating the day the Court would take on the Lemmon case. Writing in a concurring opinion, Justice Samuel Nelson (1792–1873) noted, surely with Lemmon in mind, that a question remained outstanding as to the right of slaveowners to pass through a free state with their slaves without fear of losing their human property. "When that question arises," Nelson wrote, "we shall be prepared to decide it."[26]

Seven months later, the Lemmon case would be heard at its first level of appeal in New York.

Chapter 10

The First Appeal

On October 1, 1857, the Lemmon case finally reached the first level of appeal before the New York Supreme Court, General Term. The court terminology is confusing. At the time, the State Supreme Court General Term was only the first-level appeals court (and today the State Supreme Court is a trial-level court) and the New York Court of Appeals was (and still is) the State's court of last resort.

By 1857, some five years after Judge Paine's ruling, it had seemed that Virginia was in no hurry to advance its appeal, but it may have felt an increasing impetus to hasten the appeal process, considering that other free states could follow the Lemmon case example. Indeed, in the spring of that year, both Maine and Ohio had in effect codified the Lemmon ruling, legislating that anyone enslaved who sets foot in the state (except for fugitive slaves) becomes free.[1]

To make its case on appeal, Virginia had engaged the 53-year-old Charles O'Conor, a titan of the New York bar who stood at the top of his profession nationally. In the courtroom O'Conor imparted an air of truculence, fortified by a first-rate mind, meticulous preparation, and impressive oratorical skills, all of which had prompted the prominent New York politician Samuel Tilden to call him "the greatest jurist among all the English speaking race."[2] But O'Conor also happened to be a pro-slavery zealot.[3] In his courtroom advocacy, his political speeches, and his writings, he demonstrated an obsessive disdain for the Negro race, and he embraced the idea of its enslavement.

New York engaged William Evarts. At 39, Evarts also stood high in the profession. A graduate of the Harvard Law School, by 1857 he had worked for the United States Attorney's office in New York and been active in private practice with high-profile cases. Politically, he aligned with the anti-slavery Republican Party. Born in 1818, he was a Yankee patrician whose ancestors had been early settlers in Connecticut; his father was a prominent lay religious leader, and his mother was the daughter of Roger Sherman, a signer of both the Declaration of Independence and the Articles of Confederation. And there was more. If the topic of the United States Constitution came up, Evarts could have said, "Oh, yes, my grandfather signed that, too."

A funny thing happened on the way to the appeal that day, however. Before opening arguments began, John Jay, who had represented the Eight before Judge Paine, appeared as amicus curiae (a non-party "friend of the court") and asked the court to dismiss Virginia's appeal as moot.

Jay pointed out that on November 24, 1852, some five years earlier, the Lemmons had been fully compensated and had agreed, upon request, to "manumit and discharge from labor and service the eight slaves in question." This, he argued, amounted to a contract, which meant that the Lemmon family had no further interest in the case, legally or financially, leaving nothing for adjudication. In sponsoring the appeal, he added, Virginia was not actually trying to regain possession of the slaves, because they had gone to Canada—which had no extradition treaty with the United States. Because the appeal was being waged not by the actual litigants but by two regional proxies, Virginia and New York, Jay argued, it amounted to a political battle that shouldn't be fought in court.[4]

At this stage in the process, before opening arguments began, Jay and Evarts had good reason to seek a dismissal. If they could have the appeal dismissed as moot, Judge Paine's decision would stand, and the status quo would be maintained. Jay and Evarts couldn't be sure that this five-judge tribunal would uphold the decision. Even if the decision were upheld at the first appellate level, the case would then go to the New York Court of Appeals, and there was no guarantee that it would be upheld there. Either court could credibly maintain an anti-slavery posture but nonetheless draw a line in the name of interstate accommodation by allowing owners and slaves merely to pass through New York. A dismissal out of hand, on mootness grounds, would therefore be best. The dismissal would lack the gravitas of an appellate court endorsing Judge Paine's decision, but that would be fine: appellate lawyers are the first to recognize that results on appeal cannot be guaranteed, and that a bird in the hand, in the form of a dismissal, would be better than risking a reversal.

Worse yet, Jay and Evarts knew that continuing the case could mean that it would ultimately reach the United States Supreme Court, which had just delivered the infamous, pro-slavery *Dred Scott* decision. It seemed quite possible, if not likely, that the Court would pounce on *Lemmon* as a means of expanding slavery, or perhaps even nationalizing it. A dismissal rendering the appeal moot, Jay and Everts believed, would be the simplest solution: It would end the matter then and there, and would create no appellate law or precedent.

Some anti-slavery advocates disagreed, preferring a ruling on the merits. The *National Anti-Slavery Standard* summed up that view. "Give us half-a-dozen Dred Scott decisions in rapid succession . . . each worse than the other, and we shall see Northern blood up. The fear is that they will be doled out, though just as certainly given, over half-a-dozen years, and the Northern mind deadened, not excited. It is, therefore, we hope, that Mr. Jay's motion may not find favour with the Court." The newspaper want on to say that if the Supreme Court is going to overturn the Lemmon case and impose slavery, sooner is better than later. A battle, the newspaper said, is better than a siege.[5]

Keenly grasping all of this, Charles O'Conor strongly objected to a dismissal. He wanted the appeal decided on the merits—win or lose. He understood that even if he lost, it would open the path to the Supreme Court, where he would almost certainly prevail. Dismissing the appeal as moot, he argued, would be "disrespectful" to the New York Legislature, which, he said, had put a lot of effort and funding behind the case. It is hard to imagine a more cynical argument: O'Conor cared nothing about New York's expenditures in defending Judge Paine's ruling. If anything, he would have resented the thought of spending taxpayer money to free the enslaved.

Judges are not normally inclined to grant mootness dismissals that could have been granted years earlier. After five years, the stage was finally set, with the nation looking on. Speaking for the court, its Presiding Justice, William Mitchell, denied Jay's dismissal motion and allowed the appeal to go forward.

Mitchell, who, the year before, had served as a temporary judge on the New York Court of Appeals, was a widely respected jurist and editor of *Blackstone's Commentaries*. He and his colleagues obviously felt that a decision on a critical issue, let alone one of national and historic importance, should have the imprimatur of an appellate court in a real writing. He didn't want his court to be seen as ducking the case.[6]

And so, before a packed courthouse, the opening arguments began.

O'Conor went first, on behalf of Virginia—and he proceeded to speak for the whole day.

That was not unusual. In the 1850s, a lawyer's measure included rhetorical skills that could attract large audiences, and in important cases lawyers would sometimes orate for hours before judges, who rarely interrupted them with questions.[7] (Some judges chewed tobacco to keep themselves going during these performances and so were supplied with brass spittoons on the bench for spitting out the juice.) Typically, appellate judges acquainted themselves with cases by first listening to oral argument and only then reading the briefs, in contrast to the practice today, in which judges read the briefs first and then use oral argument as a brisk question-and-answer session (sometimes known as the "hot bench") that sometimes verges on outright interrogation.

In all, O'Conor advanced six points.

In opening, he argued that the common law authorized slavery and that only an express statute can defeat an owner's right to slave property. This was a non-starter. The judges would have been familiar with England's *Somersett* decision, authored by Lord Mansfield, in 1772, that slavery was repugnant to the common law.[8] They would also have known of Blackstone's *Commentaries on the Laws of England*, in which he spoke of the antagonism of natural law to slavery. In 1765, Blackstone wrote that "pure and proper slavery does not, nay cannot, subsist in England. . . . And indeed it is repugnant to reason, and the principles of natural law."[9]

O'Conor then attacked the recent anti-slavery *Foot Report* and its resolutions—which had only recently been promulgated—arguing that they were unconstitutional and "cannot retroact to affect this case." He urged that prior to the resolutions, no New York law had ever declared "that to breathe our air or touch our soil should work emancipation, *ipso facto*."

Here O'Conor was drawing a distinction between a statute and a judge's ruling. Judge Paine had ruled that *bringing* a slave to New York spells emancipation. But Judge Paine, O'Conor argued, could not have properly reached that conclusion in the absence of a *law*—and no law, including the New York law of 1841 that had repealed the nine-month exception, could be interpreted so as to deny a Virginian "an uninterrupted transitus through our [New York] territory with their negro slaves."

O'Conor even went as far as to say that interstate comity awards a free transit from one state to another and that "no American judge can pronounce slave property an exception to this rule, upon the [asserted] general ground that slavery is immoral or unjust." It is one thing, O'Conor argued, for New York to dislike or even outlaw slavery, but another to seize someone's slaves for merely bringing them in transit through the state.

O'Conor turned next to the Commerce Clause of the United States Constitution, declaring that only the Congress, and not the States, had authority to regulate interstate commerce. By confiscating a Virginian's "property" for merely passing through New York's navigable waters, he argued, New York was usurping Congress's power.

For his fourth point, O'Conor invoked Article IV of the Constitution, in its warrant that the "Citizens of each State shall be entitled to all Privileges and Immunities of Citizens in the several States." O'Conor argued that this provision was designed to prevent a state from burdening the citizens of another state. He asserted that New York had violated the clause by stopping a Virginian's vessel in transit and carrying off his Negro slaves.

His next point touched on the *Dred Scott* decision, then only seven months old. Picking up on where Justice Taney left off, O'Conor launched a virulent white-supremacist salvo. It is worth quoting in full (italics mine):

> The general doctrines of the court in Dred Scott's case must be maintained, *their alleged novelty notwithstanding*. . . . The negro was forever excluded from social union by an indubitable law of nature; what folly it would have been to endow him with political equality. Indeed, it was impossible. It never has been done: it cannot be done. . . . Whenever the Judiciary of the Union shall declare in respect to the emancipated negroes of the North that they are "citizens" of the State in which they dwell, and therefore under the Constitution "entitled in the several (other) States to all privileges and immunities of citizens," the law of nature, to which negro-philism so frequently appeals, will irresistibly demand the dissolution of the Union. We maintain that the negro was not permitted during the storm of battle to steal into a place in the fundamental institutions of our country, where, with full power to accomplish the fell purpose, he may lurk until the hour when it shall be his pleasure to apply the torch and explode our Republic forever.

For reasons that are unclear, O'Conor did not advance the Dred Scott decision to what might have been his maximum advantage. He could have cited the decision insofar as it spoke of the constitutional rights of owner-ship of slave property. Perhaps, in using the word "novelty," he was seeking a way to avoid a discussion of whether much of the decision was dicta.

In fact, the first suggestions that the *Dred Scott* decision was dicta had come from two of its own justices. In one of the two dissenting opin-ions in the case, Justice Benjamin Curtis noted that after deciding that the Circuit Court had had no jurisdiction to hear the case, the Supreme Court had no need to go on to examine its merits. Curtis wrote, "I feel obliged to say that, in my opinion, such an exertion of judicial power transcends the limits of the authority of the court. . . . I do not hold any opinion of this court, or any court, binding, when expressed on a question not legitimately before it."[10]

Likewise, in the decision's other dissent, Justice John McLean wrote that the Court's opinion lacked authority insofar as it went beyond the jurisdictional issue. "The question of jurisdiction, being before the court," he said, "was decided by them authoritatively, but nothing beyond that question."[11]

As Charles O'Conor knew well, Curtis and McLean were arguing that beyond the jurisdictional point, *Dred Scott* was dicta that need not be followed—and he may well have decided to steer well clear of that argument.

∽

After O'Conor rested his case, William Evarts rose to make his. He did so along with Joseph Blunt, representing "the people of the State of New York."[12] In a resolution adopted March 31, 1853, the general assembly in New York had resolved that the New York attorney general defend the Lemmon appeal, along with such other counsel as the governor may select. This accounted for Blunt's appearance alongside Evarts, both opposing Virginia. Blunt's presence added not only additional talent, but was also symbolic of New York lining up on the side of liberty.

Evarts did not try to meet O'Conor's arguments point by point. Instead, he followed his own script. To begin, he cited habeas corpus as the embodiment of liberty and as a basis for challenging unlawful restraint. He then addressed the question on appeal—which, as he framed it, con-cerned whether slavery, as endorsed in Virginia, could abide the laws of New York, a sovereign free state.

The answer, he said, was flatly no. New York's prohibition against slavery, he told the judges, applied to everyone: New Yorkers and non-residents alike, including Virginians. New York authorized exceptions for nobody, not even for even an instant.

Evarts presented the judges with a thought experiment. If, as O'Conor had suggested, New York should apply Virginia law, shouldn't a child born to a slave in transit in New York then be stamped a slave? But how could somebody possibly be born a slave in a free state? Evarts then turned to natural law, or the law of nations, arguing that, in effect, Virginia was making a vain appeal to "force against nature" and "law against justice."

Everts mentioned *Dred Scott* only in passing, including it as part of a string of case citations supporting bland, unassailable principles. Giving it no prominence, he treated the case almost as a toothless ally. As for comity—the respect and accommodation that one state accords another—he acknowledged the importance of the concept but emphasized its limits. Comity, he said, cannot apply when it comes to the "odious and violent injustice of slavery," of which New York had long before "purged" itself.

Evarts concluded by focusing on New York's repeal of the nine-month exception as clear evidence of legislative intent. "That the particular case of slavery during transit has not escaped the intent or effect of the legislation on the subject," he said, "appears in the express permission once accorded to it, and the subsequent abrogation of such permission." There is more than legislative silence here, Evarts was arguing: the legislature had initially allowed a modest amount of slavery by sojourners, for nine months, but then had gone out of its way to expunge the allowance.

Joseph Blunt rose next and presented his own brief for New York.

A polished writer and historian, Blunt knew his stuff. Not long before, he had helped found the Republican Party, and he was the author of *An Examination of the Expediency and Constitutionality of Prohibiting Slavery in the State of Missouri* (a prohibition he endorsed).[13]

Blunt was, of course, well aware of the *Dred Scott* decision, but he made an obvious tactical decision and chose not to dedicate a single word to it in his brief.[14] Instead, like Evarts, he focused his attention on natural law and the law of nations. In combination, the two lawyers referred to these concepts over 20 times in their briefs, and, again in their oral presentations.

༄

Comparing the arguments of the lawyers who had appeared before Judge Paine in 1852 with those at the first appellate level in 1857, it is hard not to notice a change in their thrust.

In presenting the case before Judge Paine, both sides had essentially stuck to the law, the Constitution, and the statutes. Jay and Culver did touch on the idea of freedom under "natural law," but they acknowledged that a society (or in this case, the State of Virginia) could, by statute, declare otherwise, and enact a system of slavery—in contrast to New York, which could, and did, abolish it. In good measure, the discussion before Judge Paine turned on which state's law should apply. Race had nothing to do with it.

That changed when Charles O'Conor entered the case. He put race front and center. O'Conor cited the Constitution and the statutes, of course, but as his principal point, he asserted that the Negro race was incapable of attaining political equality. His argument boiled down to this: The Eight should remain enslaved because their pigment required it.

There were other reasons for the change in approach, toward racism. In 1852, the *Dred Scott* case was still five years away. A lawyer advocating for slavery did not yet have the benefit of quoting a ruling in which the nation's highest court declared that Negroes "had no rights which the white man was bound to respect; and that the negro might justly and lawfully be reduced to slavery for his benefit."[15]

That language, basing the law on color, was an ugly shriek in our national dialogue, but to O'Conor it was musical. And he must have sensed, generally, that the rationalization for enslavement in the United States had been evolving along racial lines. Although slavery as an institution had been appreciably racist at the inception, Northerners and Southerners had for decades abided it largely on economic grounds, and were not especially proud of it. Indeed, when the North and the South combined to form the Union, the founding document, the Constitution, avoided the use of the words "slave" and "slavery."

That changed during the 19th century, when abolitionists fastened onto the immorality of the institution. Its defenders, in turn, made references to the Bible, the curse of Ham, and the God-given duty of the "dominant race" to keep things the way they were. In *Duties of Masters to Servants* (1851), for example, a prominent clergyman lectured the enslaved that cheerful obedience and contentment is the will of God, while reminding slaveowners that they are primarily responsible for the slaves' salvation.[16]

These ideas had long floated from the pulpits to legislative chambers and back. As early as 1835, addressing his state legislature, Governor George McDuffie, of South Carolina, had put it this way: "No human institution, in my opinion, is more manifestly consistent with the will of God, than domestic slavery."[17]

Many Southern judges bought into the program. In a single decision, for example, Joseph Lumpkin, Georgia's Chief Justice, justified slavery with references to the curse of Ham, the Almighty, the divine decree, sinfulness, salvation, and racial supremacy. "To be the 'servant of servants' is the judicial curse pronounced upon their race," he wrote of Negroes. "And this Divine decree is irreversible," he proclaimed.[18]

This kind of talk was not limited to Southern courts. Peleg Sprague, a federal judge in Massachusetts, told a grand jury that enforcing the Fugitive Slave Law was the will of God, and that regardless of any conscientious objections, they had an obligation to indict those accused of aiding fugitive slaves. We find little such theology in New York judicial decisions, however.[19] Charles O'Conor did try his hand at it in the Lemmon appeal—but the judges did not bite.

∽

On December 7, 1857, the court rendered its verdict, in a decision written by Justice Mitchell.

It was a model of brevity and efficiency. Mitchell began by citing the 1841 statute repealing the nine-month slavery allowance for sojourners. He pointed out that before its repeal, the statute read, "Every person brought into this state as a slave, except as authorized by this title, shall be FREE"—with that final word in capital letters.

Judge Mitchell explained the statutory repeal in a single, terse paragraph, stating that the law could not be plainer. By deleting the nine-month sojourner allowance, New York prohibited slavery on its soil, period. No allowance could be made, not even for a New York minute. In this segment of its decision, the court agreed with Judge Paine that for slavery to exist, it must have a platform of positive law (such as a statute). In New York, when the nine-month allowance had been repealed, that platform had disappeared, which meant that slavery could not be supported.[20]

Agreeing with Blunt and Evarts, Judge Mitchell went on to dispatch O'Conor's argument about comity, ruling that it does not require New York to grant out-of-staters accommodations greater than it grants to its own citizens.

Judge Mitchell then turned to O'Conor's contention that in freeing the Eight, New York had violated the Privileges and Immunities clause of the Constitution. He noted that the Constitution "gives to the citizens of a sister state only the same privileges and immunities, in our state, which our laws give to our own citizens." Critically, he continued, "As this state does not allow its own citizens to bring a slave here even, *in transitu*, and to hold him as a slave for any portion of time, it cannot be expected to allow the citizens of another state to do so."

Finally, Mitchell rejected O'Conor's "Commerce Clause" argument, ruling that while Congress has the exclusive power to regulate interstate commerce, its power does not extend to the control of people after they arrive in New York.

In his decision, Judge Mitchell deftly provided his readers a lesson in statutory interpretation. The writing has the feel of structure based on building blocks, leading to an inexorable conclusion: (1) Slavery is not tolerated in New York; (2) owing to the repeal of the nine-month sojourner allowance, a slave brought to New York, even for an instant, becomes free; (3) the Lemmons brought their slaves to New York, in transit to Texas; (4) under its own laws, New York properly seized the slaves and discharged them; (5) the only authority higher than New York law is the United States Constitution, which obligates New York to "deliver up" fugitive slaves; but (6) the Lemmon slaves were not fugitives.

The decision affirmed Judge Paine's ruling, 4–1, with one judge silently dissenting.

Needless to say, officials in Virginia were not happy. Barely a week went by before the state's governor, Henry A. Wise, wrote to the state's attorney general, John Randolph Tucker, laying out a plan for appealing this latest decision. Wise had his eyes not on the next level of appeal in New York but on the ultimate prize. "Please instruct counsel to expedite the case through the state Courts of N.Y.," he wrote, "in order that we may get the main decision in the Supreme Court of the U. States." (See figure 10.1.)

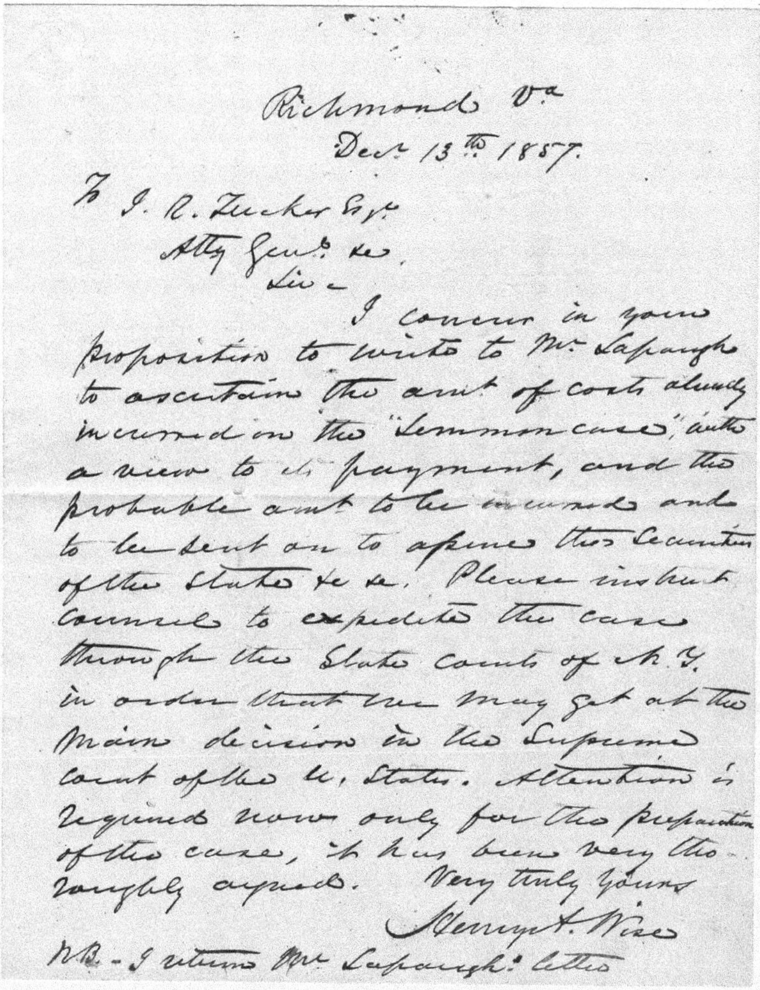
Richmond Va
Decr 13th 1857.
To J. R. Tucker Esqr
Atty Genl &c.
Sir—
I concur in your proposition to write to Mr Lapaugh to ascertain the amt of costs already incurred in the "Lemmon case", with a view to its payment, and the probable amt to be incurred and to be sent on to assure the counsel of the State &c &c. Please instruct counsel to expedite the case through the State courts of N.Y. in order that we may get at the main decision in the Supreme Court of the U. States. Attention is required now only for the preparation of the case, it has been very thoroughly argued. Very truly yours
Henry A. Wise
N.B.—I return Mr Lapaugh's letter

Figure 10.1. Governor of Virginia Henry Wise writes on December 13, 1857, to the state's attorney general, Randolph Tucker, urging that the Lemmon case be expedited to the US Supreme Court. Courtesy of the Library of Virginia (Accession 44648, Virginia Attorney General's Records Regarding the Lemmon Slave Case).

Chapter 11

High Stakes

When Judge Paine's ruling on *Lemmon* was upheld, the North generally welcomed the decision. Most in the South objected to it, of course, considering it yet another assault on their "peculiar institution." But observers everywhere, no matter what their opinion, knew that the case was far from over. The next step was another appeal, this time to the highest court in the state, the New York Court of Appeals.

Virginia soon filed a notice of that appeal. In response, in his annual State of the State message, which he delivered in early January 1858, New York's governor, John A. King, positioned himself, and New York, squarely behind the ruling and against slavery. His message was covered nationally in the press.[1]

Despite that strong show of political support, John Jay was worried about Virginia's appeal. He assumed that he had a decent chance of prevailing against Virginia in court, but even that would represent only one more step along the way to what would surely be the case's final destination: the United States Supreme Court—which, if *Dred Scott* was any guide, was likely to come to the rescue of slaveowners. Northern editorialists agreed.[2]

Jay can't have liked his prospects. If the Taney court were to overturn the *Lemmon* decision and allow transit with slaves, why would it stop there? Why not seize the opportunity also to allow sojourning with slaves, or short-term residency, or, for that matter, long-term residency? In short, the full slavery package.

Jay had already tried unsuccessfully to have the appeal dismissed as moot at the first appellate level. Now he tried again, this time in a two-step process. First, he and Louis Napoleon presented a formal application, calling it a "Memorial," asking New York Governor John King to stop financing the case.[3] If the governor agreed, the second step would be to ask the court for a mootness dismissal.

At the first appellate level, Charles O'Conor had duplicitously argued that a mootness dismissal would be disrespectful to New York's government. In their Memorial, Jay and Napoleon sought to undercut that argument, writing, "Wherefor your petitioner respectfully prays your excellency recommend to the legislature a discontinuance of all further interference with the Lemmon suit and that your memorialist, the only proper respondent in the case, may be able to procure a dismissal of the said appeal upon the simple facts without being met by the argument that the Court cannot grant the motion of your memorialist without disrespect to the other branches of government."[4] (See figure 11.1.)

On January 4, 1858, Governor King wrote back to Jay, declining his request "with great reluctance." King said he felt it necessary to publicly embrace the decision freeing the slaves. The state had gone too far to retreat, even if the United States Supreme Court might reverse the decision. As a matter of principle, he wrote, New York had "done what the people desire and demand . . . without reference to what may be decided elsewhere."

Two days later, in his annual message, King affirmed that he intended to carry on the fight—and to spend what it takes. "I am gratified," he said, that the court "expressed its judgment in favor of the constitutional power of the state to legislate as to the condition of all persons within its jurisdiction, and to banish forever, from its territory all vestige of human slavery."[5]

The exchange between Jay and Governor King is fascinating. In Governor King, Jay had an anti-slavery ally, and yet the two disagreed on how to proceed with *Lemmon*. Given their different institutional perspectives, however, this disagreement makes sense.

Jay responded tactfully to King's refusal, saying that he was disappointed and would now, as a first step, go to the legislature itself to stop financing the case.[6] It was a last-ditch effort—the only way that Jay could think of to try to head off what he and others regarded as a bad turn in the road. If New York were to cut off its funding for the defense of the case, Jay thought it might put him in a better position to ask the Court of Appeals to dismiss the appeal as moot.

On the face of it, Jay's reasoning is hard to follow. Even if New York were to stop funding the defense of the *Lemmon* appeal, that would not

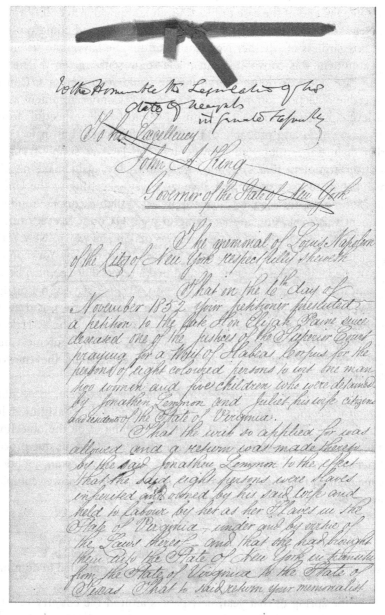

Figure 11.1. Memorial of Louis Napoleon recounting how he began the petition to free the eight enslaved people with a writ of habeas corpus, drafted for the Governor of New York and the Legislature, c. 1858. Jay Family Papers, Rare Book & Manuscript Library, Columbia University in the City of New York.

guarantee the end of the case or block Virginia's appeal. After all, Virginia, not New York, was the party maintaining the appeal and could press on with it regardless of whether New York paid for the lawyers to defend it. Jay's argument was convoluted but made some sense, given the history of the case. He was doing everything he could to undercut O'Conor's predictable objection to a mootness dismissal. O'Conor's argument at the first-level appellate court that a dismissal would be "disrespectful" to the state was cynical and probably did not count for much, but in fact Jay's earlier dismissal motion had been denied, and Jay was simply trying to defeat an argument that O'Conor would inevitably again make on Virginia's behalf to keep the appeal alive, as a way of getting to the United States Supreme Court. Jay must have appreciated that O'Conor's "funding" argument was weak, but he was trying to meet O'Conor at every turn.

The stakes were high. As the case was making its way to New York's high court, in March of 1858, Senator Preston King, of New York, on the floor of the United States Senate, argued that a reversal of *Lemmon* by the Supreme Court might allow slave power to advance slavery nationally.[7] The following year, in February 1859, as the *Lemmon* case was drawing closer to being heard by the Court of Appeals, Senator John P. Hale, of New Hampshire, referring to *Lemmon*, warned, "if the Supreme Court decide that slaves may be held in the free States an hour, they may be held forever."[8]

These were not unreasonable fears. The very next year, in deciding *Ableman v. Booth*, the Supreme Court would uphold the constitutionality of the Fugitive Slave Act of 1850, blithely brushing aside the objections of the Wisconsin Supreme Court as to the statute's egregious due process deficiencies.[9] With decisions like *Prigg*, *Dred Scott*, and *Ableman*, abolitionists maintained that the Supreme Court had helped slave power complete a sweep of all three branches of the federal government.

∽

Meanwhile, in 1858, unrest and debate over slavery continued to dominate national attention.

In the spring of that year, newspapers around the country told the story of George Anderson, who had been kidnapped in New York by a certain Oscar M. Thomas and then sold in Virginia to a slaveowner named Raglan. The case was a reminder that free Negroes were still being kidnapped and sold south into slavery. Anderson sued for his freedom, and the case was tried in New York, where the jury needed only ten minutes to find Thomas guilty of kidnapping, and the judge gave him a ten-year prison sentence. As the press noted, many similar cases were still awaiting trial.[10]

In September came what's known as the Oberlin–Wellington Rescue, which took place in Oberlin, Ohio, after federal officials arrested a fugitive named John Price. Aware that the population in Oberlin was strongly abolitionist, the federal marshal in charge of the arrest had Price taken south of the city to a station called Wellington, but before the officials could return Price to his owner, a crowd of some 600 people made their way to the station, seized Price, and brought him back to Oberlin—and soon helped him make his way to Canada on the Underground Railroad (see figure 11.2).

The year 1859 brought even more unrest and debate. In the spring, the New York state legislators Shotwell Powell, Charles S. Spencer, Almanzor Hutchinson, and James M. Northrup proposed a strongly worded anti-slavery act to their state senate. Titled "An Act to Protect the Rights and Liberties of the Citizens of the State of New York," it declared that no one could be considered chattel, that anyone charged as an escaped slave

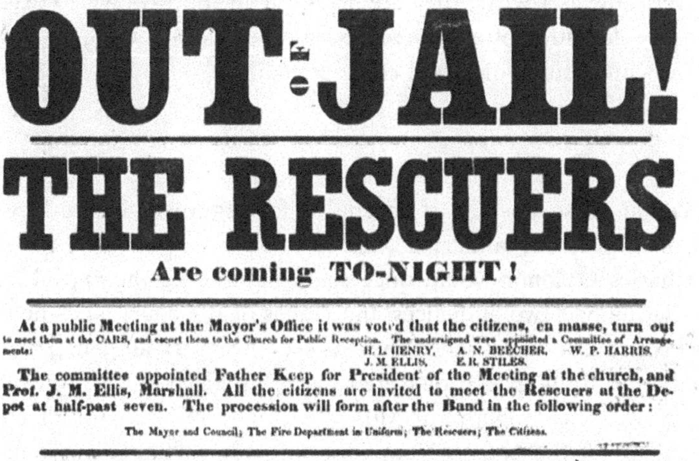

OUT-OF-JAIL!
THE RESCUERS
Are coming TO-NIGHT !

At a public Meeting at the Mayor's Office it was vot'd that the citizens, en masse, turn out to meet them at the CARS, and escort them to the Church for Public Reception. The undersigned were appointed a Committee of Arrangements:
H. L. HENRY,   A. N. BEECHER,   W. P. HARRIS.
J. M. ELLIS,   E. R. STILES.

The committee appointed Father Keep for President of the Meeting at the church, and Prof. J. M. Ellis, Marshall. All the citizens are invited to meet the Rescuers at the Depot at half-past seven. The procession will form after the Band in the following order :

The Mayor and Council; The Fire Department in Uniform; The Rescuers; The Citizens.

Let there be a grand gathering !
Oberlin, July 6.   By order of Committee of Arrangements.

Figure 11.2. A broadside calling for public celebration of the return of the Oberlin–Wellington Rescuers, 1859. Courtesy of Oberlin College Archives.

had a right to trial by jury, and that anyone who deprived a person of liberty under a claim of service was guilty of a felony. It also provided that anyone brought into New York with his or her alleged master or mistress becomes free—a codification, in effect, of Judge Paine's *Lemmon* decision.[11]

There were expressed concerns about the fate of the Lemmon appeal. In August, Ohio's governor, Salmon P. Chase, joined others in expressing a worry that in the hands of the Supreme Court the case could become the pathway to extending slavery into the free states.[12]

Two months later, in October, John Brown took matters violently into his own hands, leading his famous raid on Harpers Ferry, Virginia. In the South, the raid provoked outrage, but in parts of the North it was celebrated. On October 30, in what has come to be known as "A Plea for Captain John Brown," Henry David Thoreau defended Brown, saying that he supported him and his raid "not to gratify any personal animosity, revenge, or vindictive spirit" but out of "sympathy with the oppressed and the wronged."[13] On November 22, speaking in Boston's Tremont Temple, Ralph Waldo Emerson joined in, declaring, "If Brown were to be hanged, he would make the gallows as glorious as the cross."[14] And on the day of Brown's execution, the poet Henry Wadsworth Longfellow, an ardent critic of the Fugitive Slave Law, wrote, "This will be a great day in our history; the date of a new Revolution, quite as much needed as the old one. Even now as I write, they are leading Old John Brown to execution in Virginia for attempting to rescue slaves! This is sowing the wind to reap the whirlwind, which will come soon."[15]

∼

The *Lemmon* case was at last scheduled for argument in the New York Court of Appeals on January 24, 1860.

Charles O'Conor would once again be arguing the appeal, and he knew that he had two audiences: the judges of the court, and the public. As the court date approached, he worked the latter audience hard. On December 19, in a speech delivered to an audience at a Union meeting of the New York Academy of Music, he made his case for the natural subservience of the Negro. New York was not particularly sympathetic to slavery, but this particular audience was bent on saving the Union, even if it meant subordinating their anti-slavery attitudes, and O'Conor was able to rouse his listeners by playing that card well (see figure 11.3).

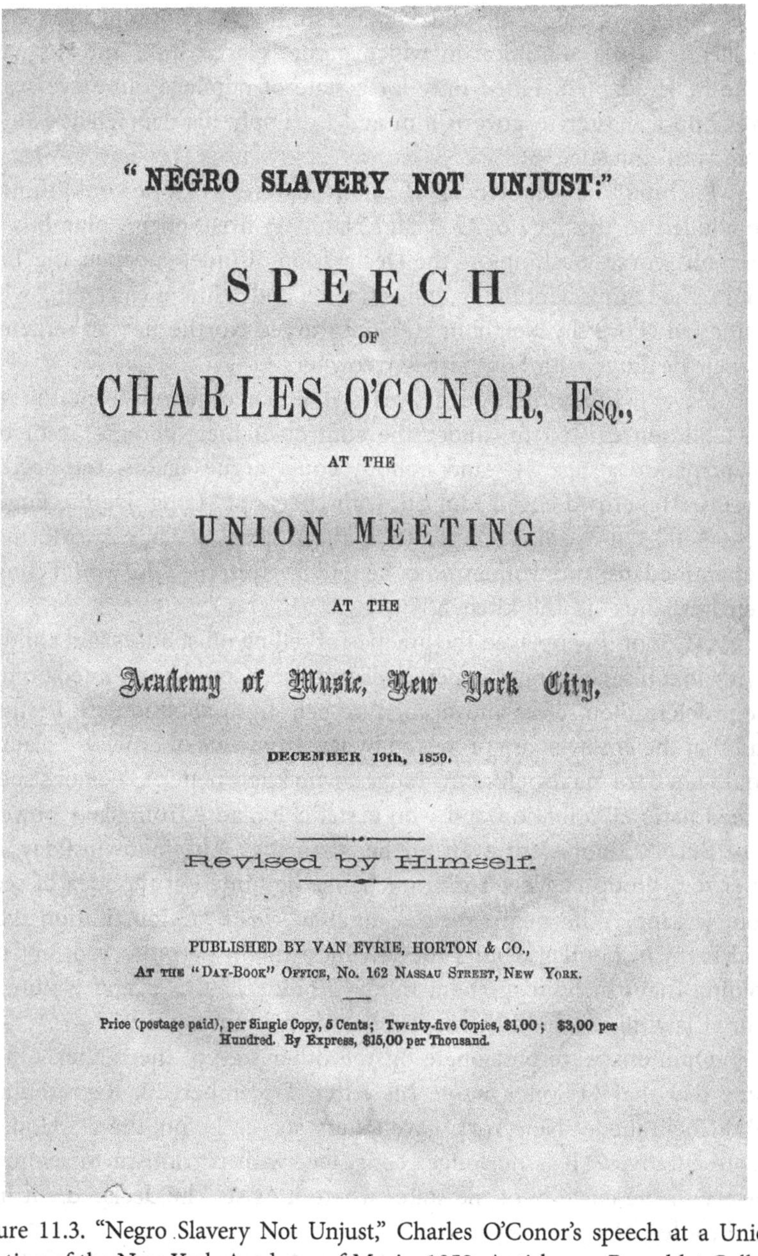
"NEGRO SLAVERY NOT UNJUST:"

SPEECH

OF

CHARLES O'CONOR, Esq.,

AT THE

UNION MEETING

AT THE

Academy of Music, New York City,

DECEMBER 19th, 1859.

Revised by Himself.

PUBLISHED BY VAN EVRIE, HORTON & CO.,
AT THE "DAY-BOOK" OFFICE, No. 162 NASSAU STREET, NEW YORK.

Price (postage paid), per Single Copy, 5 Cents; Twenty-five Copies, $1,00; $3,00 per Hundred. By Express, $15,00 per Thousand.

Figure 11.3. "Negro Slavery Not Unjust," Charles O'Conor's speech at a Union meeting of the New York Academy of Music, 1859. Antislavery Pamphlet Collection, Robert S. Cox Special Collections and University Archives Research Center, UMass Amherst Libraries.

"Now, gentlemen," he said, "I maintain that it is not injustice to leave the negro in the condition in which nature placed him, and for which alone he is adapted. Fitted only for a state of pupilage our slave system gives him a master to govern him and to supply his deficiencies: in this there is no injustice."[16]

Pitching to his audience, O'Conor rang every bell he could think of. He alluded to the Law of God and Nature, Christopher Columbus, the tomb of George Washington, the Declaration of Independence, the Taney Court, The Omniscient Being, Julius Caesar, and "Him of Nazareth," whose injunction "Love thy Neighbor" O'Conor urged Northerners to remember in their dealings with Southern slaveowners.

Slavery, O'Conor argued, was not much different from the state that children existed in, under the control of their parents, until their emancipation at age 21—and nobody could argue against the need for parents. The crowd egged him on, with cheers of "Long live the Fugitive Slave Act!" On a roll, O'Conor took cheap shots at Shakers, Mormons, Mohammedans, and women, who, he said, if given the vote would consign their husbands "to the kitchen."

O'Conor downplayed the practice of selling off spouses and children, saying that if such things happened, slaveowners could be counted on to fix the problem themselves and needed no help from abolitionists. Lastly, he said that the enslaved are protected by law from acts of cruelty, a claim he would not dare make before the judges, who knew better. O'Conor's speech gained national attention and won ecstatic applause from slave power.[17]

But O'Conor went even further than that. The following day, in a letter to a group of New York merchants, he hinted at the idea of secession, writing, "The negro race is upon us. With a Constitution which held them in bondage, our Federal Union might be preserved; but if so holding them in bondage be a thing forbidden by God and Nature, we cannot lawfully so hold them, and the Union must perish."[18]

Opinions were passionate on the other side of the matter. On the same day that O'Conor wrote his letter, December 20, Representative John Cochrane, of New York, gave a fiery speech before the US House of Representatives. "It is no longer consistent with patriotism to relinquish slavery to the custody of the states where it exists," he declared. "It must be throttled."[19]

In January of 1860, not long before the *Lemmon* appeal was heard, the public battle over slavery was in full view. On January 18, for example, an exchange took place on the floor of the House of Representatives between Congressman John J. McRae, a Democrat from Mississippi, and Congressman Luther C. Carter, a Republican from New York.

McRae began by giving a full-throated defense of slavery on grounds that had become increasingly common among its proponents. "It is a universal institution of God and of man, nature and Christianity, earth and heaven," he said, "having its origin in the law of God, sustained by the Bible, sustained by Christianity, sustained by the laws of all nations, sustained by all history in all parts of the world."

Carter countered: "I acknowledge no right of property in men under any circumstances whatever, according to the spirit and intent of the national Government," he said, and continued, "The sovereign right in this country is in the people and in the States. They cannot carry their peculiar kind of property from one State into another where it is not recognized as property." As if quoting from the *Lemmon* decision, he added, "Under the fugitive slave law, as I understand it, no man can be reclaimed as a fugitive slave if his master carries him out of the State in which he is held as a slave."[20]

As the voices grew louder, so did O'Conor's political stock among those who supported slavery—including the editors of the *Correspondence*, a newspaper in Augusta, Georgia, which recommended that O'Conor be nominated as president of the United States.

Four days later, having worked up a full head of steam, O'Conor would go before the judges of New York's high court and argue for *Lemmon*'s repeal.

Chapter 12

Privileges and Immunities

The *Lemmon* case reached the New York Court of Appeals, in Albany, on January 24, 1860 (see figure 12.1).

In their written briefs, the attorneys on both sides presented a well-framed legal issue.[1] New York did not question Virginia's right to allow slavery within its borders, nor did Virginia question New York's right to abolish it. Lemmon was a middle case: Could New York, a sovereign state functioning under a constitutional compact, prohibit out-of-state slaveowners from bringing their slaves through New York?

The case was like no other before it. It was the first time that New York's high court had been asked to construe the statute by which the legislature had repealed the nine-month allowance for owners sojourning with their slaves.

On principle, most New Yorkers would have supported the *Lemmon* ruling, but powerful commercial interests in the state were broadcasting three fears at the time. If Virginia were to lose on appeal, they argued, New York would lose business involving Southern slave products, from the fields to the mills and affecting factories, distributors, retailers, financing banks, and others. The outcome might also contribute to the dissolution of the Union, held dear for genuine reasons of patriotism—and if that were to happen, which seemed increasingly likely already, many Americans in the North and South might lose their lives in a civil war.

The elephant in the courtroom, of course, was *Dred Scott*. Because the Supreme Court had handed it down in 1857, well after Judge Paine

Figure 12.1. In 1860, the New York Court of Appeals was in the State Capitol. It would have looked much like this later picture. New York State Archives, New York State. Education Dept. Division of Visual Instruction. Instructional lantern slides, ca. 1856–1939. Series A3045-78, No. D47 AlS5.

had made his ruling in 1852, Virginia could claim that Judge Paine's ruling was no longer valid and had to be overturned. The argument was easily worded: If, as *Dred Scott* had declared, slaves were indeed property, then how could New York get away with prohibiting slaveowners from traveling through the state with them, just as they had the right to do with any of their other property?

In making that argument about the *Lemmon* case, of course, slave power hoped to win its day in court. But it also had a larger hope: overturning the Lemmon ruling would help slavery itself advance into the free states.

New York's high court bench was not monolithic, and no one expected a unanimous decision, least of all the lawyers. None of the eight judges on the court saw it as his sworn duty to uphold slavery or to advocate abolition.[2] Moreover, because New York had abolished slavery some 33 years earlier, most of the judges on the court had never written or even participated in a slavery case.

There were two remarkable exceptions: Judges Thomas Clerke and Henry E. Davies, both of whom had sat on the first-level appeals court that had reviewed Judge Paine's ruling three years earlier, and both had affirmed it. This repeat performance is extraordinary. After having decided the case at the first appellate level, they were now sitting on a higher court, reviewing their own decision—a practice not prohibited until 1867. Given their history with the case, Clerke and Davies might have been expected to uphold the ruling again at this higher level of appeal, although there were no guarantees. And how any of the other judges would rule was anybody's guess.

The courtroom was full when the oral arguments began.[3] Representing Virginia, of course, was the state's standard bearer, Charles O'Conor. Representing New York was William Evarts, who spoke for not only the state but also the larger anti-slavery interests of the free states, some of which had barred slaveowners from traveling with their slaves within their borders. Alongside Evarts, just as he had been during the first level of appeal, was Joseph Blunt.

Technically, Erastus Culver remained the attorney of record on behalf of the Eight. But after he had moved to the bench, his law firm duties were taken over by Chester A. Arthur, the future president, whose name was substituted for Culver's on the Court of Appeals docket. Arthur played no direct role in the case, but later in life he would refer proudly to his affiliation with the case, which most of his obituaries mention (see figure 12.2).

Evarts and O'Conor had the main billing when *Lemmon* reached the Court of Appeals. (See figures 12.3 and 12.4.) Onlookers were eager to hear the arguments of both men, whom the *New York Herald* described as the "recognized champions" on each side. But there was no doubt whom they were rooting for. "Several ladies were present," the paper noted, "and were accommodated with seats near the clerk's desk. It was evident that their sympathies, as well as those of the majority of the sterner sex present, were with Mr. Evarts' side."[4]

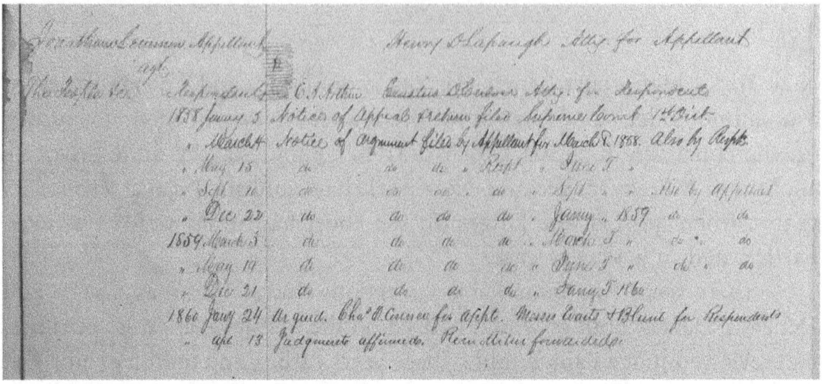

Jonathan Lemmon Appellant — Henry D Lapaugh Atty for Appellant
agt
The People &c Respondent — C A Arthur — Atty for Respondents
1858 Jany 5 Notice of Appeal & return filed Supreme Court 1st Dist
" March 4 Notice of Argument filed by Appellant for March 8 1858. Also by Respt
" May 15 do do do Respt " June 7
" Sept do do do " Sept " " Also by Appellant
" Dec 22 do do do do " Jany " 1859 do do
1859 March 5 do do do do " March 7 " do " do
" May 19 do do do do " June 7 " do " do
" Dec 21 do do do do " Jany 5 1860
1860 Jany 24 Argued. Chas O'Conor for Applt. Messrs Evarts & Blunt for Respondents
" Apl 13 Judgment affirmed. Remittitur forwarded.

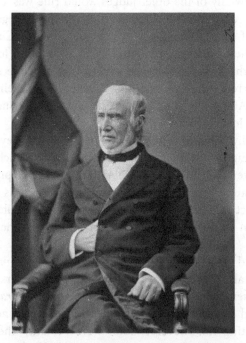

Figure 12.2. From the docket of the New York Court of Appeals in the Lemmon case, showing C. A. Arthur as Attorney for the Respondents. New York State Court of Appeals, Minutes of Causes, vol. 3 (New York State Archives series J2006).

Figure 12.3. Portrait of Charles O'Conor (1804–1884). Library of Congress, Prints and Photographs Division, Brady-Handy Photograph Collection, LC-DIG-cwpbh-05061.

Figure 12.4. Portrait of William Evarts (1818–1901). Library of Congress, Prints and Photographs Division, Brady-Handy Photograph Collection, LC-BH832-30075.

O'Conor rose first, losing no time in acquainting the judges with the importance of the case (as if they were unaware) and that it mattered "in every portion of the civilized world."[5] He then laid out his deplorable views of Negroes and enslavement. "Negroes," he began, "alone and unaided by the guardianship of another race cannot sustain a civilized social state. . . . It follows that . . . the negro must remain in a state of pupilage under the government of some other race." Enslavement, he argued, offered Negroes at least the possibility of self-improvement. "I do not know that they can be said to have made any progress," he continued. "If they have, certainly it has been through the beneficent operation of the slave trade, and their pupilage under the system now established in the slaveholding States of this Union. . . . Through these instrumentalities alone have any of the race attained the blessings of civilization, the light of Christianity, and the advantages which must ever follow as consequences from these, even to the lowest types of humanity." Rather than center his argument on the law, O'Conor felt he could convince the judges that they should reverse Judge Paine's ruling simply by arguing that Negro enslavement was natural and necessary.

He did not ignore the law completely, however, knowing that Northern judges considered England's *Somerset* case a landmark in repudiating slavery. The case was not without its complications and ambiguities, but it was widely celebrated as one of the common law's most inspirational expressions of freedom. O'Conor would have none of it. He attacked *Somerset* as "misleading dogma," a case of "negrophilism," and as irrelevant to the case at hand. The decision, O'Conor claimed, was nothing more than the dictum of a judge, Lord Mansfield, who was "much more renowned for his tendencies to usurp the power of making law than for any inclination to diminish prerogative or to defend the liberty of his white fellow subjects."

With this ad hominem attack on Judge Mansfield, perhaps O'Conor felt he could persuade the judges that *Somerset* had been wrongly decided—a tall order, bordering on heresy for many. But it may be that he was simply belittling the case to please his larger audience—Virginia and the allied forces of slave power in the South. That may be why he also dismissed the writings of Blackstone, the dean of English law, on the questions of slavery and liberty, calling the writings "paradoxical nonsense."

On and on he went.

O'Conor did eventually address an issue that would have been of great interest to the judges—interstate comity, which, he argued, grants to residents of the respective states free transit "with their families and rights of property." A state can accord interstate comity, he contended, without disturbing its own domestic relations. For the judges, this argument was at the core of the case, and they would struggle with it.

O'Conor then turned to the statute by which New York had repealed the nine-month allowance for sojourning with slaves. The repeal had created all sorts of hardships and dangers for slaveowners wishing to come to New York, he claimed. Imagine the plight of a gentle Virginia mother, he told the judges, "whose babe was nursed by a fond and affectionate negro woman—born in the family, bred up under its protection, cherished and cared for by all its members with kindness and affection."

O'Conor then moved on to the *Foot* resolution, passed by the New York legislature in 1857, and declaring that New York would not tolerate slavery within its borders in any form or for any time. O'Conor dismissed the resolution as "treasonable" and insisted that it could not be used to fortify the statute or the repeal of the nine-month exception. That argument was unlikely to sway the judges much, but O'Conor then raised two additional arguments that were sure to capture their attention.

First, he reminded them that control of interstate commerce lies exclusively within the power of Congress. By prohibiting the transit of slaves, he said, New York was usurping that power.

Second, he invoked the Privileges and Immunities clause of the United States Constitution, which under Article IV declares that "the citizens of each state shall be entitled to all privileges and immunities of citizens in the several states"—a provision designed to prevent states from discriminating against other states' citizens. New York's ban on slave transit in New York, O'Conor argued, would "pen up" slaveholder travel to their own states.

In the whole of his oral argument, which lasted some three hours, not once did O'Conor mention *Dred Scott*.

A puzzlement. Even in his written brief he devoted only a single sentence to the case, just as he had done at the previous level of appeal. "The general doctrines of the court in Dred Scott's case must be maintained," he wrote, "their alleged novelty notwithstanding." Again, he did not explain what he meant by "novelty."

Dazzled, no doubt, by his own racist flourishes, O'Conor concluded his argument with his version of patriotism, declaring that it was "the duty of every American citizen," when it came to Negro enslavement, "to vindicate its essential justice and morality in all courts and places before men and nations."

∿

In response, Blunt went first, officially representing New York. He opened crisply, saying that slavery was irreconcilable with the state's jurisprudence.

By joining the Union, he said, New York was obligated to obey the Fugitive Slave Clause as part of the Constitution, insofar as it required New York to deliver up fugitive slaves. But that stipulation, he stressed, referred to fugitive slaves only, and did not include slaves in transit with their owners. Because the Lemmon Eight were brought to New York by their owners, he continued, they fell outside the stipulation—exactly as Judge Paine had ruled.

Evarts and Blunt both addressed New York's statute, in which the legislature initially allowed slavery for a nine-month sojourn. When the state had repealed the allowance, in 1841, they argued, the point had been settled—nothing more needed to be said on the topic.

They then took on the question of the Privileges and Immunities Clause, arguing that New York was *not* discriminating against the Lemmons as slaveowners. All the state was doing, they argued, was granting the Lemmons the same privileges and immunities as it did for its own citizens—who were likewise prohibited from even sojourning with slaves in New York without confiscatory consequences.

Should New York, out of a sense of courtesy (that is, interstate comity), recognize Virginia's choice to allow slavery? Yes, both men said—but not on New York soil, where its practice would violate New York's "absolute policy and comprehensive legislation." New York fulfills its obligation by respecting Virginia's right to allow slavery within its own borders—but not to import slavery into New York.[6]

Evarts also dealt in basics, elaborating on the purpose of the writ of habeas corpus. The writ by which the Lemmon case began, he said, belongs to every person restrained of liberty within New York, "under any pretence whatsoever"—which, by definition, includes enslavement. The practice of slavery (or its abolition) is undisputedly a matter for each state, he continued. For centuries under Anglo-American law, habeas corpus had been the time-honored gateway to freedom, unless there was legal cause for the restraint on liberty. Concerning the Eight, under New York law, he told the judges, there was no such cause. Nor did any federal law justify the restraint on their freedom in New York.

On a broader theme, Evarts labeled slavery a violation of the law of nature, sustained only by physical force backed up by local (municipal) law. When the municipal law is vacated, as when New York abolished slavery, he argued, there is nothing for slavery to rest upon, and "the captive is free." Evarts spoke eloquently of New York as a free state: "It has no code of the slaveowner's rights or of the slave's submission," he said, "no processes for the enforcement of either, no rules of evidence or adjudication in the premises, no guard-houses, prisons or whipping-post to uphold the slaveowner's power and crush the slave's resistance."

Evarts then dealt with one of the other side's most compelling arguments: that allowing mere transit, in recognition of Southern law, would be a very small price for New York to pay to preserve union, harmony, commerce, and peace.

Not so simple, Evarts contended. If, in this instance, New York were to recognize Southern law even briefly, in preference to its own, then unintended consequences would follow. He then recited for the judges a list of brain-teasing hypotheticals worthy of a final examination prepared by a law professor teaching conflicts of laws:

If a slaveowner died on New York soil, a New York probate court would have to administer the slave as assets.

If a slave gave birth to offspring in New York, the state would have a native-born slave.

If a slaveowner maimed or killed a slave while in transit in New York, and if the act were done with no intent to kill but merely to enforce obedience, capriciously or otherwise, the act would not be criminal and would not result in an assault or manslaughter charge.

If a slave while in transit in New York were to commit a crime, the testimony of a fellow slave would be prohibited at a trial in New York.

And so forth. The list went on and could have been almost endless.

In his rebuttal O'Conor tried to mock the illustrations, contending that New York could avoid them all by simply enacting its own rules of evidence. Evarts must have smiled when he heard that, because it proved his very point—that New York had the power to set up its own rules, on its own soil, including a prohibition against traveling with slaves. The point was not lost on the judges.

Interestingly, it was Blunt alone who mentioned *Dred Scott* in the oral arguments. He may have felt that the judges could not or would not ignore the case, even if O'Conor had. Blunt began this part of his argument with a five-minute primer in decision-writing, pointing out that courts decide only what is before them, free of unnecessary discourse (or "surplusage," as it's sometimes called in legal circles). Any gratuitous discourse that goes beyond what is necessary to decide a case, he told the court, is dictum and need not be followed.

With the primer behind him, Blunt then turned to *Dred Scott*. Dred Scott had lost his case, Blunt noted, because as a Negro Dred Scott was ruled incapable of bringing the suit. Okay, Blunt continued—but if someone lacks the capacity to sue, then courts dismiss the case and do not go on to discuss how the case should be decided if it were properly brought. In *Dred Scott*, once the Supreme Court had concluded that Dred Scott had no capacity to sue, there was a lack of jurisdiction—and everything that followed in the ruling, including Taney's most punishing language, was incidental and not binding as precedent. "That is sound doctrine," Blunt declared. "It is law. It is the law of that court. It is the law of all courts, and is familiar to your honors."

Interestingly, in rebuttal, O'Conor did not utter a word about *Dred Scott*, even to defend its value as precedent.[7] Perhaps, as at the first appellate level, he did not want to be drawn into an esoteric and risky discussion as to how much of the decision was dictum.

❧

The oral arguments in the *Lemmon* appeal ended up lasting two full days.[8] After the lawyers wrapped up, the judges adjourned the proceedings and took the case under advisement. A decision, everybody knew, would probably come within a few weeks.

The following day, the *New York Daily Herald* published an account of the arguments and the case. In it, the paper made clear just how high many New Yorkers felt the stakes to be. "It is a case of the deepest interest," the paper wrote, "and on its decision, at this critical moment, depends, to a great degree, the peace of the country."[9]

Chapter 13

The Voice of Humanity

The Court of Appeals would end up taking more than two months to render its Lemmon decision.

In the interim, however, New York remained active in its anti-slavery efforts. Just a few days after the Court of Appeals had heard oral argument, a select committee of the New York State Assembly took up a citizens' petition to end "slave hunting" in the state—the practice, based on federal law, of returning escaped slaves to their owners in the South after slave catchers had seized them. The petitions asked that New York reverse decades of practice and simply refuse to return runaway slaves.

Of all the anti-slavery reports and resolutions produced during this period, this was the boldest. Unsurprisingly, it prompted outrage in the South. Commenting on the petition, a Mississippi newspaper wrote, "See what the vile wretches propose to do."[1]

A moving force behind it was the formidable Susan B. Anthony, who had urged readers to rise up against the fugitive-slave laws. "If you are disheartened, and feel that the cause of freedom is retrograding," she wrote, "then the more pressing is my appeal to you, to take the petition in hand, and go forth among the people."[2] Anthony invited the public to get copies of a petition from her and to circulate them for signatures. Direct the petitions, she said, to Shotwell Powell (1808–1896), a Quaker farmer-turned-assemblyman who had been named to head the select committee.[3]

On February 11, Powell released a rousing report (see figure 13.1). "The time has arrived," he wrote, on behalf of the committee, "when the

147

Figure 13.1. *Report of the Select Committee on the Petitions to Prevent Slave Hunting in the State of New York*, 1860.

voice of humanity, in our State, will not be hushed. . . . [The enslaved] ask the protection of the greatest republican State in the world, in behalf of her 45,000 colored citizens, whose liberty is imperiled by an unjust and despotic law of the United States."[4]

New York, Powell insisted, could not be a "free state" as long as it permitted the enforcement of the slave code "in its most abhorrent and barbarous features." Nor should it worry about offending "our Southern brethren," a phrase often used by Unionists worried about maintaining national harmony—or, more cynically, the flow of money and profits from the South. "Of the ten millions of our brethren of the south," he continued, "about four millions are slaves and free persons of color, who would hail with delight such a statute."

Powell was no fool. He knew that the courts in New York and other Northern states had consistently recognized the constitutional obligation to return fugitive slaves. So what was his motivation? He wanted to spur the New York Legislature into resisting the federal fugitive-slave laws by passing some form of personal liberty legislation, as other free states had done. Two of the boldest personal liberty laws came from Maine and Vermont, which had forbidden their officers from assisting in the capture of fugitive slaves, and had denied the use of their jails for holding them. Massachusetts, Connecticut, Rhode Island, New Jersey, Pennsylvania, Michigan, Illinois, Indiana, and Wisconsin all had various forms of personal liberty laws, which Powell outlined in a comprehensive appendix.[5]

Powell's proposal went beyond Judge Paine's ruling in *Lemmon*, which had discharged slaves "brought" into New York by a master or owner. Powell's report, however, proposed freedom for any one "who shall come" into New York—an unconditional grant of freedom and official protection to any slave, even fugitives, who set foot on New York soil.

Unfortunately, it was all too much for the Democrats in the New York Assembly. (At the time, Democrats were pro-slavery.) The bill's chief assailant was Theophilus C. Callicot (1826–1920), a Virginia-born assemblyman representing Brooklyn. Callicot assailed the bill as unconstitutional, an assessment probably shared by some moderate Assembly Republicans— but his assault on it was vitriolic. He warned his colleagues that if they passed the bill, they would be morally guilty of perjury and treason. Not only that, he said—appealing to the base elements in his party—New York would attract fugitive slaves and become a "Negro paradise."[6]

Callicot's speech was a remarkable demonstration of how, even in 1860, a member of the New York Legislature could speak with racial venom worthy of the most obdurate slaveholder:

Sir, the proposition to put negroes on a footing of political equality with white men is repugnant to the sense of the American people. . . . First, then, I assert that colored persons are not citizens of the United States, and not being such citizens they have no right to claim the full privileges of citizenship of this State. . . . Let us not be misled by the teachings of fanatics whose morbid sympathies impel them to fight against the laws of God and nature, and to seek the reduction of the superior and the inferior races to the same level.[7]

On the other side, Delaware County Assemblyman Barna R. Johnson (1825–1908) rose and fought back eloquently:

Are we to be compelled by law to aid the master to catch his slave, and help him with his human chattel, on to the land of chains, and stripes, and slavery hopeless, cruel, unmitigated slavery? Is it fair for a quarter of a million of slaveholders to rule with a rod of iron, not only the four millions of slaves, and the free people of color, and the five millions of Southern whites, who would rejoice in the abolition of slavery, but the twenty-millions of free people at the North also?[8]

Delivered back to back, Callicot's and Johnson's speeches epitomized the nation's breach. By and large, New York was politically and culturally much closer to Johnson than to Callicot—but the Assembly nonetheless allowed Powell's proposal to die. Even anti-slavery Republicans found it too radical, and on shaky constitutional footing.

On February 27, 1860, while the Lemmon case was still under review by the Court of Appeals, Abraham Lincoln gave a speech at Cooper Union, in New York (see figure 13.2).

Lincoln was not yet the Republican Party's presidential nominee—that would happen in May. But in his speech, which has become justly famous, he nonetheless firmly staked out his position on slavery. It was akin to the one Judge Paine had set forth in *Lemmon*, when he had ruled that no one can have "property in slaves.

But what of *Dred Scott*, which had been decided after Judge Paine's ruling? Did not the highest court in the land speak of slaves as property?

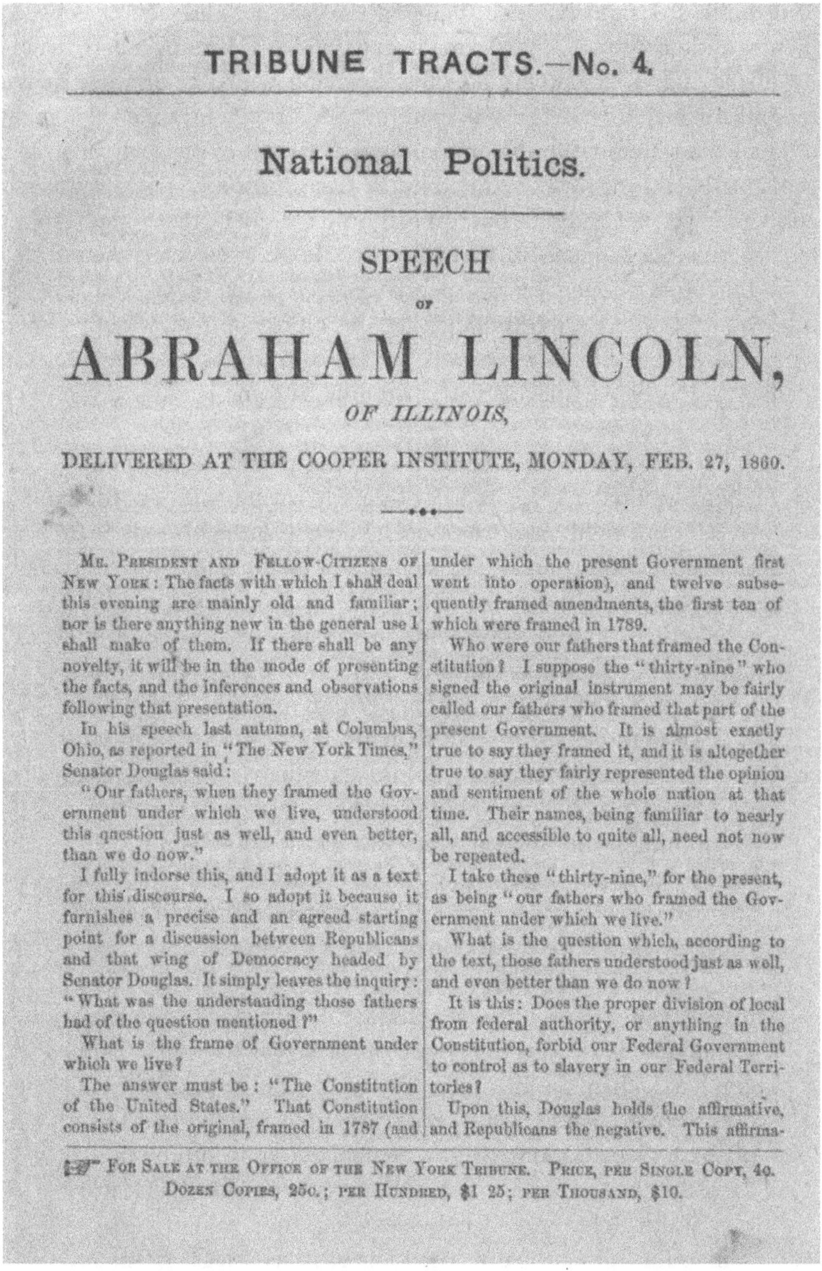

TRIBUNE TRACTS.—No. 4.

National Politics.

SPEECH

OF

ABRAHAM LINCOLN,

OF ILLINOIS,

DELIVERED AT THE COOPER INSTITUTE, MONDAY, FEB. 27, 1860.

—•••—

MR. PRESIDENT AND FELLOW-CITIZENS OF NEW YORK: The facts with which I shall deal this evening are mainly old and familiar; nor is there anything new in the general use I shall make of them. If there shall be any novelty, it will be in the mode of presenting the facts, and the inferences and observations following that presentation.

In his speech last autumn, at Columbus, Ohio, as reported in "The New York Times," Senator Douglas said:

"Our fathers, when they framed the Government under which we live, understood this question just as well, and even better, than we do now."

I fully indorse this, and I adopt it as a text for this discourse. I so adopt it because it furnishes a precise and an agreed starting point for a discussion between Republicans and that wing of Democracy headed by Senator Douglas. It simply leaves the inquiry: "What was the understanding those fathers had of the question mentioned?"

What is the frame of Government under which we live?

The answer must be: "The Constitution of the United States." That Constitution consists of the original, framed in 1787 (and under which the present Government first went into operation), and twelve subsequently framed amendments, the first ten of which were framed in 1789.

Who were our fathers that framed the Constitution? I suppose the "thirty-nine" who signed the original instrument may be fairly called our fathers who framed that part of the present Government. It is almost exactly true to say they framed it, and it is altogether true to say they fairly represented the opinion and sentiment of the whole nation at that time. Their names, being familiar to nearly all, and accessible to quite all, need not now be repeated.

I take these "thirty-nine," for the present, as being "our fathers who framed the Government under which we live."

What is the question which, according to the text, those fathers understood just as well, and even better than we do now?

It is this: Does the proper division of local from federal authority, or anything in the Constitution, forbid our Federal Government to control as to slavery in our Federal Territories?

Upon this, Douglas holds the affirmative, and Republicans the negative. This affirma-

☞ FOR SALE AT THE OFFICE OF THE NEW YORK TRIBUNE. PRICE, PER SINGLE COPY, 4c. DOZEN COPIES, 25c.; PER HUNDRED, $1 25; PER THOUSAND, $10.

Figure 13.2. A pamphlet of Abraham Lincoln's Speech delivered at the Cooper Institute, New York (Tribune Tracts no. 4), February 27, 1860. The Gilder Lehrman Institute of American History, GLC02812.

"Not quite so," Lincoln said. "Waiving the lawyer's distinction between dictum and decision . . . it was made in a divided Court, by a bare majority of the Judges, and they not quite agreeing with one another in the reasons for making it . . . it was mainly based upon a mistaken statement of fact—the statement in the opinion that 'the right of property in a slave is distinctly and expressly affirmed in the Constitution.'"[9] Lincoln was too good a lawyer not to point out, even if only obliquely, that Judge Taney's most pernicious language in *Dred Scott* could be considered dictum.

Lincoln's Cooper Union speech covered a lot of ground, but he brought it to a close by arguing that the North and the South would simply never be able to arrive at a lasting compromise on the question of slavery. His explanation is worth quoting at some length:

> What will convince [Democrats to work with Republicans]? This, and this only: cease to call slavery wrong, and join them in calling it right. And this must be done thoroughly—done in acts as well as in words. Silence will not be tolerated—we must place ourselves avowedly with them. . . . We must arrest and return their fugitive slaves with greedy pleasure. We must pull down our Free State constitutions. The whole atmosphere must be disinfected from all taint of opposition to slavery, before they will cease to believe that all their troubles proceed from us.
>
> I am quite aware they do not state their case precisely in this way. Most of them would probably say to us, "Let us alone, do nothing to us, and say what you please about slavery." But we do let them alone—have never disturbed them—so that, after all, it is what we say, which dissatisfies them. They will continue to accuse us of doing, until we cease saying.
>
> I am also aware they have not, as yet, in terms, demanded the overthrow of our Free-State Constitutions. Yet those Constitutions declare the wrong of slavery, with more solemn emphasis, than do all other sayings against it; and when all these other sayings shall have been silenced, the overthrow of these Constitutions will be demanded, and nothing be left to resist the demand. . . . Holding, as they do, that slavery is morally right, and socially elevating, they cannot cease to demand a full national recognition of it, as a legal right, and a social blessing.

Accompanying the published version of Lincoln's speech was a set of notes, written by Charles C. Nott and Cephas Brainerd, that Lincoln approved of as "extremely valuable." And in one of those notes, commenting on the remark that the slave states had yet to demand "the overthrow of our Free-State Constitutions," the authors wrote, "That demand has since been made." And who had made it? Charles O'Conor, in arguing Virginia's side of *Lemmon* before the New York Court of Appeals.

The authors of the note went on to discuss *Lemmon* and the threat posed should it reach the Supreme Court. "The State of Virginia, not content with the decision of our own courts upon the right claimed by them, is now engaged in carrying this, the Lemon [*sic*] case, to the Supreme Court of the United States, hoping by a decision there, in accordance with the intimations in the Dred Scott case, to overthrow the Constitution of New-York."[10]

Many New Yorkers had this precise worry. With *Dred Scott*, the first shoe had dropped—and the second would likely follow if and when *Lemmon* reached the Supreme Court.

John Jay, as we know, certainly had that worry. So on March 27, 1860, with the case still pending decision before the Court of Appeals, he filed an amicus application—for the third time, and now *after* the case had been heard—seeking to dismiss the Lemmon appeal as moot.[11] But the court denied the motion, and the judges continued to craft their writings.

A little over a week later, on April 6, Representative Alfred Wells, of New York, brought concerns about *Lemmon* to the floor of Congress. If Charles O'Conor had his way, Wells declared, soon in every state of the Union one might hear "the crack of the overseer's lash."[12]

Chapter 14

The Final Ruling

On April 14, 1860, the New York Court of Appeals issued its decision. By a 5–3 vote, the majority upheld Judge Paine's ruling.

The decision consisted of three opinions. The first, the primary opinion for the majority, was written by Judge Hiram Denio, and the second, also for the majority, by Judge William Wright; both were joined by three other judges. The third opinion, a dissent, was by Judge Thomas Clerke, who was joined by the court's other two judges.[1]

Judge Denio wrote in exemplary "judicious" style. He began with the statute. When New York had repealed the nine-month allowance for sojourning with slaves, he said, the statute left no room for debate: Having been brought to New York by their owners, the Eight acquired absolute and unconditional freedom as soon as they disembarked from *City of Richmond* and set foot in New York.

Judge Denio next ruled that if New York expressly repudiates the laws and practices of another state, there can be no occasion for "comity." He then noted, as a matter of constitutional history, that the *only* case in which slaves would not be granted their freedom upon arriving in a free state would be if they arrived as fugitives. In that case, the federal law was clear: The national government could compel their return. But, Judge Denio noted, the Eight had not arrived as fugitives.

Next, he addressed O'Conor's "privileges and immunities" argument based on the idea that no state may discriminate against citizens of other states. Denio posed a hypothetical: If a state were to allow some forms of gambling that New York prohibits, would anyone expect New York to

155

allow people to carry their state laws into New York and engage in acts that New York had banned? Certainly not. So why should they expect anything different for somebody arriving in the state with slaves?[2]

He concluded by declaring that New York had not usurped Congress's power to regulate interstate commerce. The Lemmons, he wrote, were not passing through waters of New York in a vessel having a coasting license granted under the act of Congress regulating the coasting trade, nor did Congress pass any act to regulate commerce between the states when carried on by land, or otherwise than in coasting vessels.

Nowhere in his opinion did Judge Denio mention *Dred Scott*.

∾

Judge William Wright saw the case as involving the sovereignty of a state to determine the civil status of every person within its boundaries—in New York's case, as free and unenslaved.

Judge Wright began by describing enslavement as "repugnant to natural justice and right, [with] no support in any principle of international law, and . . . antagonistic to the genius and spirit of republican government." Slavery, he added, citing Montesquieu, "not only violates the laws of nature and of civil society; it also wounds the best forms of government; in a democracy where all men are equal slavery is contrary to the spirit of the Constitution." No person, he continued, Black or white, can be held in New York "for any moment of time, in a condition of bondage." Like Judge Denio, he acknowledged that the Constitution allowed an exception, but for fugitive slaves only.

Judge Wright then took up the questions of positive law and comity. Slavery, he wrote, may exist only if supported by local, positive enactments, such as in the Southern states and formerly in New York.[3] In support of this position, he turned deftly to *Prigg*, the slavery case decided by the Supreme Court some 18 years earlier, nullifying a Pennsylvania statute that criminalized the abduction of alleged fugitive slaves. *Prigg*, however, had also emphasized that slavery was a local matter. Within its own boundaries, the ruling had declared, a state need not recognize the slavery laws of another state, although it could choose to as a matter of "comity."[4]

Next, Judge Wright recounted the history of Negro enslavement in New York, noting that the practice was not recognized by English common law and had never had any foundation in the law of nature.[5] He next turned to *Butt v. Rachel*, a case in which the Virginia Supreme Court, in

1815, had granted freedom to an American Indian woman who had been claimed as a slave. A Virginia statute of 1691 stated that no American Indian woman could be a slave in Virginia, even if she had been a slave elsewhere (for instance, in Jamaica) and had been brought as a slave to Virginia. The case held, in effect, that the woman had become free as soon as she had set foot on Virginia soil.[6]

When it came to *Dred Scott*, Judge Wright was unimpressed and undaunted. "The exclusive right of the State of Missouri to determine and regulate the status of persons within her territory," he wrote, "was the only point in judgment in the Dred Scott case, and all beyond this was obiter." None of Justice Taney's thunderings in *Dred Scott*, Judge Wright implied, had any bearing on the fate of the Eight.

What a moment! As if with his pinky, Judge Wright brushes aside the pernicious language in the *Dred Scott* decision as dicta, unworthy of any importance in the Lemmon decision.[7]

∾

Judge Clerke's dissent is surprising. He had sat on the first-level appeals court that sustained Judge Paine's ruling, agreed with it, and was now serving on a higher court reviewing his own ruling.

Why did he change his mind? All we know is that at the previous level of appeal, he said he had been "erroneously influenced" by Judge William Mitchell, who had written the decision—a candid admission, perhaps, that he voted one way in 1857, perhaps feeling some pressure, but now thought otherwise.

Like the majority, Judge Clerke examined the statute in question and concluded that New York's legislature had intended to free every slave *brought* to its soil, even in transit. Unlike the majority, however, he believed that under the United States Constitution, New York lacked the power to enact such a law.

Clerke did not question New York's right to abolish slavery and to prohibit lengthy sojourning with slaves. Although New York might, and did, repudiate the idea of slaves as "property," he wrote, Virginia was free to conclude otherwise. Here he noted that when the Constitution was drafted, all of the states considered slaves at least partly as property.

Insofar as the case might be termed one of "choice of law," he argued that New York was not free to impose its definition of property on Virginia when it comes to mere transit, and that New York may not stop Virginia's slave-owning residents from passing through New York. By the "law of nations," he argued, "citizens of one government have a right of passage through the territory of another, peaceably, for business or pleasure; and the latter acquires no right over such person or his property."

Judge Clerke then turned to the "privileges and immunities" argument. Here he compared the states of the Union to foreign countries, saying, in substance, that if one country allows the "privilege" of transit to another, the Union demands at least as much, given the American compact among its states.[8]

A good legal technician, Clerke knew that if the test were comity alone, New York could decline to recognize Virginia law, since comity is voluntary. Instead, he contended that New York's obligation was based on comity, plus. The plus converts the voluntary into the obligatory.

After all was said and done, the New York judiciary had spoken—not unanimously, but with five of the eight judges joining in two forceful majority writings. And their holding, as stated by Judge Denio in his majority opinion, was clear: "Upon the whole case," he wrote, "I have come to the conclusion that there is nothing in the National Constitution or the laws of Congress to preclude the State judicial authorities from declaring these slaves thus introduced into the territory of this State, free, and setting them at liberty."

∞

After the Court of Appeals released its decision, those opposed to slavery around the country worried aloud, broadcasting what might happen if Virginia were to appeal to the Supreme Court.

"Since the Dred Scott case," the Cleveland Morning Leader wrote on April 18, "there is hardly any extravagance in favor of Slavery not to be expected from that court." Three days later, in a Vermont newspaper called Aurora of the Valley, an editorialist predicted that an appeal would give the Supreme Court "the opportunity still further to apply its new doctrine of the nationality of slavery."[9]

On the floor of Congress, Representative James M. Ashley (1824–1896), of Ohio, weighed in. If the Lemmon case went to the Supreme Court, he warned, the country should expect another Dred Scott—a pro-slavery decision that, with a Democratic president in power, would be "enforced by the strong arm of the Executive department of the Government, with the army and navy and purse of the nation at its command."[10]

Virginia never initiated an appeal to the Supreme Court. This is inexplicable. Charles O'Conor himself wrote to Virginia's governor, John Letcher, suggesting that he appeal. "The Lemmon Slave Case has just been Affirmed," O'Conor told Letcher on April 14, 1860, "five Judges for Affirmance, two dis-senting, and one not voting. If speed is an object in reference to the present Term of the Supreme Court, it would be well to direct the Writ of Error at once." (See figure 14.1.)

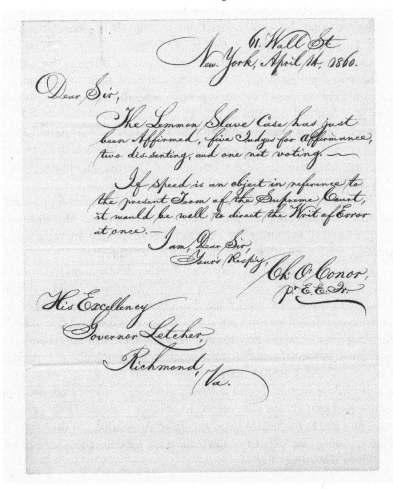

Figure 14.1. A letter from Charles O'Conor to Virginia's governor John Letcher, urging him to appeal the Lemmon case to the US Supreme Court, April 14, 1860. Courtesy of the Library of Virginia, Executive Papers, Governor John Letcher, Accession 36787.

What happened? Why didn't Governor Letcher act? Some had earlier accused him of being soft on slavery, but he had publicly disavowed any affinity for abolition and he was elected.[11] In his January 7, 1860, inauguration speech, he chastised Massachusetts, Vermont, and Wisconsin for obstructing the Fugitive Slave Act, criticized the Republican Party for what he called its utter repudiation of *Dred Scott*, and even advocated that Virginia send a delegation to recalcitrant Northern states to insist that they repeal their personal liberty laws.

It's true that the lower-court *Lemmon* appeals had been sponsored not by Governor Letcher but by his predecessor, Governor Wise, and there may have been some bad blood between them. But now that Letcher was the state's governor, it fell to him to carry the fight to the Supreme Court—a fight approved by slave power generally, not to mention the voters who had just put him in office.[12]

Eight months passed between when the Court of Appeals handed down its ruling, in April, and when the Civil War broke out, in December, but during that period Governor Letcher and Virginia did nothing by way of appeal, allowing the filing deadline to expire.

Nonetheless, as late as late February of 1861, after Mississippi, Florida, Alabama, Georgia, Louisiana, and Texas had all seceded, the *Richmond Dispatch* was still expecting the case to be heard by the Supreme Court, assuming, mistakenly, that Virginia had filed an appeal.[13]

Perhaps, after the ruling, Governor Letcher felt he could live with the stand-off that it had created—one in which Southerners could not bring their slaves to New York and a handful of other like-minded states, but otherwise could continue to keep slaves at home and expect free states to return fugitives who had fled enslavement and had been apprehended in those states. Perhaps he didn't feel passionately enough about expanding slavery to want to lead the charge.

Or maybe somebody just dropped the ball. Perhaps, after the filing deadline had passed, one aide turned to another and said, "I thought *you* were going to file the notice," and the other responded, "Wait, I thought *you* were doing that." That wouldn't make for appealing history—but it's how things sometimes happen in the real world.[14]

On April 23, less than two weeks after the *Lemmon* ruling, the Democrats held their first convention, in Charleston, South Carolina. Charles O'Conor was there, fresh from his performance in New York. As talented as he was,

Figure 14.2. Portrait of John Letcher (1813–1884). Library of Congress, Prints and Photographs Division, LC-USZ62-38891.

few Southerners had expected him to convince the Court of Appeals to rule in favor of slave power, although the 5–3 vote was probably closer than most observers had expected. He had burnished his pro-slavery credentials, and now, at the convention, he was again being mentioned (along with many others) as a candidate for either the presidency or the vice-presidency.[15] Eventually, however, he wound up endorsing John Breckenridge, Virginia's staunchest pro-slavery candidate, for the presidency.[16]

For months afterward, as the presidential campaign proceeded, O'Conor spoke out vehemently in favor of slavery, using the rhetoric of a religious warrior. "A moral war has been made upon [slavery] by infidels," he declared in July.[17] New York, in his view, would be critical to the election's outcome. "I trust that in the coming contest," he said in October, "New York will be redeemed from her thraldom to Black Republicanism, and become once more a bulwark to the Union."[18] (Slavery advocates commonly employed the term "Black Republicans" as a slur against the Republican Party, given its anti-slavery origins and platform.)

But the wind was blowing in Lincoln's direction, and by the end of October, just several days before the November 6, 1860, election, O'Conor adopted a different tone. Sensing that Lincoln might win, and unable to endure the thought of the South being subjugated by abolitionists, O'Conor began to talk of secession.

Lincoln won, carrying some 40 percent of the popular vote, with 30 percent going to Stephen Douglas, the Democratic Party candidate; 18 percent to John C. Breckenridge, the Southern Democrat; and 12 percent to John Bell, the Constitution Union candidate. Lincoln's electoral vote was far larger than the other three combined.

The election, and what it portended, brought on a host of grievances from the South. The *Lemmon* decision ranked high. One North Carolina newspaper, the *Newbern Weekly Progress*, decried "the monopoly, by the Lemmon and other Northern State Judicial decrees, of the rivers, waters, and coasts of the United States, which make it impossible for Southern men to travel on them, as Northern men travel on them, with their house-holds, &c." The same paper also focused its aggrieved attention on "the now threatened conversion of the Supreme Court of the United States into a political tribunal, to decide slave questions by geography—by latitude and longitude—instead of by law."[19]

Concerned over the growing threat of disunion, a large group met in New York on December 15, 1860, and chose O'Conor as their leader, seemingly unaware that he had earlier counseled a Southern audience to secede.

It didn't matter. Nine days later, South Carolina seceded, the first state to do so. And in its Declaration of Secession, it pointed its finger at *Lemmon*. "In the State of New York," the authors wrote, "even the right of transit for a slave has been denied by her tribunals."[20]

Mississippi, Florida, Alabama, Georgia, Louisiana, and Texas soon followed South Carolina's lead, and together they began calling themselves the Confederate States of America. Within months, Virginia, Arkansas, North Carolina, Tennessee, and Kentucky would join them—but not before the original states of the Confederacy had produced a new constitution that itself addressed the outcome of *Lemmon*.

"The citizens of each State," it read, "shall be entitled to all the privileges and immunities of citizens in the several States; and shall have the right of transit and sojourn in any State of this Confederacy, with their slaves and other property; and the right of property in said slaves shall not be thereby impaired."[21]

The die was cast. On April 12, 1861, almost a year to the day after the Court of Appeals had upheld the liberation of the Eight, Confederate forces fired on Fort Sumter, and the Civil War began.

～

And so marks the end of the Lemmon case in its contemporary life.

What of it? The Eight have long passed on, and so have all the players in the drama. Slavery laws have been wiped from our books. So why dwell on it?

The most obvious answer is that although slavery has been cast out of our country by constitutional decree, it left consequences that we are still grappling with. When slavery was abolished after the Civil War, it produced offspring in the form of Jim Crow laws—and when those were abolished, more than a half century ago, we inherited or put into place a number of systemically racist policies and practices, the abiding pernicious effects of which we are still coming to terms with today. Slavery may be over, but the movement for racial justice certainly is not.

The conventional wisdom tells us that history repeats itself, and if we don't learn from our past mistakes we will repeat them. As the saying goes (sometimes attributed to Mark Twain), history doesn't repeat itself, but it often rhymes. We can spot an exact repetition, but it usually doesn't work that way. A variant emerges, different enough to create a new trap. Today's racial injustices may manifest in new ways, but they are rooted in many of the same prejudices used to justify enslavement.

On the surface, the Lemmon case dealt with certain specific and often technical aspects of the law. Ultimately, however, the case was about how we see our relations with one another, and where the governments fit into the picture. Those are timeless concerns.

In *Lemmon*, the lawyers and judges spoke of "privileges and immunities," of "due process," and of "property." Each of these phrases is open wide to interpretation. Take, for example, the majestic phrase in the Constitution guaranteeing that the government may not deny anyone "life, liberty, or property without due process of law." In the *Lemmon* era, the phrase had taken on a meaning that depended on where you lived. In one part of the country, "property" included people, and the government stood ready to protect one person's ownership of another, as it would protect ownership of a horse or a bag of oats.

But what about the first part of the phrase, protecting life and liberty? No, not in a slavery regime. How could it be otherwise, given the basic idea that one person could sell or mortgage another?

It is fair to look back and ask: Couldn't these laws have been upended by the courts? Shouldn't they have been? How could judges have sat by and approved of sales at the auction block in which children were sold off from their parents, and spouses from one another? At the earliest stages of our country, this was accepted everywhere, and had been going on for two hundred years before *Lemmon*.

It makes sense to ask how a court system could be set up to allow that to happen. The judges and lawyers in one part of the country were of the same stock as the other. Many even sat next to one another in class in college. But when they went back home, all bets were off.

When we set things up, our framers knew there would be regional differences, and it came as no surprise that the laws of one region would, in time, bump up against those of another. The Constitution tries to deal with this by saying that if you are a citizen of state X and you find yourself in state Y, the government in state Y cannot discriminate against you. In *Lemmon*, this question of turf came up when the Lemmons brought the Eight to New York, having good title of ownership under Virginia law. Should that title disappear merely by bringing their "slave property" into a free state? Lawyers might call this a "conflicts of law" case, and in Lemmon, it came down to whether someone entering New York could carry with them not only their shoes and overcoats but also their *laws*.

Today, a rough analogy might be when someone from a 70 mph highway speed limit state crosses into a state with a 60 mph speed limit. When you are pulled over for speeding, the officer will not care that you can go 70 mph at home. That is how the *Lemmon* judges saw things, and it's why they freed the Eight.

The problem, of course, is that despite what we can now see as the manifest injustice of slavery, a century and a half ago, the country had no broad consensus on its morality. If the human race ever agreed on anything, enslavement was not it. If Grant had surrendered to Lee, in the South there would have been a very different version of what was "right," at least as a matter of law.

Lemmon is worth thinking about for another reason. Politics is the art of compromise, and when groups disagree on fundamental questions, how far do we—or should we—go in the name of compromise? When we revisit the story of the Lemmon Eight, and the many actors who fought for and against them in the courts, we throw that question into relief, and we're reminded that it's just as pertinent today as it was in 1850. What compromises are we making today, in our laws and in our legislative chambers, and in society at large, that 200 years from now will seem as misguided as the compromises we made concerning slavery?

∾

It seems fitting and proper to end this story with a brief tribute to its heroes. Their efforts, their dedication, and their humanity all buoy the spirit.

When Louis Napoleon learned that there were eight enslaved people on a steamer in New York harbor, he sprang into action. He could not read or write but he knew he had to get before a judge who might liberate the Eight, even though it was a long shot. Without his efforts there would simply have been no case. Those efforts also enable us to appreciate that the fight for freedom was waged not only by whites and by Black elites who weighed in productively on the political, cultural, and religious dimensions of the struggle, but also the lesser-known Black people who played a critical role in the anti-slavery battle. Napoleon was one in this spectrum of African Americans who themselves advanced the cause of freedom.

We might also imagine what it was like for Judge Elijah Paine, who stuck his neck out writing a decision liberating the Eight. He got some praise for it, but also heaps of scorn.

Think of Erastus Culver, John Jay, and William Evarts, the lawyers who dedicated themselves to the cause and guided the case through the courts. Think, too, of the now-forgotten heroes who helped transport the Eight out of New York and to Canada via the Underground Railroad, so that they could live out their lives in freedom.

Think, most lastingly, of Emeline—to me, the bravest and noblest character in this whole story. She was only 23 when the *Lemmon* case began, and at that point had lived her whole life in bondage. Nonetheless, she stood up to her owner in a court of law, risking everything before a judge she did not know, in order to win freedom for herself and her family. Staring down the arrayed forces against her, and through her tears, she did not yield. Instead, she fought the good fight, and she prevailed.

Let Emeline's example be a lesson to us all. Plenty of good fights remain to be fought—and, like hers, they can be won.

Afterword

We know how the case turned out, but what became of the people involved? I've done everything I can to find out, and here's what I've learned.

Louis Napoleon, as one of the most active conductors on the Underground Railroad, helped thousands escape slavery. His records and those of Sidney Howard Gay, with whom he collaborated, are at Columbia University. I even got to speak with Napoleon's great-granddaughter Angela Terrell.

After Judge Paine's ruling, the Lemmons did not go to Texas, as originally planned, but returned to Virginia. **Juliet Lemmon** died in 1909 and is buried in Botetourt County, Virginia. **Jonathan Lemmon** died in 1890 and is buried in Allegheny County, Virginia. Two of the Lemmon sons served in the Confederate army.

William Evarts went on to become United States Attorney General; then Secretary of State, in the Hayes administration; and finally a United States Senator from New York. He prosecuted Jefferson Davis for treason—with Charles O'Conor serving as counsel for the defense. Evarts later defended President Andrew Johnson in his impeachment trial. Evarts's great-grandson Archibald Cox served as a US Solicitor General and special prosecutor during President Richard Nixon's Watergate scandal.

Today, portraits of both Evarts and O'Conor, facing one another, hang in the entryway of the New York Law Institute, a landmark site that houses an extensive collection of legal volumes and documents.

Judge Elijah Paine died less than a year after his decision liberating the Eight. He was survived by a teenage son, Horatio, who enlisted with the Union forces in 1861, as a surgeon, and later became the superintendent of Roosevelt Hospital, in New York.

Richard (formerly Levi) Johnson, the brother of Nancy, one of the Eight, enlisted with the Union forces in the 102nd USCT (United States Colored Troops) from Michigan. He was wounded in the arm. He died in 1921, at about age 98.

Erastus Culver was elected Brooklyn City Judge in 1854. While on the bench, he issued a writ of habeas corpus liberating 24-year-old "Jeems" Stead, who had escaped from bondage. President Lincoln later appointed him Minister to Venezuela. He later returned to Greenwich, Washington County, New York, where he was president of the Greenwich Bank. He died in 1889 at age 86.

But what became of **the Eight**? This was the question I most sought to answer.

It wasn't easy. I began my search by trying to locate historical records of people formerly enslaved who had found their way to Canada at around the time the Eight left New York. Surely, I thought, there must be records maintained by historians or by a society or library in Canada. And indeed there are, in Buxton, Ontario, which was a terminus of the Underground Railroad and today is home to a museum and a historical repository.

I reached out to Bryan Prince, who operates the Buxton Museum with his wife, Shannon—and so began a friendship. Many conversations and emails followed. Bryan Prince is a descendant of slaves who came to Canada before the Civil War. He has written about the Lemmon case and is the author of *A Shadow on the Household*, which tells the story of one of the many formerly enslaved couples who escaped to Canada in the antebellum period. The more I worked with him, the more I began to consider him *the* source for records of people who escaped slavery and settled in Canada.

When I asked Bryan if he had any idea what became of the Eight, he told me he didn't—but he then suggested that I try looking for Louis Wright, one of Emeline's twin sons, who Bryan thought might have gone to Michigan after the Civil War. Neither of us knew whether Wright spelled his first name Louis or Lewis, but I now at least had something to work with.

I knew that Wright had been born in either 1845 or 1847. Searching online with those birthdates, I soon found a few dozen Louis Wrights and a couple hundred Lewis Wrights. Gradually I narrowed down the pool, and eventually, on a marriage certificate, I found a 26-year-old Lewis Wright who, all of the evidence suggested, had to be my man.

That was not the end but the beginning of my search. Finding Wright in Michigan at age 26 was one thing; finding progeny many decades later was another. Fortunately, I managed to figure out that Wright and his wife, Rebecca Ann Scipio, had six children, which gave me six family lines to trace.

After a lot of research and a lot of luck, I found my way to Tyler West and his father, Randy, who live in Lansing, Michigan. I called Randy and did my best to convince him that I was not a scam artist and it seemed to work; after a few minutes, he told me that, yes, he was descended from Lewis Wright. Not only that, he told me that he had a picture of Lewis and his twin, Robert, whose fate we know nothing about. (The Wests and I now fondly call Lewis and Robert the Wright Brothers.) (See figure A.1.)

Figure A.1. Robert Wright, standing, and Louis/Lewis Napoleon Wright, undated. Courtesy of Stella Porter, granddaughter of Louis Napoleon Wright, and her niece Luanne Wills-Merrell.

Lewis went by the full name Lewis Napoleon Wright. How did he happen to get that middle name? Is it too much to suppose that he took it on to honor Louis Napoleon, who helped give him freedom? I like to think so, even if that's pure conjecture.

Not long after Randy West and I found each other, he arranged for me to join the first of several Zoom sessions that we had with his extended family. One of these sessions even included Joan Lemmon Johnson, a descendant of Juliet and Jonathan Lemmon. Meeting the Wests and their extended family during these calls—and knowing they were descended from Lewis or Robert, and almost certainly from Emeline—was one of the great thrills of my lifetime.

Acknowledgments

Many months ago, Dennis Glazer and I were working on an exhibit for the Historical Society of the New York Courts concerning the Lemmon case. We created panel exhibits to be displayed in courthouses around the state, with an introduction by the Chief Judge of New York, Janet DiFiore, to whom Dennis—a prominent lawyer in his own right—was married. Working with Dennis was one of the prompts for writing this volume and I thank him heartily for that. Around that time I had mentioned to my daughter, Betsy (a law professor specializing in intellectual property and acquainted with scriptwriters) that the Lemmon case has enough drama to make a movie of it. When I asked about the chances of that happening, she replied, "First you have to write a book."

And so . . .

No case stands in isolation, and that is certainly true of the Lemmon decision, which, in historical context, required a lot of research to put it in perspective. That brought me to scholarly writings, including those from friends, who were generous with their time in talking with me, like John Kaminski, Stephen Schechter, and John Gordan, along with Francis Murray, who had assembled valuable historical materials for the website of the Historical Society of the New York Courts, and historians Sarah L. H. Gronningsater, Dan Hulsebosch, Wilma Dunaway, Dwight T. Pitcaithley, Don Papson, Dennis Maika, and Christopher L. Webber, with whom I conversed and was able to draw upon their writings.

Professor William Nelson was especially helpful, opening his legal history seminar to a session involving my ongoing chapters in this volume, enabling me to gain good insights from him and from the participants.

In starting to piece things together, I began writing chapters dealing with aspects of the Lemmon case, preserving source materials in footnotes, aided by Emily Miller. I had mentioned my project to Susan McCloskey, who offered to edit the footnotes, which by then had taken on a life of their own. She did so marvelously.

From time to time Bob Lehner looked at the narrative and would make helpful suggestions. I sent chapters along to my friend Charlie Pierce, who responded with encouraging comments. As the work progressed, I would talk about it to friends, including Jack Schachner, Dr. Sam Basch, Rabbi Daniel Polish, Howard Levine, Alan Schoenberger, Larry Plapler, and George Marlow, all cheering me on, as did Dr. Ray Raymond, with his keen insights. After the work began to jell, I turned to Toby Lester to help edit the volume. Given his considerable editorial talent and congeniality, the manuscript became more cogent. We spent many a day alternating the cursor on a "cloud" from our respective screens, and emerged as well with a lasting friendship.

The Lemmon troupe began their journey from Bath County, Virginia, and it took them 17 days to get to Richmond. I took the journey via my desktop computer, stopping online at libraries along the way to gain insights as to what the towns and villages along the way were like in the 1850s. I received good help from Tricia Johnson of the Fluvanna County, Virginia, Historical Society; Catherine Southworth of the Goochland County, Virginia, Historical Society; Janet M. Stanton and Kevin Scott Tanner at the Waynesboro, Virginia, Public Library; Emily Talbot of the Botetourt Historical Society and Museum; Kevin Shupe of the Library of Virginia; Kelly Sheely, museum curator of the Waynesboro Heritage Foundation; Nancy Sorrells of Lot's Wife Publishers; and Geoff Huth at the New York State Office of Court Administration.

Dawn Tinnell at the Library of Virginia was able to unearth letters from Charles O'Conor urging Virginia's Governor to appeal the Lemmon case to the Supreme Court.

Trying to learn about Judge Elijah Paine, who had been a member of Harvard College's class of 1814, I turned to the staff at Harvard's Widener Library asking if they might have anything about him, and to my delight they came up with some interesting background material about him.

From Albany, California, Margaret Paine Hasselman sent us an image of Elijah Paine.

In pursuing other original source materials, I had wonderful help from Brant M. Vogel and Robb K. Haberman at the rare book room at Columbia's Butler Library in looking at the Jay Family documents, and Michael Widener at the Yale Law School library looking at documents including those written by William M. Evarts (1818–1901); from the library at the New York Law Institute in Manhattan; and from the John Jay Homestead State Historic Site in Katonah, New York, and the Jay Estate historic site in Rye, New York, as well as information and records from Kenneth Cobb of the New York City Municipal Archives.

I also had memorable encounters with people who helped me dig out important items: Attorney Taylor M. Baker of Hot Springs, Virginia, located the site of the Lemmon homestead, pinpointed its place in the region, and helped me with other local historical information. Scott Miller and Jean Miller furnished me with a picture of the cabin in which the Eight likely lived.

Throughout, I had been hoping to find progeny of the Eight—a long shot by any reckoning—and had almost given up on the idea when I asked Bryan Prince, curator at the Buxton Museum in Chatham, Ontario, whether he might provide a sliver of a lead, and so he did, resulting in my being able to trace the line, through the present, of Emeline's son, Lewis, one of the Eight. In turn, I met, and zoomed with his descendants, in Michigan.

As one of the lawyers fighting for freedom on behalf of the Eight, Erastus Culver played a critical role in the saga, and I thank his lineal descendant, Henry Ryder, for providing me with a copy of Culver's image. I am grateful for the enthusiasm and encouragement of Richard Carlin, Senior Acquisitions Editor at SUNY Press, the production editor, Susan Geraghty, and the copyeditor James Harbeck.

I was able to work hand in hand with the Historical Society of the New York Courts in planning and furthering every facet of this work, given the countless hours I spent with its incomparable executive director, Marilyn Marcus, with thanks as well to Daniel Sierra in setting up innumerable Zoom and other sessions.

I give special mention to Allison Morey, programs director of the Historical Society of the New York Courts. Allison has made prodigious efforts in sorting out images for copyright concerns, and in gaining publication permissions. Allison labored painstakingly, for many days and hours, dealing with the complicated—and highly technical—task of compiling, organizing, sizing, spreadsheeting, and preparing the images for inclusion. I am hugely grateful for her efforts.

I am grateful to Anthony Maranzano for his technical support and computer wizardry.

Karen Johnson was also a valuable resource. More than once, she came to my rescue, with her abundant typing and computer skills.

My wife, Julia, as always, has been my constant consultant and inspiration. She shared with me the joys of discovery, and the disappointments of going down blind alleys—thankfully there were more of the former. She often adjusted her schedule to meet my needs, and she gave me enduring, loving support and encouragement from beginning to end. I cannot count the number of times I looked to her for her reaction as to a paragraph, a chapter, or an idea. "How does this sound?" I asked her countless times. Her keen judgement and her insightful observations are very much a part of this volume, and I am an eternally grateful recipient and beneficiary.

Notes

Dramatis Personae

1. Lemmon v. People, 20 N.Y. 562, 599 (1860).

Chapter 1

1. William ("Billy") Douglas (sometimes Douglass) was born in 1767 in Fauquier, Virginia, in 1767 and died in Bath County, Virginia in April, 1837. His slaves are listed in the 1830 census (see www.ancestry.com/imageviewer/collections/8058/images/4411233_00371?pId=819480; for the number of slaves in Virginia in 1830, see www2.census.gov/library/publications/decennial/1830/1830b.pdf). For a fine article on the Lemmon case generally, see Thomas J. Davis, "Napoleon v. Lemmon: Antebellum Black New Yorkers, Antislavery, and Law," *Afro-Americans in New York Life and History*, vol. 33, no. 1 (2009), 27.

2. When Billy Douglas wrote his will in 1836 Juliet had been recently married (on June 9, 1835) to Adam D. Stewart (sometimes Stuart). See search.ancestry.com/cgi-bin/sse.dll?dbid=3723&h=1002550&indiv=try&o_vc=Record:OtherRecord&rhSource=3723.7&_phstart=successSource. After Stewart's death, Juliet married Jonathan Lemmon in 1840. Jonathan was 32; Juliet, widowed, was 23. See, generally, Nicholas Guyatt, review of *They Were Her Property: White Woman as Slave Owners in the American South* by Stephanie E. Jones Rogers, *New York Review of Books*, November 18, 2021, 43. Upon marriage, slaves became the property of the husband; see Wallace v. Taliaferro, 6 Va. 447, 461 (1800). Juliet married Jonathan Lemmon on April 16, 1840; see search.ancestry.com/cgi-bin/sse.dll?dbid=60214&h=219833&indiv=try&o_vc=Record:OtherRecord&rhSource=3723. Jonathan Lemmon's ancestry goes back as far as a grandfather born in Germany in 1738 and settling in Virginia (search.ancestry.com/cgi-bin/

sse.dll?indiv=1&dbid=60525&h=47597596&ssrc=pt&tid=85116699&pid=48569
399591).

Unlike Juliet's people, Jonathan's people had no history of slaveholding. In 1820, when Jonathan was 12, his family's homestead on the Cowpasture River in Botetourt, Virginia, consisted of 13 people and no slaves among them. In 1830, when Jonathan was 22, the household increased to 15, with none enslaved. For 1820 see search.ancestry.com.au/cgi-bin/sse.dll?indiv=1&dbid=7734& h=22390&tid=&pid=&queryId=b7973d2120b220b32dbee1deff1e3347&use PUB=true&_phsrc=XCb591&_phstart=successSource. For 1830 census, see search. ancestry.com.au/cgi-bin/sse.dll?indiv=1&dbid=8058&h=818092&tid=&pid=& queryId=b7973d2120b220b32dbee1deff1e3347&usePUB=true&_phsrc=XCb590&_ phstart=successSource. The family name was spelled variously as Lemon, Lemmon, Leman, and Lehman.

3. Juliet's mother was Nancy Griffith. For that maternal line, see www. ancestry.com/family-tree/person/tree/67941200/person/30172934914/facts. As for her paternal line, as one of Billy Douglas's children: The Douglas family was prominent; for its history (the descendants of William de Douglas), see www. genealogy.com/ftm/d/o/u/William-H-Douglas/GENE1-0026.html. At his death Billy Douglas owned over 2000 acres of land. He was the third of nine children born to Benjamin Thomas Douglas (1742–1816) and Charity Tennill (1742–1832). See douglashistory.co.uk/famgen/familychart.php?familyID=F45924&tree=tree1.

4. A. Leon Higginbotham, Jr. In the Matter of Color (1978) at 53, citing Tucker v. Sweney, Jeff. 5 (Va. Gen. Ct., 1731). See The Last Will and Testament of William Douglas, January 2, 1836, Office of the Clerk of the Circuit Court of Bath County in Will Book 4 at page 356. There is an abstract of the will and the inventory in Jean R. Bruns, Abstracts of the Wills and Inventories of Bath County, Virginia 1791–1842, at 179 (will) and 191 (inventory), at www.ancestry. com/search/collections/49016/?name=william_douglas&event=_bath-virginia-usa_249&count=50&name_x=1_1.

5. Because birth records of the enslaved are sketchy at best, a fair amount of inference and deduction has gone into identifying the Eight. This is a long footnote, containing far more information than even the most assiduous reader cares to know, but I think it worth recording, open to correction of course, for future researchers, or for anyone who has the interest.

The Buxton, Ontario, National Historic Site and Museum (Buxton was a destination on the Underground Railroad) produced an informative account in "Buxton Offers Up Some 'Lemon Aid,'" by Bryan Prince (www.buxtonmuseum. com/history/eBOOKS/lemmon-slaves.pdf), furnishing interesting details including family histories of both the Lemmon family and the family of the Lemmon slaves. In a June 23, 2020 email to me, Bryan Prince provided notes on the Lemmon case that he and Shannon Prince had compiled, giving the ages and identities of the Eight, confirming that in 1852, when the case was before Judge Paine, Emeline was 23 and Nancy 20. They added that Emeline's brother Lewis was 16½ and her brother Edward, 13. Emeline's twin boys were thought to be age 7; Nancy's daughter, Ann, 2½, and Emeline's daughter Amanda, also 2½. They added "baby of Nancy to be born." Family descendants have concluded that Emeline was also known as Maria/Mariah/Miranda E. Thompson. In the same set of notes, Bryan and Shannon Prince state that Nancy's husband was named James Wright, and that they had separated (or had been separated) and he had remained in Malden Township, Canada, with his new wife, Jane.

The United States Census of 1850 listing schedules of the enslaved for Jonathan Lemon in Bath County, Virginia, is on line at search.ancestry.com/ cgi-bin/sse.dll?_phsrc%3DXCb519%26_phstart%3DsuccessSource%26usePUBJs %3Dtrue%26indiv%3D1%26dbid%3D8055%26gsln%3Dlemon%26gsln_x%3 DNP_NN%26msrpn__ftp%3Dbath,%2520virginia,%2520usa%26msrpn%3 D249%26_80100003%3Dlemon%26new%3D1%26rank%3D1%26uidh%3Dmz1 %26redir%3Dfalse%26msT%3D1%26gss%3runDangs-d%26pcat%3D35%26fh %3D0%26h%3D93176944%26recoff%3D%26ml_rpos%3D1%26queryId%3D 166b2907fd646645fe2a6e1d101c5ea4&treeid=&personid=&hintid=&queryId= 166b2907fd646645fe2a6e1d101c5ea4&usePUB=true&_phsrc=XCb519&_phstart =successSource&usePUBJs=true&_ga=2.153513976.1344185053.1592228166- 1944826924.1495160955&_gac=1.208916134.1591303120.EAIaIQobCh MIg6u8_IHp6QIVxcDICh34nQiGEAAYASAAEgKt9vD_BwE.

In the above 1850 census the names of the Lemmon slaves are not listed; only their ages, sex, and race (B or M, for Black or Mulatto) are given. The document adds some information but varies slightly from other listings of the names and ages of the Eight. For Jonathan Lemmon, the 1850 census lists seven enslaved, not eight, but their identities may be inferred. The seven listed are: First, one Black female, age 20. This would be Emeline, later inferred to be Emeline Thompson (Mariah E. Thompson in the 1880 census). We do not know how she got the name Thompson.

The second is an 18-year-old female Mulatto, who would be Nancy, described as Nancy Johnson. We do not know who Johnson was. If it was Nancy's father, he apparently was white, as Nancy is described as Mulatto. Richard Johnson (formerly called Levi) appeared at the Lemmon court proceedings in 1852 to help get the newly liberated group to Canada, and said that Nancy was his sister, which suggests that Nancy's father was named Johnson.

The third is a 16-year old Black male. This would likely be Emeline's brother, Lewis. As to him, see *Abstracts of the Wills and Inventories of Bath County, Virginia, 1791–1842*, by Jean Randolph Bruns (1991) at 191, referring to p. 454 of *Inventory of Slaves and Personal Property on the Home Plantation of William Douglas, September 15, 1837*, listing "Lewis" as part of the "inventory." Considering that "Lewis" appears to be listed as one of the enslaved born several months after Billy Douglas signed his will in 1836, he would have been around 16 in 1852, thus fitting the description of a 16-year-old brother of Emeline, as one of the Eight, as distinguished from Lewis Wright, one of Emeline's twin boys—also among the Eight—who in 1852 were about seven years old.

The fourth, a nine-year-old Black male, was likely another brother of Emeline, named Edward (Ned, Edmund). Accounts vary and may be off by a bit.

The fifth and sixth are listed as three-year-old Mulatto twins. These would be Lewis (sometimes Louis) Napoleon Wright and Robert Wright. We do not know who "Wright" was, but apparently he was white, as the twins are listed as Mulatto. In Zoom conversations in June, 2020, the descendants of Lewis Wright told me that there is a family oral history account of a "Colonel Wright." The family oral history also recognizes Emeline as Maria (or Mariah) or Miranda, adding to the evidence that Mariah E. Thompson in the 1880 Lansing, Michigan, census is Emeline. As for the age of Emeline's twins, they were listed as three years old in the 1850 census, which would have them as born around 1847 and thus age five in 1852 in the case before Judge Paine. In the 1871 marriage certificate of Lewis, however, he is listed as 26 years old, born in 1845, and in the 1880 census he is listed as age 35, meaning that he was born around 1845, and thus seven years old in 1852.

6. See Inter-university Consortium for Political and Social Research, "Population of Virginia—1840," *Historical, Demographic, Economic, and Social Data: The United States, 1790–1970*, accessed August 25, 2022, www.virginiaplaces.org/population/pop1840numbers.html. The United States Department of Commerce and Labor Bureau of the Census publication *A Century of Population Growth, from the First Census of the United States to the Twelfth, 1790–1860*, ed. W.S. Rossiter (1909), chapter 14, "Statistics of Slaves," 132–141, has some interesting data concerning the population and proportion of the enslaved in Virginia around the time. In 1850, the state had some 472,000 enslaved as compared to 894,000 whites, or 53 enslaved to every 100 whites. About one in three families in Virginia (32.9%) owned slaves (table at p. 135). The average number of enslaved per slave-holding family was 8.6., in line with the Lemmon family, which had eight. For other information about Bath County during that time, see Joseph Martin, *A New and Comprehensive Gazetteer of Virginia, and the District of Columbia* (Charlottesville, VA: Moseley & Tompkins for Joseph Martin, 1835), 319, babel. hathitrust.org/cgi/pt?id=loc.ark:/13960/t3nv9r141&view=1up&seq=329&q1=bath.

7. Richard Edwards, *Statistical Gazetteer of the State of Virginia* (Richmond, VA: Richard Edwards, 1854), 173.

8. State v. Mann, 13 N.C. 263, 265–266 (1829); see also Sally Greene, "State v. Mann Exhumed," *North Carolina Law Review* 87, no. 3 (2009).

9. Commonwealth v. Booth, 27 Va. 669, 671 (1828).

10. Jane Purcell Guild, *Black Laws of Virginia: A Summary of the Legislative Acts of Virginia Concerning Negroes From Earliest Times to the Present* (Richmond, VA: Whittet & Shepperson, 1936), 45. A later statute (L. 1748, Ch 38, Sec 20)

clarified the point, making it clear that it applies to protect only white Christians. See also Tom Costa, *The Geography of Slavery in Virginia*, 2005, www2.vcdh. virginia.edu/gos/, a far-reaching catalog of writings, news articles, advertisements for runaway slaves, and other aspects of slavery.

11. Hening, ed., *The Statutes at Large*, vol. 2 (1667), 260, vagenweb.org/ hening/vol02-13.htm.

12. L 1706, ch. 160, an "Act to Incourage the Baptizing of Negro, Indian and Mulatto Slaves." For a comparison of the 1702 New York Act for Regulating Slaves with those of Virginia and South Carolina, see Mark A. Graber and Howard Gillman, *The Complete American Constitutionalism, Volume One: Introduction and the Colonial Era* (Oxford: Oxford University Press, 2015), 410–420. For an interesting article on the history of slavery and baptism, see Philip Neri, "Baptism and the Submission of Negro Slaves in the Early Colonial Period," *Records of the American Catholic Historical Society of Philadelphia* 51, no. 3/4 (September & December 1940): 220–232. Blackstone touched on the point, expressing indignation at the idea that anyone would withhold baptism for fear of losing property: "Hence too it follows, that the infamous and unchristian practice of withholding baptism from negro servants, lest they should thereby gain their liberty, is totally without foundation, as well as without excuse." William Blackstone, *Commentaries on the Laws of England*, vol. 1 (Oxford: Clarendon Press, 1765), 423.

13. Guild, *Black Laws of Virginia*, 72, citing *Virginia Laws of 1805*, ch. 12. For a book that includes a lengthy treatment as to church attendance in Antebellum Virginia, see Charles F. Irons, *The Origins of Proslavery Christianity: White and Black Evangelicals in Colonial and Antebellum Virginia* (Chapel Hill: University of North Carolina Press, 2008).

14. Guild, *Black Laws of Virginia*, 151–152. For a full treatment on the subject of the legal disabilities of slaves, see Jacob D. Wheeler, *A Practical Treatise on the Law of Slavery: Being a Compilation of All the Decisions Made on that Subject, in the Several Courts of the United States, and State Courts: With Copious Notes and References to the Statutes and Other Authorities, Systematically Arranged* (New York: A. Pollock, Jr., 1837), 190–197, known as the "Wheeler on Slavery." Legal disabilities and assertions of Negro inferiority appeared in customs and in relationships among slaveowners and slaves, as described in Bertram W. Doyle, "The Etiquette of Race Relations—Past, Present, and Future," *Journal of Negro Education* 5, no. 2 (1936): 191–208.

15. Scott v. Raub, 88 Va. 721 (1892); see also Darlene C. Goring, "The History of Slave Marriage in the United States," *John Marshall Law Review* 39, no. 2 (Winter 2006), 299.

16. Wilma A. Dunaway, *The African-American Family in Slavery and Emancipation* (Cambridge: Cambridge University Press, 2003), 61. For descriptions of slave quarters, see John M. Vlach, " 'Snug Li'l House with Flue and Oven': Nineteenth-Century Reforms in Plantation Slave Housing," *Perspectives in Vernacular*

Architecture 5 (1995): 118–129; Clifton Ellis, *Cabin, Quarter, Plantation: Architecture and Landscapes of North American Slavery* (New Haven, CT: Yale University Press, 2003); and Dennis Pogue and Douglas Sanford, "Housing for the Enslaved in Virginia," *Encyclopedia Virginia*, April 20, 2022, www.encyclopediavirginia.org/slave_housing_in_virginia.

17. See Harriet A. Jacobs, *Incidents in the Life of a Slave Girl, Written by Herself* (Boston: Published for the author, 1860); Patricia A. Broussard, "Black Women's Post-Slavery Silence Syndrome: A Twenty-First Century Remnant of Slavery, Jim Crow, and Systemic Racism—Who Will Tell Her Stories?" *Journal of Gender, Race and Justice* 16 (Spring 2013), 394; Cheryl Nelson Butler, "The Racial Roots of Human Trafficking," *UCLA Law Review* 62 (August 2015), 1464; see also Jason A. Gillmer, "Base Wretches and Black Wenches: A Story of Sex and Race, Violence and Compassion, During Slavery Times," *Alabama Law Review* 59, no. 5 (2008). Some writers describe how enslaved women were sometimes twice victimized: first by the slave masters, and then by the ensuing anger and jealousy of their wives. In other instances, the slaveowners' wives reactions might be resignation, and in some instances, complicity, considering the value of "increase" in slaves. See Stephanie Jones-Rogers, "Rethinking Sexual Violence and the Marketplace of Slavery," and Brenda E. Stevenson, "What's Love Got to Do with It," both in *Sexuality and Slavery: Reclaiming Intimate Histories in the Americas*, ed. Daina Ramey Berry and Leslie M. Harris (Athens: University of Georgia Press, 2018), 109–123, 158–188.

18. Dunaway, *The African-American Family in Slavery and Emancipation*, 121; Wilma A. Dunaway, *Slavery in the American Mountain South* (Cambridge: Cambridge University Press, 2003), 196. As to the rape of a slave not being a crime, see Jeffrey J. Pokorak, "Rape as a Badge of Slavery: The Legal History of, and Remedies for, Prosecutorial Race-of-Victim Charging Disparities," *Nevada Law Journal* 7, no. 1 (Fall 2006); A. Leon Higginbotham Jr. and Anne F. Jacobs, "The 'Law Only as an Enemy': The Legitimization of Racial Powerlessness through the Colonial and Antebellum Criminal Laws of Virginia," *North Carolina Law Review* 70, no. 4 (1992): 969; Peter W. Bardaglio, "Rape and the Law in the Old South: 'Calculated to Excite Indignation in Every Heart,'" *Journal of Southern History* 60, no. 4 (1994): 749–772. See also William Goodell, *The American Slave Code in Theory and Practice: Its Distinctive Features Shown by Its Statutes, Judicial Decisions and Illustrative Facts* (New York: American and Foreign Anti-Slavery Society, 1853), 85–86; Virginia Laws of 1792, Ch. 42, Sec. 19, "Whatsoever person shall take a woman against her will shall be guilty of a felony, provided that this act shall not extend to any person taking any woman, only claiming her as his ward or bond woman."

See also Dacia Green, "Ain't I . . . ?: The Dehumanizing Effect of the Regulation of Slave Womanhood and Family Life," *Duke Journal of Gender Law & Policy* 25 (Spring 2018); *The Making of African American Identity: Volume I, 1500–1865*, National Humanities Center, July 2009, nationalhumanitiescenter.org/pds/maai/index.htm; Thelma Jennings, "'Us Colored Women Had to Go Through a Plenty': Sexual Exploitation of African-American Slave Women," *Journal of Women's History* 1, no. 3 (1990): 45–74; "On Slaveholders' Sexual Abuse of Slaves: Selections from 19th- and 20th-Century Slave Narratives," National Humanities Center, 2009, nationalhumanitiescenter.org/pds/maai/enslavement/text6/master-slavesexualabuse.pdf; George v. State, 37 Miss. 317, 317 (1859), ruling that the crime of rape cannot exist legally among the enslaved. For a particularly moving essay dealing with the lasciviousness of slave masters toward the enslaved, see Harriet Martineau, "Morals of Slavery," in *Society in America* (London: Saunders and Otley, 1837), reprinted in *Green Bag* 21, no. 1 (Autumn, 2017), greenbag.org/v21n1/v21n1_from_the_bag_Martineau.pdf.

19. Hening, *The Statutes at Large*, vol. 3, 86–87.

20. I include this compelling suggestion as having come to me in an October 2020 email from Wilma Dunaway, who has spent years researching slavery in Appalachia and has written extensively on the subject. She said she had never seen a slaveholder's will that devised future care of slaves children to future unborn white grandchildren, and sees it as a "family retainer" that "intends to structure multigenerational family obligations for his bastard slave children and probably a concubine or two."

21. Va. Rev. Code, Vol. I, at 424 (1819) mandated that "any slave or free colored person found at any school for teaching reading or writing, by day or night, may be whipped, at the discretion of a justice, not exceeding twenty lashes." In 1849, Virginia declared unlawful every assemblage of Negroes for the purpose of instruction, in reading or writing, or in the night time for any purpose, and that any justice could order such Negro to be punished with stripes. See Code of Virginia: With the Declaration of Independence and Constitution of the United States; and the Declaration of Rights and Constitution of Virginia, Offences Against Public Policy Title 54, Sec. 32, p. 108 (1849); see also Goodell, *The American Slave Code in Theory and Practice*, 320; and George M. Stroud, *A Sketch of the Laws Relating to Slavery in the Several States of the United States of America* (Philadelphia: Henry Longseth, 1856), 60–61. (Interestingly, Stroud asserts that in Virginia, slaveowners were free to instruct their own slaves and that the prohibition against instruction applied to the efforts of third persons only. He offers no citation for that.)

22. Peter v Hargrave, 46 Va. 12 (1848). The Last Will and Testament of James Hargrave, dated January 1, 1835 is on file in the Circuit Court of Dinwiddie County, Virginia, with thanks to Kelly LaBlanc for sending it to me.

23. Maria v. Surbaugh, 23 Va. 228, 229 (1824).

Chapter 2

1. See J. T. McAllister, *Historical Sketches of Virginia Hot Springs, Warm Sulphur Springs, and Bath County, Virginia* (Salem, VA: Salem Publishing Company,

1908), books.google.com/books?id=qKAimJxSj-oC; Karl E. Ashburn, "Slavery and Cotton Production in Texas," *Southwestern Social Science Quarterly* 14, no. 3 (1933): 257–271. The Texas State Historical Association reports that there were some 397 free Blacks in Texas 1850, compared with over 58,000 slaves. See "Free Blacks," *Texas State Historical Association*, October 22, 2020, www.tshaonline.org/handbook/entries/ free-blacks. See, generally, Alice L. Baumgartner, *South to Freedom, Runaway Slaves to Mexico and the Road to Civil War* (New York: Basic Books, 2020).

2. Randolph B. Campbell, *An Empire for Slavery: The Peculiar Institution in Texas, 1821–1865* (Baton Rouge: Louisiana State University Press), 100–101; Randolph B. Campbell, ed., and William S. Pugsley and Marilyn P. Duncan, comp., *The Laws of Slavery in Texas* (Austin: University of Texas Press, 2010). See also Coshandra Dillard, "On This Texas Island, Pirates Kept the Atlantic Slave Trade Going—Even after It Was Abolished," *Timeline*, April 10, 2018, timeline.com/ galveston-island-texas-pirate-slave-trade-bdb45657f08.

3. David J. Brown, "A Brief History of Staunton, Virginia," from David J. Brown, ed., *Staunton, Virginia: A Pictorial History* (Staunton, VA: Historic Staunton Foundation, 1985), www2.iath.virginia.edu/staunton/history.html; see also Joseph Addison Waddell, *Annals of Augusta County, Virginia* (Richmond, VA: J. W. Randolph & English, 1888), 271, books.google.ca/books?id=JzQXOZl-glQC. The route to Cloverdale would have been closely linked to modern-day Route 629.

4. "Jerome N. Bonaparte Travels Through Waynesboro," in George Hawke, *A History of Waynesboro, Virginia to 1900* (Waynesboro, VA: Waynesboro Historical Commission, 1997), 91.

5. Bethany Nemec, "Oregon Trail Mileposts," *End of the Oregon Trail*, April 3, 2019, historicoregoncity.org/2019/04/03/oregon-trail-mileposts/.

6. In 1810, Waynesboro had a population of 250. By 1860, that number grew to 457. The town maintained a steady stream of visitors, due to its position on Three Notch'd Road. With thanks to Kelly Sheely, Museum Curator of the Waynesboro Heritage Foundation, for emailing me a copy of *The First Industrial Complex in Waynesborough, Virginia and the Men Who Developed It* (Waynesboro, VA: Waynesborough Historical Society, 2017) containing this information, p. 23. See also Joseph Martin, *A New and Comprehensive Gazetteer of Virginia, and the District of Columbia* (Charlottesville, VA: Moseley & Tompkins for Joseph Martin, 1835), 319, babel.hathitrust.org/cgi/pt?id=loc.ark:/13960/t3nv9r141.

7. See Virginia C. Johnson, *Virginia by Stagecoach* (Charleston, SC: History Press, 2019), 54; the tavern may have been in private hands as of 1850, according to "D.S. Tavern, Near Charlottesville, Albemarle County, VA," *Old Virginia Taverns*, December 15, 2019, oldvirginiataverns.com/2019/12/15/d-s- tavern-near-charlottesville-albemarle-county-va/.

8. Edward Tayloe Wise, *Albermarle County, 1850–1860; An Overview*, graduate research paper, University of Richmond, November 1989, www.jmrl. org/ebooks/Albemarle%20County%201850-1860.PDF.

9. See Lindsay Nolting and J. Stephen Pence, "Rivanna River History," *Rivanna Conservation Society*, February 1996, www.rivannariver.org/wp-content/uploads/2015/02/RCS-Rivanna-River-History.pdf.

10. Timberlake is listed as owning 37 slaves in 1837: www.ancestry.com/discoveryui-content/view/2244577:8058?tid=&pid=&queryId=0739415e6aa1e0340e281a49629ce862&_phsrc=yxt74&_phstart=success.

11. Mack Curle, "Roads and Taverns in Goochland—Three Chopt Road," *Goochland County Historical Society Magazine* 35 (2003): 14–15.

12. October 24, 1850 census, Goochland, Virginia, www.familysearch.org/ark:/61903/3:1:S3HY-6S87-FHR?i=46&cc=1420440.

13. The September, 1852 article, "North American Slavery," is in *Household Words*, no. 130 (September 18, 1852): 1–6, babel.hathitrust.org/cgi/pt?id=hvd.hnxu39&view=1up&seq=13. References to Dickens's 1842 *American Notes* are from *American Notes* (New York: John W. Lovell, 1883), 693–714.

14. For modern readers there is an extraordinary disconnect here. Upon Dickens's arrival in Richmond, the *Richmond Enquirer* reported on the unbounded adulation the city felt for Dickens. "He had caused us to feel for the humblest . . . and all to feel for all—for the youthful tenant of the Work-house, and for the poor and pious Nell. This . . . creates in us all a sympathy for each other a participation in the interests of our common humanity, which constitutes the great bond of equality." And yet, when Dickens's *American Notes* reached Richmond, the *Richmond Enquirer* responded not with renewed appreciation for his humanity but with fury. (Compare *Richmond Enquirer*, March 24, 1842, 3, written before Dickens arrived in Richmond, with *Richmond Enquirer*, November 15, 1842, 3, written after Dickens had published *American Notes*.) That the paper could see no connection between the unfortunate 14-year-old Nell and the plight of the people its own inhabitants enslaved speaks volumes. As to the justifications for slavery that Dickens heard during his visit, based on claims of how the enslaved loved their masters, see Arthur A. Adrian, "Dickens on American Slavery: A Carlyean Slant," *PMLA* 67, no. 4 (June 1952), 315–329.

15. "Statement of Mr. Lemmon," *Baltimore Sun*, November 19, 1852; "Mr. Lemmon's Statement," *Richmond Dispatch*, November 22, 1852. The distance by road between Richmond and Norfolk today is about 93 miles. In 1851, the Norfolk Directory (p. 5) gave the distance as 140 miles, and the distance from Norfolk to New York, by sea, as 300 miles.

16. We thank Bryan Prince of the Buxton National Historic Site and Museum for this document, given to him by a descendant of Jonathan and Juliet Lemmon. It reads: "State of Virginia, City of Richmond to wit: This day personally appeared before me James Ennis a Justice of the Peace in and for said City John S. Armentrant, Joseph Lemmon and Oliver F. Metheney and make oath that a negro woman named Emeiline and her three children, Bob, Lewis and Amanda—a negro Girl named Nancy & her child Ann—a negro man named Lewis and a

negro Boy named Ned are the property of Johnathan Lemon and were raised by him in the County of Bath [in] this said state. Given under my hand & seal this 1st day of November 1852."

17. William S. Forrest, *The Norfolk Directory, for 1851–1852* (Norfolk, 1851).

18. Don Papson and Tom Calarco, *Secret Lives of the Underground Railroad in New York City: Sydney Howard Gay, Louis Napoleon and the Record of Fugitives* (Jefferson, NC: McFarland, 2015), 43–50, discovered this interview of Nathan Lobam, entitled "The Banana Man," in which a reporter for the *Troy Daily Record* of May 6, 1874, interviewed Lobam, "a pleasant looking colored man" who sold bananas out of a cigar store on First Street in Troy, New York. In the telling, Lobam referred to Napoleon Gibbs, conflating two Underground Railroad agents, Louis Napoleon and Jacob Gibbs—a minor error after 20 years in an otherwise impeccable account.

19. *Baltimore Sun*, September 1, 1851, 4; *New York Evening Post*, September 3, 1851, 2; September 5, 1851, 4. See also "Exploring a Common Past, Part III: Tracking Escape: A Case Study," *National Park Service*, www.nps.gov/parkhistory/online_books/ugrr/exugrr4.htm, describing the capacity of the steamer *City of Richmond*; the *City of Richmond*'s 444 ton weight is from *De Bow's Review* 6 (June 1853), 580.

20. The booking from New York to the *Memphis* was done through J. H. Brower and Co. of 45 South St. in Manhattan. In a letter to the *New York Journal of Commerce* (published in the *New York Times* of November 22, 1852), Brower explained that he had warned the "purser" of the ship *City of Richmond* (evidently Ashmead) that it was unwise to leave the slaves in New York City and that the Lemmons would do well to take their slaves to some secure location until they were safely aboard the *Memphis*. Brower warned the purser that given the abolitionist elements in New York, the slaves could be seized or "kidnapped."

21. For Jonathan Lemmon's account, see his November 17, 1852, statement in the *Richmond Dispatch*, November 22, 1852, 2; *Tri-Weekly Commercial*, Wilmington, NC, November 23, 1852; *Chronicle and Sentinel*, Augusta, GA, November 23, 1852, 2; *Middlebury (VT) Register*, December 1, 1852, 1. In his statement, Lemmon claimed that the hacks dropped him off at 3 Carlisle Street. What might have been the vicinity of 3, 5, or 8 Carlisle Street has become a vacant lot. In his account, Jonathan Lemmon stated that he and the group had planned to board the *Memphis* on Saturday morning, November 6, 1852, but that the slaves were in court and the *Memphis* had sailed away without him and the group. There is no reason to doubt that. An advertisement for the *Memphis*, however, states that the vessel leaves every Monday—meaning that it would depart for New Orleans not on Saturday, November 6, but on Monday, November 8; see *New York Spring and Commercial List and New York Price Current*, November 11, 1852, 1. This is an oddity I include merely for completeness.

Chapter 3

1. Culver's anti-slavery speech before Congress on January 30, 1846, is online at hdl.handle.net/2027/aeu.ark:/13960/t3cz3r39m. In the family, some members spelled the name as Colver. For his stance against slavery in the Oregon territory, see *New York Evening Post*, August 7, 1846, 3. The *Lancaster (PA) Examiner* of December 24, 1845, reported on his calling for the abolition of slavery in the District of Columbia. For other newspaper articles as to his denunciation of slavery, see *The Liberator*, March 16, 1838, 3; *Brandon (VT) Telegraph*, October 13, 1841, 3; *Green Mountain Freeman*, August 31, 1848, 1. For good biographies of Culver, see Frances Murray, former archivist and librarian for the New York Court of Appeals: "Erastus D. Culver," *Historical Society of the New York Courts*, history.nycourts.gov/figure/erastus-culver/; and "Erastus Dean Culver," *University of Vermont Obituary Record*, no. 1 (Burlington: University of Vermont, 1895), 41, books.google.com/books?id=gIQfAAAAYAAJ&pg=PA41&lpg=PA41. Culver was a graduate of University of Vermont in 1826, and represented Washington County, New York, in the State Legislature in 1838 and 1841, and the United States Congress from 1845 to 1847 (see obituary, *New-York Tribune*, October 16, 1889, 7; *Rutland Weekly Herald*, October 17, 1889).

2. In the 1850 census, he is listed as living in Manhattan's 5th ward, age 48, having been born in New York, his occupation "polisher and varnisher." He is listed as Mulatto, and in a residence or house with Samuel Livingston, Mulatto, age 27, Sarah Livingston, Mulatto, age 25, and their daughter, 5-year-old Sarah Livingston. Census online at www.ancestry.com/imageviewer/collections/8054/images/4189778-00424?pId=7246282. The 5th Ward covered the area of Manhattan's lower Broadway, around Lispenard and Duane Streets; see Library of Congress map at www.loc.gov/resource/g3804n.fi0001l0l/?r=0.062,0.226,0.274,0.161,0. Thirty years later, however, in the *New-York Tribune* obituary (March 30, 1881, 2), he is said to have been born of slave parents in Virginia and remained in slavery until 1828 when he came North.

3. *Fayetteville (NC) Weekly Observer*, July 29, 1834, 2. His decision was affirmed in Jack v. Martin, 12 Wend. 311 (1834), insofar as it upheld the constitutionality of the Fugitive Slave Act of 1793, although somewhat equivocally, by New York's high court [14 Wend. 507 (1835)].

4. *New York American*, July 18, 1834, 2.

5. Paine had been a law partner of Henry Wheaton and assisted in Wheaton's preparation of the 12 volumes of Wheaton's *Supreme Court Reports* (1816–1827). In 1827 Paine published volume 1 of the *Reports of Cases Argued and Determined in the Circuit Court of the United States for the Second Circuit*, with a second volume published posthumously in 1856. In 1828, the State Legislature created the Superior Court of the City of New York—a trial-level court. It was abolished

under the Constitution of 1894 and its jurisdiction was folded into the New York State Supreme Court. See "More Whig Nominations," *New York Evening Post*, October 17, 1849, reporting Paine's nomination for New York Superior Court as a Whig candidate. For the creation of the court see Jona. Prescott-Hall, *Reports of Cases Argued and Determined in the Superior Court of the City of New-York* (New York: Oliver Halstead, 1831), vii, babel.hathitrust.org/cgi/pt?id=ien.3555900 2390478&view=1up&seq=11. Paine also wrote, with William Duer, a two-volume work published in 1830, *The Practice in Civil Actions and Proceedings at Law in the State of New York in the Supreme Court and Other Courts of the State*. Paine represented Wheaton in what was said to be the Supreme Court's first copyright case in 1834. See Paul DeForest Hicks, *The Litchfield Law School: Guiding the New Nation* (Westport, CT: Prospecta Press, 2019), 57; see also p. 88, describing Paine's decision in the Lemmon case.

6. The announcement of Paine's marriage to Louisa Tileston was published in the *Columbian (MA) Centinel* on November 29, 1834 and the *New York Evening Post*, November 27, 1834, 2. Both announcements were brief, giving no details. The *Post* mentions only that the wedding was performed by "Rev. Mr. Schroeder" and that she was the daughter of Lemuel Tileston of Haverhill, Massachusetts. At the time, Rev. J. F. Schroeder was an Episcopalian clergyman associated with New York's Trinity Church and it is likely that it was he who officiated. Their first son, Elijah, born April 11, 1836, died on January 2, 1837. For ancestry records of the Paine/Payne family, including Elijah and his immediate family, see Henry D. Paine, ed., *Paine Family Records: A Journal of Genealogical and Biographical Information Respecting the American Families of Payne, Paine, Payn &c.*, vol. 2 (Albany: J. Munsell, 1883), archive.org/stream/painefamilyrecor02pain_0/paine-familyrecor02pain_0_djvu.txt. The death of their first-born, Elijah, on January 2, 1837, was reported in the *New York Evening Post*, January 3, 1837, 2.

7. Dr. Martyn Paine, "Biographical Sketch of Hon. Elijah Paine," in Elijah Paine, *Reports of Cases Argued and Determined in the Circuit Court of the United States for the Second Circuit: Comprising the Districts of New-York, Connecticut, and Vermont* (New York: Banks, Gould, & Co, 1856), vii.

8. "Death of Hon. Elijah Paine," *Burlington Weekly Free Press*, May 6, 1842, 3; *Bennington Evening Banner*, August 22, 1919; "The Men of Vermont," *Rutland Weekly Herald*, February 27, 1862, 6. Elijah Paine Sr. also charted the town of Williamstown, VT; "A Search for the Colonial," *Barre Daily Times*, May 31, 1919, 3. Paine Sr. was one of the so-called "Midnight Judges" that included John Marshall and others appointed by President John Adams under the Act of 1801, during the very end of his presidency. See Kathryn Turner, "The Midnight Judges," *University of Pennsylvania Law Review* 109, no. 4 (1961): 502. Elijah Paine Sr. was also president of the Vermont Colonization Society; see *African Repository and Colonial Journal* 14 (May 1838): 155–157, and 15 (February 1839): 44–48, books. google.com/books?id=rCJLAQAAMAAJ&pg=RA2-PA44&lpg=RA2-PA44; see also

Vermont Watchman and State Journal, Montpelier, VT, January 31, 1842, 3. As for the historic role of Elijah Paine Sr. in founding Northfield, VT, see *Barre (VT) Daily Times*, March 19, 1942, 8; *Vermont News and Advertiser*, Northfield, VT, July 20, 1932, 7. He was also one of the commissioners appointed by Vermont to meet with New York counterparts concerning territorial jurisdiction between New York and Vermont; see John P. Kaminski et al., eds., *The Documentary History of the Ratification of the Constitution: Ratification of the Constitution by the States: Vermont* (Madison: Wisconsin Historical Society Press, 2020), 12–26, asset.library. wisc.edu/1711.dl/67AZXDTE53WZX8M/R/file-9cdcb.pdf.

9. Obituary of Martyn Paine, *Burlington Free Press*, November 14, 1877.

10. She authored *Tent and Harem: Notes of an Oriental Trip* (1859), an elegantly written volume. Judge Paine had two other sisters, Sophia Paine Dunn (1803–1861) and Sarah, who died in infancy. Another younger brother, George Paine (1807–1836), died at age 29 after studying law in New York with Chancellor James Kent. Later, George was editor and one of the proprietors of the *Providence (RI) Journal*; see Jonathan Fox Worcester, *A Memorial of the Class of 1827, Dartmouth College* (Hanover, NH: Centennial Anniversary of the College, 1869). Information as to Judge Paine's sisters is from Abby Maria Hemenway, ed., *The Vermont Historical Gazetteer*, vol. 2 (Burlington, VT: A. M. Hemenway, 1871), 1151, archive.org/details/bub_gb_xkEOAAAAIAAJ/page/1150/. Elijah Paine's mother was Sarah Porter Paine (1769–1851). Her portrait is at the Hood Museum, Dartmouth College, New Hampshire. See also *Argus and Patriot*, Montpelier, VT, October 29, 1879, 4, for further information on the Paine family.

11. *St. Johnsbury (VT) Caledonian*, November 16, 1841, 3.

12. Sim's Case, 61 Mass. 285 (1851).

13. The court record reflects that "eight colored persons were thereupon brought up before him, viz.: Emeline, aged twenty-three; Nancy, aged twenty; Lewis, brother of Emeline, aged sixteen; Edward, brother of Emeline, aged thirteen years; Lewis and Edward, twins, boys of Nancy, aged seven years; Ann, daughter of Nancy, aged five years, and Amanda, daughter of Emeline, aged two years." The identities were off, slightly. Emeline, not Nancy, was the twins' mother.

14. "Speech of Hon. E.D. Culver," *National Anti-Slavery Standard*, May 21, 1859, 1–2; *Liberator*, May 20, 1859. The location on Carlisle Street remains unclear, described variously as number 3, 5, and 8. In the *Buffalo Evening News* (November 12, 1852, 2) the report states that it was 3 Carlisle Street, "the house of P. Egan" and "not a German house as has been stated." Erastus Culver's firsthand account is the most reliable. Possibly, the Lemmon family lodged upstairs, and the Eight below, in what Culver described as a Dutch bakery. Evidently, Judge Paine had earlier directed that the Eight, after they were located, remain under the aegis of the police, notably officer William Thompson, to whom Culver was referring when he warned the officer to not be rough with Nancy (*Daily Republic*, Washington, DC, November 10, 1852, 2).

Chapter 4

1. Judge William Jay's outspoken anti-slavery publication cost him reappointment to the bench as Westchester County Judge. Bowing to Southern commercial interests, New York Governor William C. Bouck refused to reappoint Jay in 1843, although he had served with distinction for 25 years. *Liberator*, April 7, 1843, 1; Corey M. Brooks, *Liberty Power: Anti-Slavery Third Parties and the Transformation of American Politics* (Chicago: University of Chicago Press, 2016), 25.

2. "Hail Columbia Happy Land," *Albany Evening Journal*, April 5, 1852, 2; "U.S. Commissioner's Office," *New York Daily Times*, April 5, 1852, 1. After being sent south, Horace Preston was bought back for $1200 and came home. See Samuel May, *The Fugitive Slave Law and Its Victims* (New York: American Anti-Slavery Society, 1861), 22.

3. "A Card from the Legal Counsel of Horace Preston, Claimed as a Fugitive Slave by William Reese," *New York Daily Herald*, April 7, 1852, 2. The "card" from Culver and Jay dated April 3, 1852—the equivalent of today's letter to the editor—was published in the *New York Tribune* of April 5, 1852, 4. Alongside that, on the same page, the *Tribune* itself excoriated the commissioner. See also *New York Sun*, April 5, 1852, as quoted in "The Fugitive Slave Case," *New York Daily Herald*, April 7, 1852, 2, the *Sun* calling (vainly) for Morton's dismissal. Morton gave an unconvincing response, duly rebutted by another lawyer present at the proceedings. "The Case of Horace Preston: Card of Commissioner Morton," *National Era*, April 15, 1852, 2. Morton (1793–1855) went on to become mayor of Hoboken, New Jersey. See also Daniel S. Farbman, "Resistance Lawyering," *California Law Review* 107, no. 6 (2019): 1915–1916 for an account of the Preston case.

4. In the Matter of George Kirk, a fugitive slave, 4 N.Y. Leg. Obs. 456, 1 Parker Crim. Rep. 67, 1 Edm. Sel. Cas. 315, 9 Month. L. Rep. 355 (N.Y. Sup. Ct. 1846).

5. "The Slave Free!" *New-York Tribune*, October 28, 1846, 4. See also *Washington (DC) Union*, October 29, 1846, 3 (two articles). See "Sydney Howard Gay's 'Record of Fugitives,'" *Columbia University Library*, exhibitions.library.columbia.edu/exhibits/show/fugitives, stating that Napoleon worked at the premises. See Papson and Calarco, *Secret Lives of the Underground Railroad in New York City*, 43–47, as to Kirk, Gay, Napoleon, and the Anti-slavery Building; see also Otis Kidwell Burger, "Forefather's Papers Bring Abolition Fight Alive," *amNY*, September 17, 2015, www.amny.com/news/forefathers-papers-bring-abolition-fight-alive/ as to the Gay records.

6. "The Police of New-York on a Slave Hunt," *New-York Tribune*, October 30, 1846, 2. For a touching account by someone who helped in George Kirk's escape, see Willis F. Johnson and Ray B. Smith, *History of the State of New York Political and Governmental*, vol. 2, 1821–1864 (Syracuse, NY: The Syracuse Press, 1922), 288–190. See John Freeman Gill, "Preserving New York's Ties to the Under-

ground Railroad," *New York Times*, January 8, 2021, for an article dealing with New York's Underground Railroad and mentioning the Kirk case.

7. Kirk, 9 Month. L. Rep. at 366, citing Prigg v. Pennsylvania, 41 US 539 (1842). In deciding the Kirk case in 1846, Judge Edmonds was a judge on the Court of Oyer and Terminer (First Circuit). In 1847 the courts were reorganized, and at a June 7, 1847, election, he was elected a judge of the Supreme Court (see *Brooklyn Evening Star*, June 9, 1847, 2; *New York Daily Herald*, June 11, 1847, 2). In the Belt case (1848), he was sitting as a judge of the New York State Supreme Court, which was and still is a trial-level court, below two levels of appeal. In a letter of January 15, 1853, Jay described his role in the Kirk case to David Lee Child, husband of abolitionist writer Lydia Maria Child. Jay mentions the account of "Mrs. Child," whose stirring description of the Kirk case and of her admiration for Jay and his heroic role in it appeared in the *New-York Tribune* of November 4, 1846. There is also an excellent account of the Kirk case in Papson and Talarco, *Secret Lives of the Underground Railroad in New York City*, 43–50.

8. See, generally, *Baltimore Sun*, December 27, 1848; "The Fugitive Slave," *Brooklyn Daily Eagle*, December 27, 1848, 3; "The Abduction Case," *Evening Post*, December 27, 1848, 2; "Decision of the Slave Case by Judge Edmonds," *Evening Post*, December 29, 1848, 2. The news accounts do not give Joseph Belt's age. *The Liberator* of December 29, 1848, 3, describes him as "a negro boy."

9. In the Matter of Joseph Belt, an alleged fugitive from service, in the State of Maryland, 7 N.Y. Leg. Obs. 80, 1 Parker Crim. Rep. 169, 2 Edm. Sel. Cas. 93 (N.Y. Sup. Ct. 1848). Belt left the courtroom through a crowd assembled around City Hall and was understood to have headed for New England, perhaps to Lynn, Massachusetts, his first stop after fleeing from Maryland and before coming to New York. In an interesting postscript, the police and the kidnappers brought charges against one another. The police charged Belt's abductors with kidnapping; Clayton, one of the kidnappers, filed a criminal complaint against the police for false arrest. His complaint was dismissed summarily by Judge Garreson. We do not know what became of the kidnapping charges. See The People on the Complaint of Sidney Clayton v. Samuel Wolven and Russel Hulse, 7 N.Y. Leg. Obs. 89 (N.Y. Sup. Ct. 1848); "The Joseph Belt Case Again," *National Anti-Slavery Standard*, January 25, 1849, 4. The *National Anti-Slavery Standard* called the Belt case "one of the most important ever decided in a Free State, and must give another staggering blow to the slave power in this country." See "Slave Case," *National Anti-Slavery Standard*, January 4, 1849, 2.

10. Richmond Dispatch, November 11, 1852, 4, quoting the *New York Journal of Commerce*.

11. The quoted exchange between Juliet Lemmon and the two mothers is from the *New-York Tribune*, November 19, 1852, 4. See also "Claim of Emancipation for Eight Slaves Brought Into a Free State," *New York Daily Times*, November 9, 1852, 6; "The Slave Case in New York," *Richmond Dispatch*, November 11,

1852, 4, quoting the *New York Journal of Commerce*; *Daily Republic*, Washington DC, November 11, 1852, 2. See also *Louisville (KY) Courier Journal*, November, 12, 1852, 2. The quotation concerning the "tender mercies of the abolitionists" is from the *Richmond (VA) Whig*, November 16, 1852, 4, quoting the *New York Mirror* of November 9, 1852.

In the November 22, 1852, issue of the *New York Tribune* at p. 5, Jonathan Lemmon denied the conversation between Juliet Lemmon and the young women, Emeline and Nancy. He also denied selling off any slave's husband. Responding, the *Tribune*'s editors asked Lemmon how it came to pass that the children were separated from their fathers, that if Lemmon did not sell them away, who did, and what were the prospects of the children ever seeing their fathers again. Lemmon never answered. See also *National Anti-Slavery Standard*, November 25, 1852, commenting on the exchange. For further discussion of this point, see "Buxton Offers Up Some 'Lemon Aid,'" www.buxtonmuseum.com/history/eBOOKS/lemmon-slaves.pdf, quoting *The Danville Advertiser*, February 12, 1853, stating that Emeline's first husband was Tom Reynolds, sold off by his master, named Wood, to Cobb Reynolds. In another account, Lapaugh asked that the Lemmons be allowed "outside the influence of others" personally to ask the Eight if they would not want to return to the Lemmons. Culver said he "would be perfectly happy that he should do so—that they were free people and [Lapaugh] could ask them anything he chose—he might do it in open court, if he pleased, and had no doubt their reply would be, that they would rather remain in New York than go to Texas" (*Pennsylvania Freeman*, November 18, 1852). They were separately asked (the article continued) and they declined.

As for selling off family members, see Andrew Fede, *People Without Rights: An Interpretation of the Fundamentals of the Law of Slavery in the U.S. South* (Abingdon: Routledge, 2012); Margaret A. Burnham, "An Impossible Marriage: Slave Law and Family Law," *Law & Inequality* 5 (1987): 209–219; and Neal K. Katyal, "Men Who Own Women: A Thirteenth Amendment Critique of Forced Prostitution," *Yale Law Journal* 103 (December 1993): 791. See also "On Slaveholders' Sexual Abuse of Slaves," National Humanities Center, nationalhumanitiescenter.org/pds/maai/enslavement/text6/masterslavesexualabuse.pdf. As one court put it, "With us, nothing is so usual as to advance children by gifts of slaves. They stand with us, instead of money." Jones v. Mason, 26 Va. 577, 582 (1827). For an elaboration on the paternalism toward slaves, see Peter v. Hargrave, 46 Va. 12, 22 (1848), written by Supreme Court of Virginia Justice Briscoe Gerard Baldwin (1789–1852). For a first-hand description of the travail in separating families, see *Mission to the Fugitive Slaves in Canada, for the Year 1858–1859* (London: Colonial Church and School Society, 1859), and Damien Alan Pargas, *Slavery and Forced Migration in the Antebellum South* (New York: Cambridge University Press, 2015), 89, as to the doleful cry of those separated saying, "buy me too." For a personal account by a woman who told of her husband and child being sold, see Isaac Williams, *Aunt*

Sally: or, The Cross the Way of Freedom. A Narrative of the Slave-life and Purchase of the Mother of Rev. Isaac Williams (Cincinnati: American Reform Tract and Book Society, 1858), 66, 78, docsouth.unc.edu/neh/sally/menu.html. As a measure of racist thought at the time, one reporter commented that "a natural love of liberty for themselves and the unconscious children clinging to them outweighed [Juliet Lemmon's] arguments. One of the women, and two of the boys about age 7, are Mulattoes, and appear to possess a degree of intelligence above their class" (*New York Times*, November 9, 1852, 2).

After a good deal of research, comparison of often conflicting records, and discussions with the descendants and with author and Buxton Historian Bryan Prince, the evidence strongly suggests that the twin boys, Lewis Louis and Robert Wright, either 5 or 7 years old, were the sons of 23-year-old-Emeline (Maria/ Mariah/Miranda E. Thompson), and that Nancy was the Mulatto woman to whom the reporter referred. It is equally safe to say that the father of the twin boys was white or light-skinned, and may have been named Wright, although his identity remains unknown. For further elaboration on the identities of the Eight, see chapter 1, note 5.

12. The 1817 statute (L. 1817, ch. 137) was enacted in parts in 1830 (1 *R. S.* 656). The repeal is in L.1841, ch. 247.

13. Prigg v. Pennsylvania, 41 US 539, 612 (1842).

14. R. v. Knowles, ex parte Somerset (1772) Lofft 1, 98 E.R. 499, 20 S.T. 1. Somerset v. Stewart, 1 Lofft 1, 1, 98 Eng. Rep. 499, 499 (K.B. 1772). Lord Mansfield (1705–1793) was William Murray, 1st Earl of Mansfield, PC, SL, chief justice of the Court of King's Bench, and one of England's most eminent jurists. Volumes have been written about the Somerset case. See Daniel J. Hulsebosch, "*Somerset's Case* at the bar: Securing the 'Pure Air' of English Jurisdiction within the British Empire," *Texas Wesleyan Law Review* 13, no. 1 (Fall 2006). Hulsebosch, a first-rate scholar, states that, "by the time Somerset's lawyers made their appearance at the bar of King's Bench in 1772, English schoolboys had for a long time been taught, among other lessons of Whig history—or English history as the story of the progress of freedom—that their kingdom had too pure an air for a slave to breathe." See also Mark S. Weiner, *Black Trials: Citizenship from the Beginnings of Slavery to the End of Caste* (New York: Knopf Doubleday, 2007), 70–88, for a fine, lengthy treatment of the case. See also Derek A. Webb, "The Somerset Effect: Parsing Lord Mansfield's Words on Slavery in Nineteenth Century America," *Law and History Review* 32, no. 3 (August 2014); Aviam Soifer, "Status, Contract, and Promises Unkept," *Yale Law Journal* 96, no. 8 (July 1987).

15. "The Slave Case in New York," *Richmond Dispatch*, November 11, 1852, 4, quoting the *New York Journal of Commerce*; *National Anti-Slavery Standard*, November 25, 1852, quoting the *New York Day Book*. Nathaniel R. Stimson founded the *Day Book* in 1848 to "promote the proslavery cause among New York City's commercial interests." See Eric Conrad, "Whitman and the Proslavery

Press: Newly Recovered 1860 Reviews," *Walt Whitman Quarterly Review* 27 (2010), 227, citing C. Peter Ripley, ed., *The Black Abolitionist Papers*, vol. 5, *The United States, 1859–1865* (Chapel Hill: University of North Carolina Press, 1992), 402n.

16. *New-York Tribune*, November 15, 1852, 4, referring to the *New York Journal of Commerce* as an "exemplar of cotton piety and humanity." *Liberator*, November 19, 1852, 2 ("You that have tears"); see *Richmond Dispatch*, November 11, 1852, 4; *Daily Republic*, Washington, DC, November 11, 1852, 2; *Baltimore Sun*, November 11, 1852, 1 (indignation at Judge Paine's ruling).

17. The Antelope, 23 U.S. (10 Wheat.) 66 (1825).

18. *New York Times*, November 10, 1852, 8.

19. "Claim of Slaves Brought Into a Free State, for Their Freedom," *New York Daily Times*, November 10, 1852, 8. The oral arguments of counsel are reported in 5 Sandford 681 (1852). See also, for counsels' arguments, *New York Herald*, November 10, 1852, 1; *National Anti-Slavery Standard*, November 11, 25, 1852. Henry Lauren Clinton would later recount his role in the Lemmon case in his book *Extraordinary Cases* (New York: Harper & Brothers, 1896), 173–181. For an account of the attorneys' colloquy with Judge Paine before he adjourned the case for his decision, see *National Anti-Slavery Standard*, November 11, 1852. For a biography of Clinton, see *Appleton's Cyclopaedia of American Biography* 7 (1901), 71, babel.hathitrust.org/cgi/pt?id=ucl.l0100651298&view=1up&seq=105, including role in the prosecution of William "Boss" Tweed. Clinton also wrote *Celebrated Trials* (New York: Harper & Brothers, 1897).

Chapter 5

1. For accounts of the earliest years of slavery in New Netherland, see Dennis J. Maika, "Slavery, Race, and Culture in Early New York," *de Halve Maen* 73, no. 2 (Summer 2000); Dr. Charles T. Gehring, ed., *Annals of New Netherland: The Essays of A.J.F. van Laer* (Albany: Consulate General of the Netherlands, 1999), www.newnetherlandinstitute.org/files/1213/5067/2997/1999.pdf; Joyce D. Goodfriend, "Burghers and Blacks: The Evolution of a Slave Society at New Amsterdam," *New York History* 59 (April 1978): 124–143. See also *The Memory of the Netherlands*, geheugen.delpher.nl/en/, a database containing paintings, drawings, photographs, sculptures, ceramics, stamps, posters and newspaper clippings of Dutch institutions, much of which deals with Dutch New York. For a work on segregated burial grounds in Dutch New York, see Robert J. Swan, *New Amsterdam Gehenna: Segregated Death in New York City, 1630–1801* (New York: Noir Verite Press, 2006). For more recent scholarship on the subject, see Dennis J. Maika, "To 'Experiment with a Parcel of Negros': Incentive, Collaboration, and Competition in New Amsterdam's Slave Trade," *Journal of Early American History* 10 (2020): 33–69; "Slavery in New Netherland," New Netherland Institute, www.

newnetherlandinstitute.org/history-and-heritage/digital-exhibitions/slavery-exhibit/slave-trade/.

2. For example, Hudgins v. Wrights, 11 Va. 134 (1806); Fulton's Ex'rs v. Gracey, 56 Va. 314 (1859). For a further discussion as to when the presumption applies, see Charles Mangum, *The Legal Status of the Negro* (Chapel Hill: University of North Carolina Press, 1940), 2. See, generally, for a history of Negro slavery in the United States, George Bancroft, *History of the United States of America, from the Discovery of the Continent* (New York: D. Appleton, 1888), 119f.

3. L. 1702, ch. 123, archive.org/details/coloniallawsnew00stagoog/page/n547. Colonial law in New York also had placed testimonial restrictions on the enslaved, as appears in the Laws of 1706, ch. 160.

4. L. 1708, ch. 171, passed September 18, 1708. For general background, see Edwin Olson, "The Slave Code in Colonial New York," *Journal of Negro History* 29, no. 2 (1944). See also Carl Nordstrom, "The New York Slave Code," *Afro-Americans in New York Life and History* 4, no. 1 (1980): 7.

5. L 1706, ch. 160, an "Act to Incourage the Baptizing of Negro, Indian and Mulatto Slaves." See also Joyce Goodfriend, "The Souls of New Amsterdam's African Children," in *Opening States: Law, Jurisprudence, and the Legacy of Dutch New York*, ed. Albert M. Rosenblatt and Julia C. Rosenblatt (Albany: State University of New York Press, 2013), 27–35.

6. In his article, Edwin Olson goes into considerable detail describing 18th-century laws in New York to keep slaves in line, including those governing assembly and behavior, with violations typically calling for public whipping. Olson, "The Slave Code in Colonial New York." Public whipping was used for even the most minor infractions. In 1740, the New York City Common Council decreed that any "Negro, Indian, or Mulatto slave 'be publicly whipped for the offense of selling fruit.'" *Minutes of the Common Council of the City of New York*, vol. 4 (New York: Dodd, Mead, 1905), 498.

7. After a series of fires, rumored to have been started by slaves, Judge Daniel Horsmanden (1691–1778), of the Supreme Judicial Court of New York, sponsored dubious charges against scores of people, mostly slaves, and then sat as one of the judges at the ensuing trials. By the time it all ended, officials had burned 13 Black men to death at the stake, hanged 17 more, and sent 70 others to slavery in the Caribbean. (Horsmanden's performance prompted the authors of New York's first constitution to include a mandatory retirement provision for judges at age 60.) See, generally, Jill Lepore, *New York Burning: Liberty, Slavery, and Conspiracy in Eighteenth-Century Manhattan* (New York: Vintage, 2005); William Cullen Bryant and Sydney Howard Gay, *A Popular History of the United States*, vol. 3 (New York: Scribners, 1879), 234; Peter Charles Hoffer, *The Great New York Conspiracy of 1741: Slavery, Crime and Colonial Law* (Lawrence: University Press of Kansas, 2003); David McAdam et al., eds., *History of the Bench and Bar of New York* (New York: New York History Company, 1892), 133, n. 2; George Pellew,

John Jay: American Statesman, vol. 9 (Boston: Houghton Mifflin, 1890), 7. The other two judges with Horsmanden, at trial, were James De Lancey (1703–1760) and Frederick Philipse II (1698–1751).

8. In Section 35 of the New York Constitution of 1777.

9. Blackstone, *Commentaries on the Laws of England*, vol. 1, 127.

10. For a guide to the records of the Manumission Society, see "New-York Manumission Society Records," New-York Historical Society Museum & Library, accessed February 24, 2020, dlib.nyu.edu/findingaids/html/nyhs/manumission/ manumission.html. See *Loudon's New York Packet*, February 21, 1785, 2, as to the founding of the "Society for the promoting of the manumission of Slaves."

11. David T. Morgan, *The Devious Dr. Franklin, Colonial Agent: Franklin's Years in London* (Macon, GA: Mercer University Press, 1996), 63; John P. Kaminski et al., eds., *The Documentary History of the Ratification of the Constitution*, vol. 19, *Ratification of the Constitution by the States: New York*, no. 1 (Madison: Wisconsin Historical Society Press, 2005), 253; John Kaminski, *A Necessary Evil?: Slavery and the Debate Over the Constitution* (New York: Rowman & Littlefield, 1995), 127. As for Alexander Hamilton's attitude toward slavery, see Rob N. Weston, "Alexander Hamilton and the Abolition of Slavery in New York," *Afro-Americans in New York Life and History* 18, no. 1 (1994): 31.

12. The Constitution has five slavery clauses, although not using the word slavery: Article I, sec. 2, cl. 3 (three-fifths clause); Art. I, sec. 9, cl. 1 (slave trade clause); Art. I, sec. 9, cl. 4 (capitation tax clause); Art. IV, sec. 2, cl. 3 (fugitive slave clause); Art. V (prohibiting amendments of the two slavery-related provisions in article I, sec. 9, before 1808). In addition, Paul Finkelman lists several constitutional provisions that protect enslavement indirectly, including the use of the militia to suppress insurrection (Art. I, sec. 8); prohibiting taxes on exports (Art. I, sec. 9, 10); the electoral college (Art. II, sec. 1); the admission of new states (Art. IV, sec. 3); protection from domestic violence (Art. IV, sec. 4); and the laborious amendment process (Art. V). Paul Finkelman, *Slavery and the Founders* (Abingdon: Routledge, 2014), 7–8. See also Carl T. Bogus, "Race, Riots, and Guns," *Southern California Law Review* 66 (1993), contending that fear of slave insurrection played a part in promulgating the Second Amendment. As to slave trading, see, generally, Nicholas Guyatt, *New York Review of Books*, November 18, 2021, 43, reviewing Joshua D. Rothman, *The Ledger and the Chain: How Domestic Slave Traders Shaped America*.

13. For Pinckney's comment, see Jonathan Elliot, ed., *The Debates in the Several State Conventions*, vol. 4 (Philadelphia: J.B. Lippincott, 1836–1859), 286; Charles Pickney, "Speech in the South Carolina House of Representatives," Columbia, SC, January 17, 1788, Center for the Study of the American Constitution, archive.csac.history.wisc.edu/sc_cotesworth_pinckney.pdf; John Fiske, *The Critical Period of American History, 1783–1789* (Boston: Houghton Mifflin, 1892); Clinton Rossiter, *1787: The Grand Convention* (New York: Macmillan, 1966): 267–268. For

an interesting catalog of quotations, see Walter E. Williams, "What the Founders Said About Slavery," walterewilliams.com/quotations/slavery/. For Emerson's comment see Ralph Waldo Emerson, "Lecture on Slavery: 25 January 1855," in *Emerson's Antislavery Writings*, ed. Len Gougeon and Joel Myerson (New Haven: Yale University Press, 1995), 91–106; David Waldstreicher and Matthew Mason, *John Quincy Adams and the Politics of Slavery* (Oxford: Oxford University Press, 2017), 84.

14. Prigg v. Pennsylvania, 41 US 539, 612 (1842).

15. Stephen L. Schechter, ed., *The Reluctant Pillar: New York and the Adoption of the Federal Constitution* (Lanham, MD: Rowman & Littlefield, 1985), 62–64.

16. Kaminski et al., *The Documentary History of the Ratification of the Constitution*, vol. 19, *New York*, 253; Kaminski, *A Necessary Evil?*, 127. For a penetrating discussion of the motivations of the delegates in Poughkeepsie, and their attitudes toward slavery, and as he aptly put it, whether they and others supported slavery to protect union, or supported union to protect slavery, see Mark Boonshoft, "Doughfaces at the Founding: Federalists, Anti-Federalists, Slavery, and the Ratification of the Constitution in New York," *New York History* 93, no. 3 (2012): 187–218.

17. Kaminski et al., *The Documentary History of the Ratification of the Constitution*, vol. 19, *New York*, 409.

18. For Senator Pinkney's remarks, see Elliot, *The Debates in the Several State Conventions on the Adoption of the Federal Constitution*, vol. 4, 316; John Elster, "Arguing and Bargaining in Two Constituent Assemblies," *University of Pennsylvania Journal of Constitutional Law* 2, no. 2 (March 2000): 345.

19. Washington was a slaveowner and was said to have pursued a fugitive slave owned by his wife. See Erica Armstrong Dunbar, *Never Caught: The Washingtons' Relentless Pursuit of Their Runaway Slave, Ona Judge* (New York: Simon & Schuster, 2017). Author Jesse J. Holland has counted 12 of the first 18 American presidents as slaveholders. Jesse J. Holland, *The Invisibles: The Untold Story of African American Slaves in the White House* (Lanham, MD: Lyons Press, 2016), 5.

20. Richard J. Follett, *The Sugar Masters: Planters and Slaves in Louisiana's Cane World, 1820–1860* (Baton Rouge: Louisiana State University Press, 2005). See also Khalil Gibran Muhammad, "The Sugar that Saturates the American Diet Has a Barbaric History as the 'White Gold' that Fueled Slavery," *New York Times Magazine*, August 14, 2019, www.nytimes.com/interactive/2019/08/14/magazine/sugar-slave-trade-slavery.html. See also Adam Hochschild, *New York Times Book Review*, November 15, 2021, reviewing *The 1619 Project*, edited by Nikole Hannah-Jones, Caitlin Roper, Ilena Silverman, and Jake Silverstein, stating that one of the book's contributors, Matthew Desmond, "points out that the cotton plantation 'was America's first big business,'" and that "on the eve of the Civil War the monetary value 'of enslaved people exceeded that of all the railroads and factories in the nation.'"

21. Allen Johnson, "The Constitutionality of the Fugitive Slave Acts," *Yale Law Journal* 31, no. 2 (1961): 179–182; L. Brophy, "Jim Crow in the *Yale Law Journal*," *Connecticut Law Review* 49 (May 2017): 3; James Forman Jr., "Juries and Race in the Nineteenth Century," *Yale Law Journal* 113, no. 4 (January 2004): 895. For punishments that awaited runaways, see Paul Finkelman, "The Crime of Color," *Tulane Law Review* 67, no. 2063 (1993).

22. Hudgins v. Wrights, 11 Va. 134, 141 (1806).

23. Referring to Georgia and South Carolina, see Joseph Brevard, *An Alphabetical Digest of the Public Statute Law of South Carolina* (Charleston: John Hoff, 1814), 2:230, quoted in Stroud, *A Sketch of the Laws Relating to Slavery*, 123.

24. Link v. Beuner, 3 Cai. R. 325 (1805); Oatfield v. Waring, 14 Johns. 188 (1817).

25. "February 16, 1817–February 18, 1817," in *Minutes of the Common Council of the City of New York, 1784–1831*, vol. 9 (New York: City of New York, 1917), 493; "February 18, 1818," in *Minutes of the Common Council of the City of New York, 1784–1831*, vol. 3 (New York: City of New York, 1917), 691.

26. "July 27, 1818," in *Minutes of the Common Council of the City of New York, 1784–1831*, vol. 9, 742.

27. John R. Van Atta, *Wolf by the Ears: The Missouri Crisis, 1819–1821* (Baltimore: Johns Hopkins University Press, 2015), 77. For insights into the presence of Blacks in New York City at the time, see Laura Copeland, "The Rise and Fall of Moses Simons: A Black Lawyer in the New York City Criminal Court, 1816–1820," *Afro-Americans in New York Life and History* 37 (2013): 81–114.

28. Under John Jay's leadership as governor in 1799, New York began its gradual abolition process with a statute decreeing that children born after July 4, 1799, to enslaved mothers would be born free, but were required to serve their mothers' masters, without compensation, until age 25 (for females) and age 28 (for males). This, however, continued enslavement for those born *before* July 4, 1799—a condition remedied in 1817 by a statute declaring a final end to slavery in New York for all, on July 4, 1827. For an excellent, step-by-step description of the legislative journey toward New York's gradual abolition of slavery from 1799 to July 4, 1827, including the important role played by New York Governor Daniel Tompkins in the 1817 statute, and the varying accounts of the number of people who on that day gained their freedom, see Craig A. Landy, "When Men Among Us, Shall Cease to Be Slaves," *Judicial Notice*, no. 12 (2017): 42–54. As to the events in New York on July 4, 1827, see Shane White, " 'It Was a Proud Day': African Americans, Festivals, and Parades in the North, 1741–1834," *Journal of American History* 81, no. 1 (1994): 38–45.

29. Peter J. Galie, *Ordered Liberty: A Constitutional History of New York* (New York: Fordham University Press, 1996), 76–77; Robert E. Cray Jr., "White Welfare and Black Strategies: The Dynamics of Race and Poor Relief in Early New York, 1700–1825," *Slavery & Abolition* 7, no. 3 (1986): 273–289; Phyllis

Field, *The Politics of Race in New York: The Struggle for Black Suffrage in the Civil War Era* (Ithaca, NY: Cornell University Press, 1982), 37; Nathaniel H. Carter and William L. Stone, *Reports of the Proceedings and Debates of the Convention of 1821* (Albany: E. and E. Hosford, 1821), 374. According Landy, "When Men Among Us, Shall Cease to Be Slaves," in 1825, only 68 were qualified to vote out of 12,559 Black inhabitants in New York City. In 1835, only 84 could meet the property requirement out of a Black population of 15,061, while in 1845, 255 could vote out of a total of 12,913 Black residents. Ten years later, of the 11,840 Blacks living in New York City, a mere 100 could cast a ballot.

30. Shane White, *Somewhat More Independent: The End of Slavery in New York City, 1770–1810* (Athens: University of Georgia Press, 1991). See also David N. Gellman, *Emancipating New York: The Politics of Slavery and Freedom, 1777–1827* (Baton Rouge: Louisiana State University Press, 2006), 195. By way of contrast, from 1700 to 1860, the number of slaves in the United States grew from just under 700,000 to almost 4 million. Virginia typified the increase, having some 293,000 enslaved in 1790 and 472,000 in 1860. Edgar J. McManus, *Black Bondage in the North* (Syracuse: Syracuse University Press, 1973), 211, citing the Second US census of 1800 (see "Slave, Free Black, and White Population, 1780–1830," userpages.umbc.edu/~bouton/History407/SlaveStats.htm); W. S. Rossiter, ed., *A Century of Population Growth: From the First to the Twelfth Census of the United States: 1790–1860* (Washington, DC: US Government Printing Office, 1909), Statistics of Slaves, table 60, pp. 132–141.

31. Philip S. Foner, *Business & Slavery: The New York Merchants and the Irrepressible Conflict* (Chapel Hill: University of North Carolina Press, 1941), 7, quoting the *New York Journal of Commerce*, December 12, 1849, and October 25, 1850. See also Leslie M. Harris, *In the Shadow of Slavery: African Americans in New York City, 1626–1863* (Chicago: University of Chicago Press, 2003), 273, stating that while New York merchants were opposed to the expansion of slavery into the territories, they created the Union Safety Committee in 1850 to preserve their economic ties with the South.

32. Jacqueline Bacon, *Freedom's Journal: The First African-American News-paper* (Lanham: Lexington Books, 2007). The article's content is available online at "The First American Newspaper Appears, 1827," college.cengage.com/history/ayers_primary_sources/first_african_american_newspaper.htm. For a penetrating discussion of the role of the Blacks as legal activists in the anti-slavery movement, see Sarah L. H. Gronningsater, " 'On Behalf of His Race and the Lemmon Slaves': Louis Napoleon, Northern Black Legal Culture, and the Politics of Sectional Crisis," *Journal of the Civil War Era* 7, no. 2 (2017): 206–241. See also Michael Stanke, "The Black Abolitionist; Saving the Past," *Afro-Americans in New York Life and History* 3, no. 1 (1979): 39; Craig Steven Wilder, "The Rise and Influence of the New York African Society for Mutual Relief, 1808–1865," *Afro-Americans in New York Life and History* 22, no. 2 (1998): 7. For the efforts of Black activists

such as Uriah Boston in New York's mid-Hudson region, see Michael E. Groth, *Slavery and Freedom in the Mid-Hudson Valley* (Albany: State University of New York Press, 2017), 127–152. On a related theme concerning when and how slaves turned to the courts, see Marion J. Russell, "American Slave Discontent in Records of the High Courts," *Journal of Negro History* 31, no. 4 (October 1946): 411–434.

33. For example, see Carol Wilson, *Freedom at Risk: The Kidnapping of Free Blacks in America, 1780–1865* (Lexington: University Press of Kentucky, 1994); David Fiske, *Solomon Northup's Kindred: The Kidnapping of Free Citizens Before the Civil War* (Santa Barbara: Praeger, 2016); Lawrence B. Goodheart, "The Chronicles of Kidnapping in New York: Resistance to the Fugitive Slave Law, 1834–1835," *Afro-Americans in New York Life and History* 8, no. 1 (1984): 7. The New York Committee of Vigilance in its first annual report stated in 1837, "That colored people were often kidnapped from the free states was generally known—but we have found the practice so extensive that no colored man is safe be his age or condition in life what it may—by sea and land, in slave states, or in those where colored men are considered free, in all the various occupations of life, they are exposed to the horrors of slavery." New York Committee of Vigilance, *The First Annual Report of the New York Committee of Vigilance for the Year 1837, Together with Important Facts Relative to Their Proceedings* (New York: Piercy & Reed, 1837). In his article "Napoleon v. Lemmon: Antebellum Black New Yorkers, Antislavery, and Law," p. 27, Thomas J. Davis aptly points out the integral role that African Americans played in the anti-slavery movement. See also Gronningsater, " 'On Behalf of His Race and the Lemmon Slaves.' "

34. N.Y. Rev. Stat. Part III, ch. 9, Tit. 1, art. 1. For an entire volume on the subject, see the oft-cited and comprehensive Thomas D. Morris, *Free Men Tell All: The Personal Liberty Laws of the North 1780–1861* (Baltimore: Johns Hopkins University, Press, 1974). See also chapter 10 of this volume, dealing with personal liberty laws of the North.

35. For example, see Jack v. Martin, 12 Wend. 311 (1834); Jack v. Martin, 14 Wend. 507 (1835); People v. McLeod, 3 Hill 635, 647 (1841). Even when the statute was enacted in 1828, there was some question as to whether the states could legislate on the subject, and, arguably, undermine federal law. For a contemporaneous discussion of this issue, see the interesting analysis of David Graham, *A Treatise on the Organization and Jurisdiction of the Courts of Law and Equity, in the State of New York* (New York: Halsted and Voorhies, 1839), 172–200. For praise of the statute, L. 1834, ch. 88, see "Important to Liberty," *The Liberator*, May 3, 1834. All was not quiet in New York City, however, given some disturbances involving anti-slavery societies and others in July of that year. See *The Evening Post*, July 12, 1834 and the *Newbern Spectator*, July 25, 1834, both carrying articles from New York newspapers.

36. Colonial law in New York placed testimonial restrictions on slaves. An Act to Encourage the Baptizing of Negro, Indian, and Mulatto Slaves, 1706 ch.

160 (passed October 24, 1706) ("Provided, always & be it declared & Enacted by ye said Authority That no slave whatsoever in this Colony shall att anytime be admitted as a Witness for, or against, any Freeman, in any Case matter or Cause, Civill or Criminal whatsoever"). As for the prohibition in southern states against Blacks (free or slave) testifying at all, see Luther Wright, "Who's Black, Who's White, and Who Cares: Reconceptualizing the United States' Definition of Race and Racial Classifications," *Vanderbilt Law Review* 48, no. 2 (March 1995): 513; Thomas D. Morris, *Southern Slavery and the Law, 1619–1860* (Chapel Hill: The University of North Carolina Press, 1996).

37. Griffin v. Potter, 14 Wend. 209 (1835).july

38. *Philadelphia Inquirer*, January 30, 1877, 4 (praising Dresser). As to Dresser's efforts on behalf of fugitive slaves and related anti-slavery efforts, see *The Colored America*, April 4, 1840, and June 19, 1841; *National Era*, October 18, 1855, and November 22, 1855; *National Anti-Slavery Standard*, July 25, 1844, August 18, 1855, June 2, 1866, and July 28, 1866. At some point, Dresser got into a dispute with John Jay. See the *National Anti-Slavery Standard*, October 26, 1843, and December 21, 1843. Dresser (1803–1877) was also involved in the George Kirk case (see chapter 4) but was replaced by John Jay II. *The National Anti-Slavery Standard*, October 29, 1846, and December 28, 1848. Dresser wrote other articles, some difficult to grasp, dealing with slavery. See *New York Day Book*, October 29, 1856, April 28, 1857 (letter dated April 24, 1857), dealing with the Lemmon case.

39. Marjorie Waters, "Before Solomon Northup: Fighting Slave Catchers in New York," *Columbian College of Arts & Sciences History News Network*, October 18, 2013, hnn.us/article/153653.

The Dixon case is important and dramatic enough to warrant a volume of its own. The best accounts are in Christopher James Bonner, *Remaking the Republic: Black Politics and the Creation of American Citizenship* (Philadelphia: University of Pennsylvania Press, 2020), 97–107; Eric Foner, *Gateway to Freedom: The Hidden History of the Underground Railroad* (New York: W. W. Norton & Company, 2015), 70–71. See also Christopher Bonner, "Trial by Jury, or Kidnapping in New York: Fugitive Slaves, Black Protest, and Legal Change in the 1830s," presentation for the American Historical Association, Denver, Colorado, January 6, 2017, aha.confex. com/aha/2017/webprogram/Paper20595.html; Daniel E. Meaders, *Kidnappers in Philadelphia: Isaac Hopper's Tales of Oppression, 1780–1843* (New York: Garland, 1994), ch. 79. Hopper's touching account of his personal involvement in the case appears also in the *National Anti-Slavery Standard*, May 23, 1844, www.accessible-archives.com/collections/national-anti-slavery-standard/.

For newspaper accounts, see *Long Island Star*, April 23, 1837 and April 24, 1837; *New York Daily Herald*, April 19, 1837 (as to court testimony); *New York Evening Post*, April 13, 1837, 2; *New York Daily Herald*, April 12, 1837, 2 and April 14, 1837 (as to escape and recapture); *Philadelphia Public Ledger*, April 14, 1837,

4 (as to attorney Horace Dresser charging Allender with false imprisonment); *Liberator*, April 21, 1837, April 28, 1837, and June 30, 1837, 3; *Vermont Telegraph*, May 17, 1837 (for a general account). Bonner states that Judge (Recorder) Riker ruled in Dixon's favor. Bonner, "Trial by Jury, or Kidnapping in New York." The *New York Daily* of August 4, 1837, states that the court ruled in favor of the slave-owner. See also Dixon v. Allender, 18 Wend. 678 (1837). Recorder's Court was a municipal level court, roughly the equivalent of today's City Courts. See James D. Folts, *"Duely & Constantly Kept": A History of the New York Supreme Court, 1691–1847 and an Inventory of Its Records (Albany, Utica, and Geneva Offices), 1797–1847* (Albany: New York State Court of Appeals and New York State Archives and Records Administration, 1991), Appendix C, www.nycourts. gov/history/legal-history-new-york/documents/History_Supreme-Court-Duely-Constantly-Kept.pdf.

40. Dresser's account is in the *Colored American* of April 18, 1840, three years later. Contemporaneous accounts do not go into any detail. *Boston Post*, October 13, 1837, 2; *Baltimore Sun*, October 13, 1837, 1; *National Gazette*, October 12, 1837, 2; *Staunton Spectator*, October 26, 1837, 3. This is not surprising, considering that many such cases were purposely concluded before friends, lawyers, or newspaper reporters learned of them. *The North Alabamian*, December 1, 1837, 3, reported that Judge Betts turned "Nat" over to his claimed owner in November 1837.

41. See "Utica Rescue," *Oneida County Freedom Trail*, www.oneidacounty freedomtrail.com/utica-rescue.html. For contemporary accounts, see the Utica, NY, newspaper *Friend of Man*, January 5, 1837, and January 26, 1837, drive.google. com/file/d/1paiWoPZe7u9njDOJIyA21Uik_A76eMtu/view.

42. An Act More Effectively to Protect the Free Citizens of This State from Being Kidnapped or Reduced to Slavery, New York State Assembly, 1840 ch. 375 (passed May 14, 1840).

43. There was, however, a wide spectrum of attitudes among workers, many of whom would serve on juries. Williston H. Lofton, "Abolition and Labor: Reaction of Northern Labor to the Anti-Slavery Appeal: Part II," *Journal of Negro History* 33, no. 3 (July 1948): 261–283.

Chapter 6

1. Prigg v. Pennsylvania, 41 U.S. 539 (1842).

2. Paul Finkelman, "Prigg v. Pennsylvania and the Northern State Courts: Anti-Slavery Use of a Pro-Slavery Decision," *Civil War History* 25, no. 1 (March 1979): 5–35.

3. Robert J. Kaczorowski, "The Supreme Court and Congress's Power to Enforce Constitutional Rights: An Overlooked Moral Anomaly," *Fordham Law Review* 73, no. 1 (October 2004): 153–243.

4. William Jay, *Miscellaneous Writings on Slavery* (Boston: John P. Jewett & Company, 1853), 236; Willian H. Seward, *The Works of William H. Seward*, ed. George E. Baker (New York: Redfield, 1853), 1:505–506; H. Robert Baker, *Prigg v. Pennsylvania: Slavery, the Supreme Court, and the Ambivalent Constitution* (Lawrence: University of Kansas Press, 2012).

5. Jamal Greene, "The Anticanon," *Harvard Law Review* 125, no. 2 (December 2011), calling Prigg one of the worst decisions in our history; Sanford Levinson, "Is Dred Scott Really the Worst Opinion of All Time? Why Prigg is Worse than Dred Scott (But Is Likely to Stay Out of the 'Anticanon')," *Harvard Law Review* 125, no. 2 (December 2011): F. 23. Much has been written about the moral dimensions (and shortcomings) of Justice Story's decision in Prigg, including criticisms by Ronald Dworkin, Robert Cover, and Kent Newmyer. For example, see Ronald M. Dworkin, "The Law of the Slave-Catchers," *Times Literary Supplement*, December 5, 1975; R. Kent Newmyer, *Supreme Court Justice Joseph Story: Statesman of the Old Republic* (Chapel Hill: University of North Carolina Press, 1985), 351; Robert M. Cover, *Justice Accused: Antislavery and the Judicial Process* (New Haven, CT: Yale University Press, 1975), 239–240; Joe Lockard, "Justice Story's 'Prigg' Decision and the Defeat of Freedom," *Amerikastudien/American Studies* 52, no. 4 (2007): 467–480 (challenging the assertion that Prigg was a "triumph of freedom"). See also William M. Wiecek, *The Sources of Antislavery Constitutionalism in America, 1760–1848* (Ithaca, NY: Cornell University Press, 1977). For articles questioning the so-called historical necessity of the fugitive slave clause and laws, see Eric W. Plaag, " 'Let the Constitution Perish': Prigg v. Pennsylvania, Joseph Story, and the Flawed Doctrine of Historical Necessity," *Slavery & Abolition* 25, no. 3 (2004): 76–101, and Paul Finkelman, "The Constitution, the Supreme Court, and History" (book review), *Texas Law Review* 88, no. 2 (December, 2009): 353–389. For an article defending Story, see Christopher L. M. Eisgruber, "Justice Story, Slavery, and the Natural Law Foundations of American Constitutionalism," *University of Chicago Law Review* 55 (Winter 1988): 279.

6. See Kentucky v. Dennison, 65 U.S. 66 (1861).

7. Louise Weinberg, "This Activist Court," *Georgetown Journal of Law and Public Policy* 1, no. 1 (Fall 2002): 112.

8. Christopher N. Lasch, "Rendition Resistance," *North Carolina Law Review* 92, no. 1 (December 2013): 149; James A. Kraehenbueh, "Lessons from the Past: How the Antebellum Fugitive Slave Debate Informs State Enforcement of Federal Immigration Law," *University of Chicago Law Review* 78, no. 4 (Fall 2011): 1465; Karla Mari McKanders, "Immigration Enforcement and the Fugitive Slave Acts: Exploring Their Similarities," *Catholic University Law Review* 61, no. 4 (Summer 2012): 921; Paul Finkelman, "Roots of *Printz*: Proslavery Constitutionalism, National Law Enforcement, Federalism, and Local Cooperation," *Brooklyn Law Review* 69, no. 4 (Summer 2004): 1399, arguing that "indeed, the genius—if we can call it that—of American federalism is that in times of crisis the States can be a check

on the national government and the national government can also be a check on the States. But if the States become a mere adjunct of the federal government, then there will be no checking possibilities, and the potential for the violation of rights is much greater"; Allan Colbern, "The House is Picking a Fight with 'Sanctuary City' Ordinances. How is This Like the Fugitive Slave Laws?" *Washington Post*, August 13, 2015; H. Robert Baker, "A Brief History of Sanctuary Cities," *Tropics of Meta*, February 2, 2017, tropicsofmeta.com/2017/02/02/a-brief-history-of-sanctuary-cities. The New York judiciary was reportedly considering a rule to bar ICE agents from arresting alleged illegals unless the officials had a federal arrest warrant. Andrew Delbanco, "The Long Struggle for America's Soul," *New York Times*, November 2, 2018; Caitlin Dickerson and Zolan Kanno-Youngs, "Border Patrol Will Deploy Elite Tactical Agents to Sanctuary Cities," *New York Times*, February 14, 2020; Caitlin Dickerson, Zolan Kanno-Youngs, and Annie Correal, "'Flood the Streets': ICE Targets Sanctuary Cities with Increased Surveillance," *New York Times*, March 6, 2020.

In 1848, six years after Prigg, observers began to see some of its consequences play out. Charles J. Faulkner (1806–1884), a member of Virginia's House of Delegates, complained that Northern courts and legislatures had seized on the decision's obiter dictum that the North need not affirmatively aid in enforcing the goals of federal fugitive slave reclamation. The North was able to do this by passive resistance, in closing its jails to slave power and prohibiting its officials from helping enforce the law (*Richmond Enquirer*, December 22, 1848). This was the early handwriting on the wall for what appeared more than a century and a half later in the form of sanctuary cities resisting certain kinds of federal immigration enforcement.

9. For a catalog of state legislation in reaction to Prigg, see Morris, *Free Men Tell All*, 219–222; Marion Gleason McDougall, *Fugitive Slaves (1619–1865)* (Boston: Ginn & Company, 1891), 65–67; Paul Finkelman, "*Prigg v. Pennsylvania* and the Northern State Courts: Anti-Slavery Use of a Pro-Slavery Decision," *Civil War History* 25, no. 1 (March 1979): fn. 50; Joseph Nogee, "The Prigg Case and Fugitive Slavery," *Journal of African American History* 39, no. 3 (July 1954): 185–205; John Coughlin, "*Prigg v. Pennsylvania* and the Rising Sectional Tension of the 1840s," master's thesis, Arizona State University, 2010; McDougall, *Fugitive Slaves (1619–1865)*, 66–70. Despite *Prigg* (and urgings by Virginia), New York did not repeal its jury trial provision for alleged fugitive slaves; see Morris, *Free Men Tell All*, 127. Governor William C. Bouck (who succeeded Governor Seward in 1843) was inclined toward repeal and harmony with Virginia. Johnson and Smith, *History of the State of New York Political and Governmental*, vol. 2, 294; "The Jury Law," *Richmond Enquirer*, February 4, 1843. This of course antagonized anti-slavery advocates (see *Bennington Banner*, February 28, 1843, 1). Although there was some legislative support for his position, others opposed it (see *New-York Tribune*, February 2, 1843), and New York left the jury trial provision on the books, symbolic, but as a practical matter inoperative.

10. James Buchanan, "Fourth Annual Message, December 3, 1860," in *American Presidents: Farewell Messages to the Nation, 1796–2001*, ed. Gleaves Whitney (Lanham: Lexington Books, 2002), 174, 177.

11. Charles Francis Adams, ed., *Memoirs of John Quincy Adams, Comprising Portions of His Diary from 1795–1848* (Philadelphia: J.B. Lippincott & Co., 1876), 11:335.

12. "Freedom and Slavery," *New-York Tribune*, March 5, 1842, 2.

13. Charge to Grand Jury-Fugitive Slave Law, 30 F. Cas. 1007, 1851 U.S. App. LEXIS 376, 1 Blatchf. 635. According to one commentator, Justice Samuel Nelson of New York "winked at slave trading in New York, and he, like Justice C. Grier of Pennsylvania, while acting as designated circuit justices, repeatedly enforced the Fugitive Slave Acts of 1793 and 1850 while counseling the North against the risks to the Union of resistance." In 1857, Nelson joined in the *Dred Scott* decision. Alexander Tsesis, "Undermining Inalienable Rights: From Dred Scott to the Rehnquist Court," *Arizona State Law Journal* 39 (Winter 2007). For a discussion as to how and why some Northern judges were motivated to take such positions, see Jeffrey M. Schmitt, "The Anti-Slavery Judge Reconsidered," *Law and History Review* 29, no. 3 (2011).

14. One researcher has noted that federal judges routinely admonished both grand and petit juries not to vote their conscience in Fugitive Slave cases. Clay S. Conrad, "Scapegoating the Jury," *Cornell Journal of Law and Public Policy* 7, no. 1 (Fall 1997): 15, citing United States v. Hanway, 26 F. Cas. 105 (C.C.E.D. Penn. 1851); Oliver v. Kauffman, 18 F. Cas. 657 (C.C.E.D. Penn. 1850); United States v. Morris, 26 F. Cas. 1323 (E.D. Mass. 1851); United States v. Cobb 25 F. Cas. 481 (N.D.N.Y. 1857); Charge to Grand Jury-Fugitive Slave Act, 30 F. Cas. 1015 (D. Mass. 1851); United States v. Scott, 27 F. Cas. 990 (D. Mass. 1851). Also see, Charge to the Grand Jury-Treason, 30 F. Cas. 1047 (E.D. Penn. 1851).

15. Unsurprisingly, Judge Nelson's remarks won praise from the South. For example, see *Richmond Enquirer*, April 1, 1851; *Washington Union*, April 11, 1851; *Times-Picayune*, April 18, 1851; *Washington Telegraph*, May 14, 1851; *Weekly Commercial*, November 7, 1851. Also, they won praise from a Buffalo, New York newspaper, *Buffalo Courier*, April 25, 1851. Northern newspapers, for the most part, disparaged the remarks as gratuitous and misguided. For example, see *The Evening Post*, April 10, 14, 21 1851; *Buffalo Daily Republic*, April 12, 1851; *Liberator*, April 25, 1851; *Vermont Watchman and State Journal*, July 24, 1851; *Daily Free Democrat*, October 30, 1851.

16. Judge Conkling's decision is reported at *Ex parte Davis*, 7 F. Cas. 45 (N.D.N.Y. 1851). A full account of the episode is online at the University of Buffalo site, "Fugitive Slave Case in Buffalo, August 1851," www.math.buffalo.edu/~sww/0history/hwny.daniel.1851.html. See also *Buffalo Commercial Advertiser*, August 15, 16, 18, 18, 1851; *Buffalo Morning Express*, August 30, 1851; *New York Daily Tribune*, September 15, 1851; *Liberator*, September 5, 1851. Particularly good accounts are in the *Buffalo Advocate* of August 21, 1851, and Samuel May's

personal account in *The Fugitive Slave Law and Its Victims*, 19. See *Fayetteville Observer*, September 8, 1851 (decision a threat to Union). Buffalo District Attorney Charles H. S. Williams, along with Harlow S. Love, prosecuted the slave catcher, Benjamin Rust, for assaulting Davis during the arrest. John L. Talcott, attorney for the slaves, later was appointed District Attorney and then became a State Supreme Court Justice. Crisfield Johnson, *Centennial History of Erie County, New York* (Buffalo: Matthews and Warren, 1876).

17. *Liberator*, June 13, 1851; *Liberator*, October 10, 1851. See also *New York Daily Herald*, May 30, 1851; *Washington Union*, May 27, 1851; *New-York Tribune*, May 30, 1851; Sean Kirst, "Syracuse, as Webster Saw It: View From a Famous Balcony on Saturday's Downtown Living Tour," *Syracuse.com*, May 15, 2015, www.syracuse.com/kirst/2015/05/syracuse_as_webster_saw_it_view_from_a_famous_balcony_part_of_saturdays_downtown.html. In September of 1839, the J. Davenports of Mississippi visited Syracuse with their slave, Harriet Powell. Abolitionists arranged for her rescue and transportation to Gerrit Smith in Peterboro, New York, after which she settled in Kingston, Ontario. See "Found!" *Vermont Union Whig*, December 7, 1839, 3. Given Syracuse's history and leanings, Daniel Webster branded it a "laboratory of abolitionism, libel, and treason." "That Laboratory of Abolitionism, Libel and Treason: Syracuse and the Underground Railroad," Syracuse University Library, September 30, 2005, library.syr.edu/digital/exhibits/u/undergroundrr/. As to the abolitionist locations in upstate New York and their role in harboring runaway slaves, particularly through Black leadership, see R. J. M. Blackett, *The Captive's Quest for Freedom: Fugitive Slaves, the 1850 Fugitive Slave Law, and the Politics of Slavery* (New York: Cambridge University Press, 2018), 360. See also Angela Murphy, "'It Outlaws Me, and I Outlaw It!' Resistance to the Fugitive Slave Law in Syracuse, New York," *Afro-Americans in New York Life and History*, 28, no. 1 (January 2004): 43.

18. Samuel J. May, *Some Recollections of Our Antislavery Conflict* (Boston: Fields, Osgood, & Co., 1869), 377. See also Johnson and Smith, *History of the State of New York Political and Governmental*, vol. 2, 283–286, including the role of Jason C. Woodruff, in whose wagon Jerry sped off on the journey northward. Woodruff would soon be elected mayor of Syracuse.

19. For a contemporaneous account of the Jerry Rescue, see "The Slave Case at Syracuse," *New York Times*, October 4, 1851, 2. See also Monique Patenaude Roach, "The Rescue of William 'Jerry' Henry: Antislavery and Racism in the Burned-over District," *New York History* 82, no. 2 (Spring 2001): 135–154; W. Freeman Galpin, "The Jerry Rescue," *New York History* 26, no. 1 (1945): 19–34. For a particularly detailed account, see Bruce W. Dearstyne, *The Spirit of New York: Defining Events in the Empire State's History* (Albany: State University of New York Press, 2015), 87–108. See also Jayme A. Sokolow, "The Jerry McHenry Rescue and the Growth of Northern Antislavery Sentiment During the 1850s," *Journal of American Studies* 16, no. 3 (1982): 427–445, observing that the Jerry rescue

was only one of as many as 35 major riots over slavery in Baltimore, New York, Boston, and Philadelphia during 1835–1860. See also "Underground Railroad in New York Report," Wilbur H. Siebert Underground Collection, 32, ohiomemory. org/digital/collection/siebert/id/17472/rec/26.

20. *Anti-Slavery Bugle*, October 18, 1851, 3.

21. *New York Times*, October 11, 1851, 3, quoting the *New York Journal of Commerce*. The unsuccessful prosecution of the Jerry rescuers did not end the story. Gerrit Smith and others brought about an indictment against Marshal Allen for kidnapping. He was exonerated.

22. *Evening Post*, May 13, 1850, 2; Blackett, *The Captive's Quest for Freedom*, 365.

23. "Escape of an Alleged Slave—Maneuvering of the Abolitionists," *New York Daily Herald*, May 18, 1852, 6.

24. "Gov. Hunt and the Fugitive-Slave Nicholas Dudley," *Semi-Weekly Standard*, May 29, 1852, 3. See also "Another Fugitive Slave Escaped," *Mississippi Palladium*, June 3, 1852, 2, saying that the Governor was prostituting his pardoning powers.

25. "Police Office," *New York Daily Herald*, July 30, 1839, 2. The entire history of the event is in Seward, *The Works of William H. Seward*, vol. 2, 449–518. See also *New-York Tribune*, February 9, 1843, 4; Stephen J. Valone, "William Henry Seward, the Virginia Controversy, and the Anti-Slavery Movement, 1839–1841," *Afro-Americans in New York Life and History* 31, no. 1 (January 2007): 65–80; Willis Fletcher Johnson and Ray B. Smith, "Chapter XVII: The Underground Railroad," in *History of the State of New York Political and Governmental*, vol. 2, 268–290.

26. For lengthy histories of the case from Virginia's viewpoint, see the *Richmond Enquirer*, January 30, February 11, April 6, and May 7, 1841. Robert Morris (1808–1855) was New York City Recorder, a municipal office (long abolished) with judicial powers. See also "Piracy, Kidnapping, False Imprisonment," *Vermont Union Whig*, September 14, 1839, 2, in which the newspaper expressed outrage at the arrest of the three sailors and applauded the court for discharging them.

27. Seward, *The Works of William H. Seward*, vol. 2, 455. See also "New York and Virginia," *Evening Post*, January 18, 1840, 2; Walter Stahr, "Seward the Lawyer," *Judicial Notice*, Fall 2014, 6.

28. *Acts of the General Assembly of Virginia, Passed at the Session Commencing 2nd December 1839, and Ending 19th March 1840, in the Sixty-Fourth Year of the Commonwealth* (Richmond: Samuel Shepherd, 1840), 155. On March 17, 1840, Virginia resolved to adopt "the most decisive and efficient measures for the protection of the property of her citizens and the maintenance of rights, which she cannot and will not, under any circumstances, surrender or abandon."

29. The history of this dispute, from Virginia's side, including Virginia's appeal to the New York Legislature to override its governor, is detailed in "The Lieutenant-Governor of Virginia to the Governor of New-York, with a report of

the Select Committee of the House of Delegates of Virginia, and a copy of the law of Virginia," in *Documents of the Senate of the State of New-York*, vol. 1 (Albany: Thurlow Weed, 1842), 23. Also see, generally, Paul Finkelman, "The Protection of Black Rights in Seward's New York," *Civil War History* 34, no. 3 (September 1988): 211–234. For a discussion of the Seward–Virginia controversy as part of the broader picture, see James Oakes, *The Scorpion's Sting: Antislavery and the Coming of the Civil War* (New York: W. W. Norton, 2014), 70. See also Stephen Valone, "William Henry Seward, the Virginia Controversy, and the Anti-Slavery Movement, 1839–1841."

30. *Documents of the Assembly of the State of New York, Sixty-Fifth Session*, vol. 1 (Albany: Thurlow Weed, 1842), 37. The Virginia Legislative Report castigating Governor Seward and New York is at *Journal of the House of Delegates of the Commonwealth of Virginia, 1839–1840*, 175, babel.hathitrust.org/cgi/pt?id=nyp.33433014925584&view=1up&seq=181. Seward remained at the opposite end of the spectrum, an enemy of slavery. In his message to the legislature in 1842, he said that New York "acknowledges no natural inequality in men, and no political inequality which may not ultimately be removed." "Message," *New-York Tribune*, January 5, 1842, 2.

31. Erika Wood and Liz Budnitz, *Jim Crow in New York* (New York: New York University School of Law, Brennan Center for Justice, 2009), 9–10. The situation was much the same in Connecticut, while in all the other England states, Blacks could vote on the same footing as whites. Bennett Liebman, "The Quest for Black Voting Rights in New York State," *Albany Government Law Review*, 11 (2018): 386–387. In the referenda of 1860 and 1869, New York again refused to remove the property qualification for Blacks. Women of any color did not get the vote until 1917, three years before it became national under the 19th Amendment in 1920. By way of contrast, in 1869, Wyoming was the first state to grant the women's vote.

32. "Equal suffrage to colored persons?—Yes, or Equal suffrage to colored persons—No. Check the box." See "State of New York," *Brooklyn Daily Eagle*, November 2, 1846. The *New York Tribune* came out strongly in favor of equal suffrage and cautioned voters to be careful. Knowing that some people might be inclined to simply vote no for a new Constitution, the newspaper pointed out that voters could turn down the Constitution but still vote for the singular amendment for equal suffrage for colored men. "Beware of a Fatal Mistake," *New-York Tribune*, November 2, 1846. The *New York Herald* on March 18, 1846, took the opposite stance: "Let Negro suffrage be extended to all the Africans in this State, and from the day it is granted, we may date the commencement of a war between the North and South, which may eventually lead to a disruption of the basis upon which the United States were founded." "The Movements of the Age—The Work Before Us," *New York Daily Herald*, March 18, 1846, 2.

33. Galie, *Ordered Liberty*, 107–110; Edward F. Underhill, *Proceedings and Debates of the Constitutional Convention of the State of New York, Held in 1867 and*

1868, in the City of Albany, vol. 1 (Albany: Weed, Parsons and Company, 1868), 380. The vote in New York City was even more lopsided against removing the property qualifications for Blacks, by a margin of 29,940 to 5,249. Leo H. Hirsch Jr., "The Free Negro in New York," *Journal of Negro History* 16, no. 4 (October 1931), 415, 423; *Evening Post*, November 7, 1846. That year, Samuel Wilberforce continued his relentless crusade against slavery. He wrote, "Many abolitionists abroad attacked slavery in the United States: 'Such is American Slavery, not as abused by the cruel and the lawless, but as established by legislative enactments and maintained by judicial decisions.'" Samuel Wilberforce, *Reproof of the American Church* (New York: William Harned, 1846), 17. As to the financial condition of African Americans in New York before the Civil War, see Arnett G. Lindsay, "The Economic Condition of the Negroes of New York Prior to 1861," *Journal of Negro History* 6, no. 2 (April 1921).

Chapter 7

1. One researcher calculated that under the Act, 332 fugitives of record were returned to slavery while 11 were declared free. Of the 332, some 141 were returned without due process of law. Stanley W. Campbell, *The Slave Catchers: Enforcement of the Fugitive Slave Law, 1850–1860* (Chapel Hill: University of North Carolina Press, 1970), 207.

2. For a fuller discussion of this provision and resistance to it, see David B. Kopel, "The Posse Comitatus and the Office of Sheriff: Armed Citizens Summoned to the Aid of Law Enforcement," *Journal of Criminal Law and Criminology* 104, no. 4 (Fall 2004): 761; Morgan Cloud, "Quakers, Slaves and the Founders: Profiling to Save the Union," *Mississippi Law Journal* 73 (2003): 417–418; Bruce Ledewitz, "Civil Disobedience, Injunctions, and the First Amendment," *Hofstra Law Review* 19, no. 1 (Fall 1990): 67; Margalynne J. Armstrong, "Are We Nearing the End of Impunity for Taking Black Lives?" *Santa Clara Law Review* 56, no. 4 (2016): 735–737; Christopher N. Lasch, "Rendition Resistance," *North Carolina Law Review* 92, no. 1 (December 2013): 179; H. Robert Baker, "The Fugitive Slave Clause and the Antebellum Constitution," *Law and History Review* 30 no. 4 (2012): 1165; Harold M. Hyman, *The Fugitive Slave Law and Anthony Burns: A Problem in Law Enforcement* (Philadelphia: J. B. Lippincott, 1975), 1–12.

3. Gautham Rao, "The Federal Posse Comitatus Doctrine: Slavery, Compulsion, and Statecraft in Mid-Nineteenth-Century America," *Law and History Review* 26, no. 1 (Spring 2008): 1.

4. *The North Star*, October 3, 1850. For a description of the alarm raised in Rochester, New York, as to the prospect of being arrested or kidnapped, see Earl Smith, "William Cooper Nell on the Fugitive Slave Act of 1850," *Journal of Negro History* 66, no. 1 (Spring, 1981): 37–40. In October, 1850, Rochester citizens rallied to protest the Fugitive Slave Act (see *Buffalo Daily Republic*, October

30, 150). Yale University has acquired a private collection relating to Frederick Douglass that will add to what we know of him and the era (Jennifer Schuessler, "Frederick Douglass, Seen Up Close," *New York Times*, July 3, 2020).

5. "Hamlet the Slave," *Buffalo Commercial*, October 4, 1850, 2.

6. See the *National Anti-Slavery Standard*, October 10, 1852. This account was also reported in *The Dublin Freeman*, October 23, 1850, and *The London Times*, October 25, 1850, 4. The latter stated: "We cannot believe that the case of the coloured man is much worse than it was; nor, on the other hand, can we allow that the Abolitionists are striking at the rights of property, dismembering the Union, violating the laws of God and the precepts of Christianity, merely because they ask the repeal of the Fugitive Slave Law."

7. "The Fugitive Slave Law," *New York Tribune*, October 7, 1850, 1; "The Fugitive Bill," *Buffalo Courier*, October 10, 1850, 2; *North Star*, October 24, 1850.

8. Papson and Calarco, *Secret Lives of the Underground Railroad in New York City*, 77; John D. Gordan III, "The Lemmon Slave Case," *Judicial Notice, The Historical Society of the New York Courts*, no. 4 (2006): 8, www.nycourts.gov/history/legal-history-new-york/documents/The Lemmon Slave Case_John Gordan. pdf; "The New Topic of Agitation," *New York Evening Post*, October 3, 1850. See Manisha Sinha, "Revolutionary Abolitionism," in *The Slave's Cause: A History of Abolitionism* (New Haven, CT: Yale University Press, 2016), 500–542; Elijah Fagan-Solis, "The Courts and Human Rights in New York: The Legacy of the Lemmon Slave Case," *Judicial Notice*, no. 6 (January 2009), 38, history.nycourts. gov/wp-content/uploads/2019/01/Judicial-Notice-06.pdf.

9. "The Boston Slave Hunt and the Vigilance Committee," *Anti-Slavery Bugle*, November 16, 1850, 2; Gordon S. Barker, *Fugitive Slaves and the Unfinished American Revolution* (Jefferson, NC: McFarland and Company, 2013), 21–36.

10. *New York Evening Post*, October 14, 15, 18, 19, 21, 22, 1850; Barker, *Fugitive Slaves*, 21–36. In the meantime, the Crafts were married by Boston abolitionist Rev. Theodore Parker. "Marriage of the Two Fugitive Slaves," *Baltimore Sun*, November 11, 1850, 1. Hughes gave a lengthy, indignant account to a Richmond newspaper of the unwelcome treatment and dizzying judicial runaround he and his partner received in Boston (see "Mr. W. H. Hughes and the Boston Abolitionists," *Richmond Enquirer*, November 29, 1850, 4). In 1860, the Crafts wrote *Running a Thousand Miles for Freedom*. See also "Stories of the Fugitive Slaves. I. The Escape of William and Ellen Craft," *New England Magazine* 7, no. 5 (January 1890), 524–531.

11. "Another Fugitive Slave Case," *Poughkeepsie Journal*, August 30, 1851, 3; "The Fugitive, Bolding," *Evening Post*, August 27, 1851; "Fugitive Slave Case in New York," *New England Farmer*, August 30, 1851; "New York, August 26th," *Charleston Mercury*, August 30, 1851; Rebecca Edwards, Torrie Williams, and Kristina Poznan, "Mid-Hudson Antislavery History Project: June 2007 Research

Report," Mid-Hudson Slavery History Project, 2007, www.mhantislaveryhistoryproject.org/documents/2007%20Research%20Report.pdf. See also *Twentieth Annual Report Presented to the Massachusetts Anti-Slavery Society by its Board of Managers* (Boston: Andrews, Prentiss & Studley, 1852), 27. For further accounts of the Bolding episode, see *Slavery, Antislavery and the Underground Railroad, A Dutchess County Guide, Mid-Hudson Antislavery History Project* (Poughkeepsie, NY: Hudson House Publishing, 2010), 46–47, giving particulars as to Bolding, and where he lived and worked. Groth, *Slavery and Freedom in the Mid-Hudson Valley*, 137–141. For a list of contributors for the fund to buy Bolding's freedom, see Helen Wilkinson Reynolds, "John A. Bolding, Fugitive Slave," *Dutchess County Historical Society Yearbook* 20 (1935), 51–55, republished in *Dutchess County Historical Society Yearbook* 94 (2015), 43, with an addition by Eileen Mylod Hayden, "John A. Bolding: The Rest of His Story." See also "Vassar in Wartime: Civil War," *Vassar College Encyclopedia*, 2004, vcencyclopedia.vassar.edu/wartime/civil-war. html; Samuel May, "The Fugitive Slave Law and Its Victims" (New York: American Anti-Slavery Society, 1861). A pro-slavery newspaper commented confidently, "No opposition is made at the North now to the arrest of fugitive slaves and their delivery to their owners. Such a proceeding indeed seems no longer to create the least excitement. The struggle is over." *Daily Courier*, September 8, 1851.

12. "Fugitive Slave Case," *Charleston Daily Courier*, August 30, 1851.

13. "The Fugitive Slave Case," *Evening Post*, August 26, 1851. Pursuant to an 1840 New York statute, the county prosecutor was to represent the slave in fugitive slave proceedings. Culver raised this point to the Commissioner. *New York Herald*, August 28, 1851. The statute is L.1840, ch. 225, passed May 6, 1840. *Documents of the Assembly of the State of New York, Sixty-Fifth Session*, vol. 1 (Albany: Thurlow Weed, 1842). Interestingly, Nathaniel Bowditch Blunt, as New York County District Attorney, joined Culver in the case, on Bolding's side. Blunt died in office in 1854. His obituary can be found in the *New-York Tribune*, July 18, 1854, 4. His older brother, Joseph Blunt (1792–1860), was New York County District Attorney in 1859 when, on behalf of the People of the State of New York, he joined with William Evarts on behalf of the Lemmon slaves before New York's high court, the Court of Appeals. He had also teamed up with Evarts on behalf of the Lemmon slaves at the intermediate appellate level in 1857 when he was a private lawyer. "The Lemmon Slave Case: The Power of a Slaveholder to Retain His Servants in This State," *New York Times*, October 3, 1857, 3; "The Lemmon Slave Case: Conclusion of the Argument," *New York Times*, October 6, 1857, 2.

14. For the full decision, see "The Fugitive Slave Case Decision," *Evening Post*, September 1, 1851, 2. See also "The Poughkeepsie Slave Case," *Liberator*, September 12, 1851. The *Louisville Daily Courier* of September 8, 1851, labeled Bolding's defense "sophistry." Commissioner Nelson noted that Bolding, once in South Carolina, could have his legal status determined by a South Carolina court.

This may seem arcane, or even fanciful, considering his dismal chance of success. It may, however, have been an inducement for the slaveowner to sell Bolding's freedom at a handsome profit.

15. See Campbell, *The Slave Catchers*, 200.

16. "Subscriptions for Bolding," *The Evening Post*, September 3, 1851, 2; *Poughkeepsie Journal*, September 13, 1851. During the negotiations to buy Bolding's freedom, his owners insisted that he first be brought back to South Carolina as their property. "New-York, August 27," *Charleston Daily Courier*, September 2, 1851, 2. This may have been a precaution or their wish to display a trophy of triumph. On Bolding's side, there was good cause for anxiety over the prospect that if he went back they would "make him howl" (so said "an antagonist in the courtroom"). "The Fugitive Bolding," *Buffalo Daily Republic*, August 30, 1851, 2.

17. The Cornhill Coffee House was located at the corner of Court Street and Court Square. When Minkins worked at the Coffee House there it might have been known as Taft's Cornhill Coffee House or Young's Cornhill Coffee House. The site was purchased by George Young, who eventually built the hotel on the location that would bear his name. Young's Cornhill Coffee House menu (December 9, 1853), cdm.bostonathenaeum.org/cdm/ref/collection/p16057coll18/id/8. Minkins was known, in Virginia, as Frederic Wilkins. There are many published accounts of Minkins's arrest and rescue on which I have drawn, e.g., Nina Moore Tiffany, "Stories of the Fugitive Slaves, II: Shadrach," *New England Magazine* n.s. 2 (1890): 280–283, babel.hathitrust.org/cgi/pt?id=umn.31951000902691n&view=1 up&seq=274; Gary L. Collison, *Shadrach Minkins: From Fugitive Slave to Citizen* (Cambridge, MA: Harvard University Press, 1997); Barker, *Fugitive Slaves*, 37–53.

18. He would eventually marry and raise a family in Montreal. He lived there until his death, in 1875. See Gary L. Collison, "Upheaval in Our Town, 1850–1854," *Concord Saunterer* 19, no. 2 (December 1987): 1–12; Sandra H. Petrulionis, *To Set This World Right: The Antislavery Movement in Thoreau's Concord Book* (Ithaca, NY: Cornell University Press, 2006).

19. See Leonard W. Levy, "Sims' Case: The Fugitive Slave Law in Boston in 1851," *Journal of Negro History* 35, no. 1 (1950): 39–74; Barker, *Fugitive Slaves*, 54–76.

20. Henry Wadsworth Longfellow, *Life of Henry Wadsworth Longfellow, with Extracts from His Journals and Correspondence*, vol. 2, ed. Samuel Longfellow (Boston: Houghton, Mifflin and Company, 1936), 192. See also Jill Lepore, "How Longfellow Woke the Dead," *American Scholar*, Spring 2011, 33, pointing out that Longfellow's poem about the ride of Paul Revere was read as a bold statement against slavery.

21. "By this remark I mean to cast no imputation upon the judicial intelligence or integrity of that court; but judges must be more than men, if they can always escape the influence of a strong popular opinion of society upon great questions of state policy and human benevolence, which have been long agitated and much discussed; and it is no matter of surprise that Chief Justice Shaw, entertaining the

opinions he did upon this question of slavery, should have found it repugnant to the spirit of their constitution." State v. Post, 20 N.J.L. 368, 377 (1845).

22. "The Fugitive Excitement," *Daily Republic*, 7, 1851, 2.

23. Commonwealth v. Aves, 18 Pick. 193 (1836).

Chapter 8

1. The account of what happened in the courtroom on Saturday morning, November 13, 1852, is from the *Pennsylvania Freeman*, November 18, 1852, 186.

2. Sewall's Case (Ind. Cir. Ct. 1829), quoted in *American Jurist and Law Magazine* 3, no. 404 (1830); Willard v. People, 4 Scammon 461, 5 Ill. 461 (1843); Com. v. Aves, 18 Pick. 193 (Mass, 1836).

· 3. See chapter 7, note 23.

4. Griffin v. Potter, 14 Wend. 209, 212 (1835). Eight years later, in his Cooper Union speech in 1860, Lincoln said, "An inspection of the Constitution will show that the right of property in a slave is not 'distinctly and expressly affirmed in it.' . . . Also, it would be open to show, by contemporaneous history, that this mode of alluding to slaves and slavery, instead of speaking of them, was employed on purpose to exclude from the Constitution the idea that there could be property in man." In the first reported case of the Supreme Court of the Territory of Iowa, In re Ralph, 1 Morris 1 (Iowa 1839), the court refused to treat a human being as property to enforce a contract for slavery and held that Iowa laws must extend "equal protection to persons of all races and conditions." This was 17 years before the United States Supreme Court infamously decided *Dred Scott v. Sandford*, which upheld the rights of a slaveowner to treat a person as property. Varnum v. Brien, 763 N.W.2d 862, 877 (Iowa 2009).

5. James Kent, *Commentaries on American Law*, Lecture 23, vol. 2 (New York: O. Halsted, 1827), 202.

6. Sands v. Codwise, 5 Johns. 536 (1808); Helm v. Miller, 17 Johns. 296 (1820).

7. Tyson v. Ewing 26 Ky. 185, 186 (1830).

8. State v. Fraser, 1 Ga. Rep. 373 (1831); Renney v. Mayfield, 5 Tenn. 165 (1817); Field v. Walker, 17 Ala. 80 (1841); De Lacy v. Antoine, 34 Va. 438 (1836). But the writ of habeas corpus was recognized in other Southern courts. Parker, 3 N.C. 528 (1805); Union Bank of Tenn. v. Benham, 23 Ala. 143 (1853); Peter v. Hargrave, 46 Va. 12, 13–14 (1848) [No redress for injuries].

9. When slavery existed in New York, its courts allowed the enslaved to use habeas corpus to test ownership, e.g., In re Mickel, 14 Johns. 324 (1827), as was true in other Northern courts, e.g., State v. Lyon, 1 N.J.L. 462 (1789), Commonwealth ex rel. Lewis v. Holloway, 6 Binn. 213 (Pa. 1814), State v. Lasselle, 1 Blackf. 60 (Ind. 1820).

10. Not only do judges and lawyers now refrain from using phrases like "natural law," the concept itself has gone out of use as a legal anchoring point. In 1918, in a widely quoted and influential passage, Justice Oliver Wendell Holmes said, "The jurists who believe in natural law seem to me to be in that naïve state of mind that accepts what has been familiar and accepted by them and their neighbors as something that must be accepted by all men everywhere." Oliver Wendell Holmes, "Natural Law," *Harvard Law Review* 32 (1918): 41. Professor Chemerinsky observes that natural law concepts were replaced by majoritarian decision-making. Erwin Chemerinsky, "The Supreme Court, 1988 Term: Foreword: The Vanishing Constitution," *Harvard Law Review* 103 (1989): 43. See also Albert M. Rosenblatt, "The Rise and Fall of Natural Law in New York," 17 (2022): 19–25.

11. Aristotle, *Rhetoric* (350 BCE), 1373b1–19, 1375a27–1377b11, using the translation by W. Rhys Roberts. One commentator has maintained that the Aristotelian dialogue between positive and natural law permeates American constitutional law. Thomas C. Grey, "Origins of the Unwritten Constitution: Fundamental Law in American Revolutionary Thought," *Stanford Law Review* 30 (1978): 844. See also Aristotle's *Nicomachean Ethics*, vol. 5, sec. 7, in which Aristotle says, "Political Justice is of two kinds, one natural, the other conventional [in some translations "legal"]. A rule of justice is natural that has the same validity everywhere, and does not depend on our accepting it or not."

12. Quoted in John W. Salmond, The Law of Nature," *Law Quarterly Review*, no. 52 (April 1895), 128–129. In a dialogue, Cicero maintained that true law is a rule of distinction "between right and wrong according to nature" and that any other sort of law ought not be called law. Cicero, *The Political Works of Marcus Tullius Cicero*, ed. and trans. Francis Barham (London: Edmund Spettigue, 1842), 47.

13. William Blackstone, *Commentaries on the Laws of England*, book 1 (Philadelphia: Lippincott Company, 1893), 199.

14. Southern courts would not have agreed with Judge Paine's decision freeing the slaves, but would agree that natural law yields to positive law even if natural law contemplates a primary condition of freedom. For example, see Groves v. Slaughter, 40 U.S. 449 (1841) and Rankin v. Lydia, 9 Ky. 467, 470 (1820), in which the court said "Slavery is sanctioned [approved] by the laws of this state, and the right to hold them under our municipal regulations is unquestionable. But we view this as a right existing by positive law of a municipal character, without foundation in the law of nature, or the unwritten and common law." Also see State v. Jones, 1 Miss. 83, 85 (1820), in which the court said, "The right of the master exists not by force of the law of nature or of nations, but by virtue only of the positive law of the state." See Birney v. State, 8 Ohio 230, 237 (1837), Stanley v. Earl, 15 Ky. 281 (1824), and Lunsford v. Coquillon, 2 Mart. (n.s.) 401 (La. 1824).In Harry v. Decker & Hopkins, 1 Miss. 36, 42–43 (1818), the court said, "Slavery is condemned by reason and the laws of nature. It exists and can only exist, through municipal regulations, and in matters of doubt, is it not an

unquestioned rule, that courts must lean 'in favorem vitae et libertatis.'" See also Justin B. Dyer, *Natural Law and the Antislavery Tradition* (Cambridge: Cambridge University Press, 2012), 38, n. 6, but compare it to George v. State, 37 Miss. 316, 320 (1859), in which the court counted as "unmeaning twaddle" any reliance on natural law as a basis for freedom from slavery. Southern courts would conclude that travel through a free state does not free a slave. For example, see LaGrange v. Chouteau, 2 Mo. 20 (1828) and the dictum Rankin v. Lydia, 9 Ky. 467 (1820). For antebellum discussion of the master's right of transit, see Thomas Cobb, *An Inquiry into the Law of Negro Slavery in the United States of America* (Philadelphia: T. & J. W. Johnson & Co., 1858), 135–140, and Louise Weinberg, "Methodological Interventions and the Slavery Case; or Night-Thoughts of a Legal Realist," *Maryland Law Review* 56, no. 4 (1997): 1340.

15. Aristotle, *Politics: Book One*, trans. H. Rackham (Cambridge, MA: Harvard University Press, 1944), 1252a, 1254b, 1255a, www.perseus.tufts.edu/hopper/text ?doc=Perseus%3Atext%3A1999.01.0058%3Abook%3D1%3Asection%3D1255a.

16. Tennent v. Dendy, Dud. 83, 23 S.C.L. 83, 1837 WL 1519 (S.C. App. L. 1837).

17. John C. Calhoun, "Speech on the Reception of Abolition Petitions. Delivered in the Senate, February 6, 1837," in *Speeches of John C. Calhoun, Delivered in the House of Representatives and in the Senate of the United States* (New York: D. Appleton & Company, 1853), 625–633. For extended discussion of the slaveholders' reliance on the "positive good" justification for slavery, see George M. Fredrickson, *The Black Image in the White Mind: The Debate on Afro-American Character and Destiny, 1817–1914* (New York: Harper & Row, 1971), 46–47; Jason A. Gillmer, "Suing for Freedom: Interracial Sex, Slave Law, and Racial Identity in the Post-Revolutionary and Antebellum South," *North Carolina Law Review* 82, no. 2 (January 2004): 613; Mark E. Brandon, *Free in the World: American Slavery and Constitutional Failure* (Princeton, NJ: Princeton University Press, 1998), 78–79; Daniel Farber, *Lincoln's Constitution* (Chicago: University of Chicago Press, 2003), 11; William W. Fisher III, "Ideology and Imagery in the Law of Slavery," *Chicago-Kent Law Review* 68, no. 3 (1993): 1051; and Ariela J. Gross, "Litigating Whiteness: Trials of Racial Determination in the Nineteenth-Century South," *Yale Law Journal* 108, no. 1 (October 1998): 151–152. See Gordon E. Finnie, "The Antislavery Movement in the Upper South Before 1840," *Journal of Southern History* 35, no. 3 (1969) (noting that before it was reversed by the "positive good" justification, there was some anti-slavery sentiment in the upper slave states). Debates in the same spirit and phrasing took place in Congress, as where William A. Sackett (1811–1895) of Saratoga Springs, New York, rose to challenge the notion that slavery is a "blessing to the master and the slave" (speech before House of Representatives, March 4, 1850).

18. George McDuffie, "The Natural Slavery of the Negro" (1835), staush. files.wordpress.com/2012/09/mcduffie-proslavery.pdf.

19. William Harper, *Memoir on Slavery: Read Before the Society for the Advancement of Learning of South Carolina at its Annual Meeting at Columbia, 1837* (Charleston, SC: James S. Burges, 1838). For the harshest criticism of Harper's slavery ideas, see "American Slavery, an Irish Question," *The Citizen, a Monthly Journal of Politics, Literature, and Art* (Dublin 1840): 489.

20. As New York's governor, William Seward supported the repeal. For his important role in it and his other anti-slavery actions, see Gronningsater, "On Behalf of His Race and the Lemmon Slaves," 212; Finkelman, "The Protection of Black Rights in Seward's New York"; "A Good Book for the South," *Vermont Chronicle*, September 1, 1841, 3; "New York Legislature," *Rutland County Herald*, June 15, 1841, 3; "New-York State Society," *Liberator*, October 1, 1841, 1; *Evening Post*, March 31, 1841, 2. For a general overview, see Seward, *The Works of William H. Seward*, vol. 4, 36; Leo H. Hirsch, "The Slave in New York," *Journal of Negro History* 16, no. 4 (October 1931): 383–414.

21. *New York Times*, November 15, 1852, 6.

22. *New-York Daily Times*, Monday, November 15, 1852, 6; the article includes the previous description of the exultation that followed the decision. *National Intelligencer* (Washington, DC), November 15, 1852, 2; *Baltimore Sun*, November 15, 1852, 1 (declining Lapaugh's request).

23. Christopher L. Webber, *American to the Backbone: The Life of James W. C. Pennington, the Fugitive Slave Who Became One of the First Black Abolitionists* (New York: Pegasus Books, 2011), 318; Papson and Calarco, *Secret Lives of the Underground Railroad in New York City*, 85. As for Rev. Pennington's own story, see James W. C. Pennington, *The Fugitive Blacksmith: or, Events in the History of James W. C. Pennington*, 3rd ed. (London: C. Gilpin, 1849), docsouth.unc.edu/neh/penning49/penning49.html. See also David E. Swift, *Black Prophets of Justice: Activist Clergy Before the Civil War* (Baton Rouge: Louisiana State University Press, 1989), 263. In another account, immediately after the decision, Lapaugh, attorney for Jonathan and Julia Lemmon, asked that the Lemmons be allowed "outside the influence of others" personally to ask the Eight if they would not want to return to the Lemmons. Culver responded, saying he "would be perfectly happy that he should do so—that they were free people and [Lapaugh] could ask them anything he chose—he might do it in open court, if he pleased, and had no doubt their reply would be, that they would rather remain in New York than go to Texas" (*Pennsylvania Freeman*, November 18, 1852). They were separately asked (the article continued) and they declined. In a newspaper article after the decision, Henry Lapaugh described, for readers, the arguments he had made before Judge Paine. See Washington (DC) *Union*, January 1, 1853, 3.

24. *New York Times*, January 15, 1852, 6; *Pennsylvania Freeman*, November 18, 1852. See also *Brooklyn Evening Star*, November 17, 1852, 2; *Daily Union* (Washington, DC), November 17, 1852, 2; *Hampshire Gazette* (Northampton, MA), November 16, 1852, 3; *New York Herald*, November 15, 1852, 5; *Norwich (CT)*

Evening Star, November 16, 1852, 2; *Baltimore American and Daily Commercial Advertiser*, November 15, 1852, 2; *Republic* (Washington, DC), November 17, 1852, 2; *Rochester (NY) Daily American*, November 15, 1852, 5.

25. "The Late Slaves," *New-York Tribune*, November 23, 1852, 4.

26. Samuel May, *The Fugitive Slave Law and its Victims* (New York: American Anti-Slavery Society, 1861), 24, archive.org/stream/fugitiveslavelaw1856mays/fugitiveslavelaw1856mays_djvu.txt.

27. Richard Johnson's account of having learned of the case and of his sister, Nancy, is in "A Family Sketch," *New York Tribune*, January 25, 1853, 5, and *The National Anti-Slavery Standard*, February 3, 1853. See also Papson and Calarco, *Secret Lives of the Underground Railroad in New York City*, 87. Historian Bryan Prince, an especially knowledgeable and reliable researcher, states in his article "Buxton Offers Up Some 'Lemon-Aid' " (www.buxtonmuseum.com/history/eBOOKS/lemmon-slaves.pdf), "While all of the slaves were closely related, it is impossible to determine the precise relationship between Emeline and Nancy as conflicting information has been reported. As well, Levi was in all likelihood the brother of Emeline, Lewis and Edward, although no last name is recorded for him until he takes the fugitive name of Richard Johnson." As to related events dealing with the liberation of the Eight, see May, *The Fugitive Slave Law and Its Victims*, 17. Garrison's newspaper, *The Liberator*, was among those watching the respective subscriptions for the Lemmons and for the Eight, cheering on the latter fund, which was far slimmer, noting that as of November 25, 1852, some $743 was raised for the slaves—a fraction of that for the Lemmons. *Liberator*, December 3, 1852, 2. An Ohio newspaper summed it up: "We regret to say that the patriots who piled up $5,240 have not generally regarded this parallel movement [for the Eight with sympathy." "The Lemmon Slaves," *Ohio Star*, December 1, 1852, 2. See *The New York Times* of April 16, 1860, describing the events of November 1852, and that immediately after the Eight were set free "their colored friends soon afterwards sent them to Canada."

28. The best account as to what took place immediately the Eight were liberated is in "Buxton Offers up Some 'Lemon-Aid,' " in which the Buxton Museum reported that immediately after Judge Paine's decision, Rev. Pennington took the Eight to Hartford. See also the *Underground Railroad in New York Report*, Wilbur H. Siebert Collection, 36, ohiomemory.org/digital/collection/siebert/id/17476/rec/26. There is also mention of this in Webber, *American to the Backbone*, 319. According to that account, the Eight, then free, were placed under the care of Black individuals named Hooker, Hawley, Brown, Gardner, and Crass. Pennington's wife, Almira, had accompanied the group from New York to Hartford. Pennington also turned to Horace Greeley for some financial help to defray the burden on the "poor laboring men" who took them in. See, generally, Fred Landon, "The Negro Migration to Canada After the Passing of the Fugitive Slave Act," *Journal of Negro History* 5, no. 1 (January 1920), 22–36.

29. "Buxton Offers up Some 'Lemon Aid.'"

30. "The Slave Case: Opinion of Judge Paine," *New-York Daily Times,* November 15, 1852; *New York Tribune,* November 15, 1852; 5 Sandford 681 (N.Y. Superior Court, 1852); *Pennsylvania Freeman,* November 18, 1852 (all references to the *Freeman* are from this issue, including "Thank God and good men" and the quote from Judge Paine as to his concern for the maintenance for the Eight, and their plight, as well as the report that the eight were driven off in the company of Louis Napoleon, and had again declined the opportunity to remain with Julia and Jonathan Lemmon). See also Wheeling, WV, *Intelligencer,* November 18, 1852, 2, as to the Eight being driven off in the company of Louis Napoleon. *Baltimore Sun,* November 15, 1852, 1: Jonathan and Juliet Lemmon "much depressed as it is said that the slaves in question were nearly all the property they owned in the world." There is a slight chronological oddity here. Judge Paine rendered his decision on November 13, 1852, but Jonathan Lemmon's statement is dated November 17, 1852 (see chapter 2, note 21). Possibly the statement was intended for the newspapers only, or it was given to Judge Paine before November 13, 1852, and formalized later. In any event it contained details not affecting the outcome. There is no indication that the attorneys for Juliet and Jonathan saw fit to make it part of the record or thought it relevant to the merits of the case.

31. *New York Courier and Enquirer* as quoted in the Louisville, KY, *Daily Courier,* November 20, 1852

32. *New York Day Book,* as reprinted in "The Slave Case," *Liberator,* December 10, 1852, 1. Thurlow Weed (1797–1882) was a prominent New York politician. When, in the *Albany Journal* of November 19, 1852, he expressed sympathy for "the unfortunate man who has been deprived of his property," Frederick Douglass responded, "God must have formed his plans invisibly in Mr. Weed. We will not deny that the case of Lemmon is a hard one. The ways of transgressors are always hard. . . . Shall we, therefore, throw over to the transgressor our wives and our children to be his property, and have their lives worn out in Texas under the lash of a brute?" *Frederick Douglass Paper,* November 26, 1852.

Another African American newspaper took on the *New York Journal of Commerce:* "Suppose the tender sensibilities of the Journal of Commerce were so far consulted, that the Constitution of the State were set aside, and the slaveholders allowed to carry their slaves to New York for the purpose of convenient shipment, that city would soon become a great mart for slaves, as well as cotton. And we suppose that this is the real desire of the Journal of Commerce, which cares nothing about the materials of trade, so long as substantial profits may be 'realized.' Were its views conclusive with the Court, we doubt not that the merchants of New York would be soon favored with the prices current of men, women, and children in the New York market." "Shall New York Be a Slave-Mart?" *National Era,* November 18, 1852, 2. See *New York Weekly Herald,* November 20, 1852, 373 (Paine's decision was "coerced by law, not governed in justice").

33. *New York Journal of Commerce* article reprinted in *The Liberator*, December 3, 1852, 1. As to New York's mercantile interest in Southern product, see Philip S. Foner, *Business and Slavery: The New York Merchants and the Irrepressible Conflict* (Chapel Hill: University of North Carolina Press, 1941), 61. See also *The Tarborough Southerner*, November 27, 1852, pointing out the harm of a decision like Lemmon to the commercial relationships between the North and South.

34. "News of the Day," *Daily Delta*, December 1, 1852, 1. The *Wheeling (WV) Daily Intelligencer*, November 18, 1852, 2, reported that "sympathy was expressed for [Jonathan and Juliet Lemmon] by the judge and counsel." There is no reason to doubt Jonathan Lemmon's claim that the decision cost him *all of his property* (as alleged in his statement of November 17, 1852, and as reported in newspapers, e.g., *Richmond Dispatch*, November 22, 1852, 1; *Baltimore Sun*, November 15, 1852, 1). This might account for any expression by Judge Paine that he had sympathy for Jonathan and Juliet Lemmon. Obviously, Paine did not confiscate the property with a vengeance, but simply did what he had to do and seemingly took no joy in it. That is my best explanation for why he contributed $100. A Southern newspaper oddly attributed Judge Paine's contribution to his own sense of injustice at the decision. "The Lemmon Slave Case," *Courier-Journal*, November 27, 1852, 2.

35. *Non-Slaveholder* n.s. 1, no. 1 (1853): 13, babel.hathitrust.org/cgi/pt?id=ui-ug.30112058450310&view=1up&seq=25. The publication called the printing of the names a "naked and shameful business advertisement" and cited a poem by John Trumbull (1750–1831), the American Hudibras, beginning, "And are there, in this free-born land, / Among ourselves, a venal band; / A dastard race, who long have sold, / Their souls and consciences for gold." Some names were accompanied by comments, making an interesting historical catalogue; see *National Anti-Slavery Standard*, December 2, 1852.

36. "The Lemmon Slave Case," *New York Times*, October 2, 1857, 3; *New-York Tribune*, October 3, 1857, 4; "The Lemmon Indemnity," *The Daily Republic*, November 27, 1852, 2. The indemnity bond was printed in the Richmond Dispatch of November 27, 1852. See also "The Lemmon Indemnity," *Richmond Enquirer*, November 30, 1852, 1.

37. *National Anti-Slavery Standard*, November 25, 1852. The quote from the North Carolina newspaper calling the Eight the victims is from the *Weekly Raleigh Register*, November 24, 1852, 3.

38. *National Anti-Slavery Standard*, December 9, 1852.

Chapter 9

1. "Slavery in America," *Aberdeen Journal, and General Advertiser for the North of Scotland*, December 8, 1852, 8.

2. William A. Link, *Roots of Secession: Slavery and Politics in Antebellum Virginia* (Chapel Hill: University of North Carolina Press, 2005), 108.

3. Governor Howell Cobb, speaking of the Lemmon case in his annual message to the Georgia Legislature, November 8, 1853. Cobb's remark that the Lemmon decision, if persisted in, would be a just cause of war is in New York Court of Appeals, *Report of the Lemmon Slave Case Containing Points and Arguments of Both Sides, and Opinions of All the Judges* (New York: Horace Greeley & Co., 1860), 12–13. See *The National Era* of January 12, 1854, 2, reacting to Governor Cobb's remark.

4. *Richmond Dispatch*, November 22, 1852

5. "Opinion of Justice Paine," in New York Court of Appeals, *Report of the Lemmon Slave Case*, 12–13. The *Baltimore Sun* of November 14, 1853, quoted the Georgia Governor as recommending that Georgia help Virginia by employing appellate counsel and that every southern state should join in the appeal. See also *Richmond Dispatch*, February 5, 1853.

6. See *Staunton (VA) Spectator and Vindicator*, March 23, 1853, 3. For Virginia Governor Johnson's message as to the need to appeal the decision, see also *Elmira (NY) Republican*, December 24, 1852, 2.

7. The case concerned Margaret Crittenden Douglass, a white woman in Norfolk, Virginia, who was indicted in June 1853 and jailed for one month by Norfolk Circuit Court Judge Richard H. Baker. News of the case was reported nationally. Judge Baker left no doubt where he stood on the question of enslavement. In his opinion, it benefitted the Negro race. He made this clear at the time of Douglass's sentencing. Speaking of the condition of the enslaved, he said, "They have been raised from the night of heathenism to the light of Christianity, and thousands of them have been brought to a saving knowledge of the Gospel. . . . Of the one hundred millions of the negro race, there can not be found another so large a body as the three millions of slaves in the United States, at once so intelligent, so inclined to the Gospel, and so blessed by the elevating influence of civilization and Christianity." If so, one might ask, why make it a crime to teach them to read? Doing so, he explained, was "a matter of self-defense against the schemes of Northern incendiaries, and the outcry against holding our slaves in bondage."

8. "The Late Fugitive Slave Case," *New York Times*, May 29, 1854, 1; "Arrest of Three Fugitive Slaves," *New Orleans Crescent*, June 3, 1854, 2, republishing an article from the *New York Express*. See also Webber, *American to the Backbone*, 343–356.

9. *New York Tribune*, April 5, 1852, 4.

10. *Anti-Slavery Bugle*, June 3, 1854, 2.

11. "Pembroke Returned a Freeman," *New York Times*, June 29, 1854, 4, stating, as to Stephen, that "on the 26th of June that bargain was closed that converted him from a chattel into a man." The sons were reportedly living in Alabama in 1893. Webber, *American to the Backbone*, 351.

12. "The Late Fugitive Slave Case," *New York Times*, May 29, 1854, 1; "Dr. Pennington's Statement," *New-York Tribune*, May 29, 1854, 5, in which Culver tells the Pennington assembly of the misleading accounts the officials gave him.

13. 60 U.S. 393 (1857). The party's name was actually Sanford.

14. Scott and his wife, Harriet Robinson Scott, brought separate suits. Their attorney proceeded only with Dred Scott's suit, with the agreement that the decision in his case would apply to his family, which included his wife and two daughters. Walter Ehrlich, *They Have No Rights: Dred Scott's Struggle for Freedom* (Carlisle, MA: Applewood Books, 2007), 43; Lea VanderVelde and Sandhya Subramanian, "Mrs. Dred Scott," *Yale Law Journal* 106, no. 4 (1997): 1033.

15. Scott v. Emerson, 15 Mo. 576, 587 (1852).

16. Ehrlich, *They Have No Rights*, 82. Today, and since 1875, Federal Circuit Courts are appellate tribunals. In 1853 diversity of citizenship cases were brought in Federal Circuit Court. On November 2, 1853, in the Circuit Court for the District of Missouri, Dred Scott filed a suit for his freedom;

17. Ehrlich, *They Have No Rights*, 82–86.

18. Ehrlich, *They Have No Rights*, 106.

19. "For this very crisis, now soon to be met, the south has been preparing for years, and Presidents devoted to southern interests have been gradually changing the character of that great tribunal, the Supreme Court, by placing Judges on the bench who will regard political considerations as paramount, and bring the Court down to the point where a decision can be given that will give the south a triumph over the free principle of the north, under a decree that slave property can be taken and held wherever the master chooses to go." "Great Question Between Freedom and Slavery," *Poughkeepsie Journal*, January 3, 1857, 2. The same lament was expressed in other anti-slavery circles: "Second Anniversary of the Michigan Anti-Slavery Society: First Day," *Anti-Slavery Bugle*, October 27, 1855, 1; *Hartford Courant*, November 19, 1856, 2; *Green Mountain (Montpelier, VT) Freeman*, November 2, 1854. Michigan gained statehood in 1837, and Detroit's Anti-Slavery Society was founded that same year. The Michigan state constitution included a ban on slavery.

20. *New-York Tribune*, March 11, 1857, 4.

21. Frederick Douglass, "Speech on the Dred Scott Decision" (speech, New York, May 14, 1857), teachingamericanhistory.org/document/speech-on-the-dred-scott-decision-2/.

22. Don E. Fehrenbacher, *The Dred Scott Case: Its Significance in American Law and Politics* (New York: Oxford University Press, 1978), 341. See also Paul Finkelman, "*Scott v. Sandford*: The Court's Most Dreadful Case and How It Changed History," *Chicago-Kent Law Review* 82, no. 3 (2007): 28–29; Robert Aitken, "Legal Lore, Justice Benjamin Curtis and Dred Scott," *Litigation* 30, no. 51 (Fall 2003).

23. *Sandford*, 60 U.S. at 454.

24. *Albany Evening Journal*, March 9, 1857; *Harper's Weekly*, March 28, 1857, 193: "Suppose in the Lemon case (all these slave cases are sour enough)

they do decide this very question? As an abstract or theoretical question, it is one of the most delicate that could be started; for if our Southern brethren are to come on to Saratoga or to Newport for the season, with their sable dependents, and if during their sojourn the domestic institution is to be hedged round and protected with all the majesty of the law, it is plain that the occasions of contest, collision, difficulty, and turmoil would be endless." *Chicago Tribune*, March 16, 1857; *New York Tribune*, March 11, 1857. The Milwaukee quote is in the *National Anti-Slavery Standard*, March 28, 1857.

25. *Baltimore Sun*, April 15, 1857; *New Orleans Times-Picayune*, April 18, 1857. See also Alix Oswald, "The Reaction to the Dred Scott Decision," *Voces Novae* 4, no. 1 (2012), a survey of how the decision was received in various parts of the country, including Georgia's reaction to the "fanaticism" of the New York Assembly's Resolutions. Two years earlier, in 1855, Judge Foot joined the Republican party, in keeping with his anti-slavery views. He denounced the repeal of the Missouri Compromise, saying that "Slavery is preparing to make, and has already commenced, one more aggression on the rights of the free States, exceedingly offensive to freemen." See Samuel A. Foot, *Reasons for Joining the Republican Party* (1855), 4, archive.org/details/reasonsforjoinin00foot/page/4/mode/2up.

26. Scott v. Sandford, 60 U.S. (19 How.) 393, 468 (1857).

Chapter 10

1. Maine, on April 15, 1857, in its Chapter 53, and Ohio, on April 17, 1857, Ch. 1772, O.L.V. 16 (1); *The Public Statutes at Large, of the State of Ohio: from the Close of Chase's Statutes, February, 1833 to the Present Time*, ed. Maskell E. Curwen, 2857 (1854–1861), at 2980.

2. Samuel J. Tilden, *Letters and Literary Memorials of Samuel J. Tilden*, ed. John Bigelow (New York: Harper & Brothers, 1908), 643. For a very good biography of O'Conor, drawing on many accounts, see Joanna D. Cowden, *"Heaven Will Frown on Such a Cause as This": Six Democrats Who Opposed Lincoln's War* (Lanham, MD: University Press of America, 2001), 127–153. As to O'Conor's Irish background in the context of slavery, see *Stroudsburg (PA) Jeffersonian*, October 25, 1860, reporting on a meeting of the Irish Republicans in New York, critical of O'Conor's views on slavery. For a good chronology of William Evarts's life, through his papers, see *Evarts Family Papers*, Archives at Yale, archives.yale.edu/repositories/12/resources/4423.

3. See *Richmond Enquirer*, March 24, 1857, 4. In his January 19, 1856, Message to the Legislature, Governor John A. King asked for an appropriation for two associate counsels to act with the Attorney General in the Lemmon case, then pending before the New York Supreme Court, General Term, then New York's first appellate level, the highest being the New York Court of Appeals, the

State's court of last resort. *Journal of the Assembly of the State of New-York; at Their Seventy-Ninth Session* (Albany: Charles Van Benthuysen, 1856).

4. See "The Lemmon Slave Case," *New York Times*, October 2, 1857, 3, for extended coverage of the mootness argument. "The People ex rel. Louis N. Bonaparte vs. Jonathan Lemmon, appellant," *New-York Tribune*, October 2, 1857, 7.

5. *National Anti-Slavery Standard*, October 10, 1857. Abolitionists had worried that by waiting for the outcome of the Dred Scott case, the New York courts would feel bound by it and rule in favor of slave power. (See *National Anti-Slavery Standard*, March 7, 1857.)

6. The question whether this was a bona fide controversy as opposed to an appeal staged to decide state interests under an "abstract question" had been raised several months earlier by Judge Mitchell, in May 1857. According to a press account, O'Conor said that he could not see how, if Lemmon was indemnified by a third party for property taken from him, he was deprived of his remedy against the unlawful holder; but he would inquire whether this was a case fairly before the court (*Buffalo Courier*, May 7, 1857, 2). In New York, dismissals for mootness have been with us for a long time; e.g., People ex rel. Lynch v. Martin, 155 N.Y. 666 (1898). If a case is "settled out of court," so to speak, a court would not want to entertain the matter, as it is "moot" and does not involve a live case or controversy. Even so, there are exceptions, as where, for example, it is a matter of public interest, likely to recur (Hearst Corp. v. Clyne, 50 N.Y.2d 707 (1980)). The court did not conduct a lengthy discussion on what came to be called "the mootness doctrine" and its exceptions, but acted instinctively and with common sense, taking on the appeal.

Others shared Jay's concern that in the hands of the United States Supreme Court, the Lemmon case could be a vehicle to expand if not nationalize slavery: "But one more decision is needed to make Slavery the actual law of the whole Republic, and render its prohibition in *any of the States* null and void;—and this we shall probably have when the Lemmon case reaches the same tribunal which has just reversed the whole policy of the Government in regard to the Territories." *New York Times*, March 7, 1857, 4; to the same effect, see *Oneida (NY) Sachem*, September 26, 1857, 2. "The Lemmon case is on its way to this corrupt fountain of law. Arrived there, a new shackle for the North will be handed to the servile Supreme Court, to rivet upon us. . . . [It] shall complete the disgraceful labors of the Federal Judiciary in behalf of Slavery. . . . The Slave breeders will celebrate it as the crowning success of a complete conquest" (quoting "The Issue Forced Upon Us," *Albany Evening Journal*, March 9, 1857, 2, in Kurt T. Lash, "The Enumerated-Rights Reading of the Privileges or Immunities Clause: A Response to Barnett and Bernick," *Notre Dame Law Review* 95, no. 2 (December 2019): 599).

7. *Brooklyn Daily Eagle*, October 2, 1857, 2; *Richmond Enquirer*, October 9, 1857, 1, opened with a lengthy, slashing editorial against abolitionists, the *New-York Tribune*, and Horace Greeley. It continued to cover the case in a later

issue, printing almost the entire brief of Charles O'Conor, representing Virginia (October 13, 1857, 4). The Tribune commented that Virginia's goal in the Lemmon case is to "convert the City of New York into a grand depot for the domestic slave trade" (*New-York Tribune*, October 5, 1857, 4). For further accounts of the appellate arguments see *New York Times*, October 6, 1857, 2, and *New-York Tribune*, October 6, 1857, 4. As a point of interest: In June, 1854, as the case was on its way to the first-level appeal, the court ruled that in order to appeal, the Lemmons, as non-residents, must post security for costs. "Lemmon Slave Case," *New York Times*, June 22, 1854, 6; *Richmond Dispatch*, June 7, 1854, 4; *Semi-Weekly Tribune* (New York), June 13, 1854, 7. At that point Virginia, and not the Lemmons, was the prime mover on the appeal, and Virginia posted the bond of the Governor of Virginia as security, to which Erastus Culver (on behalf of New York and the slaves) objected, as insufficient. "The Lemmon Case," *Richmond Dispatch*, July 22, 1854, 3; *Anti-Slavery Bugle*, July 29, 1854; "The Lemmon Case," *New York Times*, October 27, 1854, 6. In October 1854, the New York attorneys, acting for Virginia, had posted a $250 bond. "The Lemmon Case," *New York Times*, October 27, 1854, 6; "The Lemmon Slave Case," *Anti-Slavery Bugle*, November 11, 1854, 1.

8. Somersett v. Stewart, 98 ER 499, 510 (K.B.) (1772); George Van Cleve, "Somerset's Case Revisited: Somerset's Case and Its Antecedents in Imperial Perspective," *Law and History Review* 24, no. 3 (Fall 2006): 601; Paul Finkelman, "When International Law Was a Domestic Problem," *Valparaiso University Law Review* 44, no. 3 (Spring 2010): 779.

9. William Blackstone, *Commentaries on the Laws of England*, vol. 1 (Oxford: Clarendon Press, 1765), 423.

10. Dred Scott v. Sandford, 60 U.S. 393, 589–590 (1857).

11. Ibid. at 549–550. See Paul Finkelman, "John McLean: Moderate Abolitionist and Supreme Court Politician," *Vanderbilt Law Review* 62, no. 2 (March 2009): 519.

12. Although the Eight had gone to Canada immediately after Judge Paine liberated them, Evarts was technically arguing on their behalf, as they were still in the case, nominally. New York engaged Evarts pursuant to a February 24, 1855, resolution that counsel be appointed to act on behalf of Ogden Hoffman, New York's Attorney General. Not long afterward, on May 1, 1856, Hoffman died, and New York Governor Myron Clark appointed William Evarts in his place. As to Hoffman's death, see "Death of Ogden Hoffman," *Times Union*, May 2, 1856, 2. As to Evarts's appointment, see "The Lemmon Case," *Vermont Chronicle*, March 31, 1857, 3.

As for Chester Arthur's role in securing passage of a joint resolution requesting New York's Governor to appoint counsel to defend the Lemmon decision on appeal, see *Chicago Tribune*, November 19, 1886, 2; *Harrisburg (PA) Telegraph*, November 18, 1886, 1; *Leavenworth (KS) Times*, September 20, 1881, 4. There is no reason to doubt that Arthur went to Albany and spoke to the right people, but there does not appear to be documentary evidence of it. Arthur was a partner in the firm of Erastus D. Culver (Culver, Parker and Arthur). The firm was at 289 Broadway in New York (see Robert Pigott, *New York's Legal Landmarks: A Guide to Legal Edifices, Institutions, Lore, History and Curiosities on the City's Streets*, 2nd ed. (New York: Attorney Street Editions, 2014), 37). Culver went on the bench in 1853, before the case went on appeal. For Arthur's role as a young attorney in representing Elizabeth Jennings in her civil rights case, see Jerry Mikorenda, *America's First Freedom Fighter: Elizabeth Jennings, Chester Arthur, and the Early Fight for Civil Rights* (Guilford: Lyons Press, 2020). See also "Chester Alan Arthur: Civil Rights Lawyer," *Presidential History Geeks*, September 21, 2010, potus-geeks. livejournal.com/43319.html, and "Presidents and the Law: Chester Alan Arthur—Civil Rights Lawyer," *Presidential History Geeks*, September 8, 2014, potus-geeks. livejournal.com/519128.html. See also John H. Hewitt, "The Search for Elizabeth Jennings, Heroine of a Sunday Afternoon in New York City," *New York History* 71, no. 4 (October 1990): 386–415.

13. For Joseph Blunt's obituary, see *The Historical Magazine and Notes and Queries Concerning the Antiquities, History and Biography of America*, vol. 4 (Boston: C. B. Richardson, 1860).

14. The oral argument of the case was not widely covered in Southern newspapers, but the *Richmond Enquirer* wrote a lengthy essay critical of abolitionist fervor behind it. "The Lemmon Case and the New York Tribune," *Richmond Enquirer*, October 9, 1857, 1.

15. Scott v. Sandford, 60 U.S. (19 How.) 393, 407 (1857).

16. Rev. H. N. McTyeire, et al., *Duties of Masters to Servants: Three Premium Essays* (Charleston: Southern Baptist Publication Society, 1851), 39, 43, 132. For an elaboration on the theme of paternalism and God's will in slavery, see Herman N. Johnson, Jr., "From Status to Agency: Abolishing the 'Very Spirit of Slavery,'" *Columbia Journal of Race and Law* 7 (2017): 284–285.

17. George McDuffie, "The Natural Slavery of the Negro" (1835), staush.files. wordpress.com/2012/09/mcduffie-proslavery.pdf. At the Museum of the Bible in Washington, DC, is a Bible from the 1800s that was once used to convert slaves to Christianity while omitting key passages that could have led to insurrection, according to Anthony Schmidt, associate curator of Bible and Religion in America at the museum. He states that the Bible, entitled *Parts of the Holy Bible, Selected for the Use of the Negro Slaves in the British West-India Islands*, is missing large portions of text. One verse that was removed was taken from Galatians 3:28, reading, "There is neither Jew nor Greek, there is neither bond nor free, there is neither male nor female: for ye are all one in Christ Jesus." Biblical verses extolling the institution of slavery were retained, including the most famous pro-slavery verse that many pro-slavery people would have cited: "Servants, be obedient to them that are masters according to the flesh, with fear and trembling, in singleness of your hear, as unto Christ" (Ephesians 6:5).

18. Am. Colonization Soc'y v. Gartrell, 23 Ga. 448, 4640465 (1857). Also see Commonwealth v. Turner, 26 Va. 678, 681 (1827), which speaks of the "paternal curse of Noah." For general background examining the interplay between pro-slavery rhetoric and evangelical abolitionism, see Bertram Wyatt-Brown, *Yankee Saints and Southern Sinners* (Baton Rouge: Louisiana State University Press, 1985), 155–161. For an essay exploring the complicated relationship between religious thought and support for the Fugitive Slave Act of 1850, see Laura L. Mitchell, "'Matters of Justice Between Man and Man': Northern Divines, the Bible, and the Fugitive Slave Act of 1850," in *Religion and the Antebellum Debate Over Slavery*, ed. John R. McKivigan and Mitchell Snay (Athens: University of Georgia Press, 1998), 134–165.

As for the curse of Ham as biblical justification for slavery, see Thomas Virgil Peterson, *Ham and Japheth: The Mythic World of Whites in the Antebellum South* (Metuchen: Scarecrow, 1978), and Stephen R. Haynes, *Noah's Curse: The Biblical Justification of American Slavery* (Oxford: Oxford University Press, 2002), 97, which describes the biblical curse as justification for slavery, asserting that the Black race is incapable of governing itself aright and needs help from the white race. Also see "The Biblical Defense to Slavery: The Book of Genesis," *Union to Disunion*, accessed January 23, 2020, projects.leadr.msu.edu/uniontodisunion/exhibits/show/scripture-passages/the-book-of-genesis.

The biblical defense of slavery was more pronounced in the deep South than in the border states, which, as one commentator put it, considered the institution a "necessary evil" and defended the "diffusion" of slavery into the territories on the dubious ground that expansion would alleviate slavery's harshness. James Oakes, "The Great Divide," *New York Review of Books*, May 23, 2019, www.nybooks.com/articles/2019/05/23/civil-war-history-great-divide/. See also Russell B. Nye, *Fettered Freedom: Civil Liberties and the Slavery Controversy, 1830–1860* (East Lansing: Michigan State University Press, 1963), 222–223, for a discussion of writings for and against slavery, in the realm of Northern and Southern theology.

19. The closest is an 1835 ruling by New York's highest court: "Slavery is abhorred in all nations where the light of civilization and refinement has penetrated, as repugnant to every principle of justice and humanity, and deserving the condemnation of God and man." Jack v. Martin, 14 Wend. 507, 533 (1835). Interestingly, Charles O'Conor, then age 31, argued that case on behalf of the slaveowner—17 years before Lemmon. In an earlier instance, the New York Supreme Court had observed that "the progress of society in civilization, more correct notions on the subject of moral obligation, and above all, the benign influence of the Christian religion, have softened many of the rigors attendant on slavery among the ancients. But the rights of the slave in respect of marriage and the acquisition and transmission of property by way of inheritance, remain substantially on the same ground." Jackson v. Lervey, 5 Cow. 397, 402–403 (1826).

20. Tobias B. Wolff, "The Thirteenth Amendment and Slavery in the Global Economy," *Columbia Law Review* 102, no. 4 (May 2002): 1003–1009. The December 7, 1857, decision at the first appellate level in New York is reported at Lemmon v. People ex rel. Napoleon, 26 Barb. 270 (1857).

Chapter 11

1. Slave power, angered by the decision of New York's mid-levels appeals court in 1857, looked forward to vindication in the Supreme Court. *The National Era*, December 24, 1857, 3. For Governor King's message, see *The New York Times*, January 6, 1858, 2; "Message of the Governor of New York," *National Era*, January 14, 1858, 3.

2. *National Era*, April 22, 1858, 4. See also *National Era*, June 24, 1858, October 14, 1858; *Vermont Watchman and State Journal*, August 27, 1858, 2.

3. According to *The New York Times* of April 16, 1860, Jay, as amicus curiae, had asked the Court of Appeals to dismiss the appeal because the Lemmons had been reimbursed for the loss of the slaves. There does not appear to be a record of that motion.

4. It is difficult to account for Jay using the word "interference," considering that he was uncommonly articulate and well-mannered. The word seems odd under the circumstances. Perhaps Jay was trying to make the point as starkly as possible.

5. "The Governor's Message," *New-York Tribune*, January 6, 1858, 5; *Buffalo Courier*, January 6, 1858, 2.

6. I include the full letter below, with thanks to the people at Columbia University's Butler Library for allowing me to take an iPhone picture of it. Jay, accurately, referred to the Supreme Court, meaning the State Supreme Court, General Term, then New York's first-level appellate court, and not the Supreme Court of the United States. To avoid confusion, in the square bracket I substituted the words mid-level appellate court for the Supreme Court.

Also, I put the word "triumph" in italics to reveal that I was not certain of its legibility, but it fits the context.

New York January 9, 1858

I beg to thank your excellency for your note of the 4th January in reply to my letter and the memorial of Louis Napoleon. I regret that your excellency views the propriety of State interference in the matter of the Lemmon Slave appeal from so different a standpoint from that which I occupy. I know the anxiety of the Counsel employed by Virginia to carry the case to Washington and the certain *triumph* [*illegible*] they there anticipate not only over the state of New York but over all the free States—and in my view the appeal should be stayed where it is, not simply as a matter of legal practice upon the grounds stated in my suggestion to [New York's first-level appeals court] but as a matter of State policy and State duty to the whole country.

[?] knowing the regard of the American people for adjudged law that regard the removal of Judge Paine's decision by the Supreme Court at Washington a national misfortune.

I make these remarks not with the expectation of changing views—now finally embodied in your message but to explain why it is that in opposition to your suggestion to the legislature to make another appropriation for continuing the appeal I shall feel it my duty as the counsel for the Lemmon Slaves to stay the appeal if possible and to address to the Legislature the petition of Louis Napoleon which was originally addressed to Your Excellency. In so doing I feel that no assurances are necessary to satisfy you that although forced by my conviction into an attitude of opposition on a point of expediency I am with undiminished attachment and regard.

Your Excellency's very faithful servant,
John Jay

7. See "Congressional Globe, 35th Congress, 1st Session," *A Century of Lawmaking for a New Nation: U.S. Congressional Documents and Debates, 1774–1875*, memory.loc.gov/cgi-bin/ampage?collId=llcg&fileName=048/llcg048.db&recNum=219.

8. See "Congressional Globe, Senate, 35th Congress, 2nd Session," *A Century of Lawmaking for a New Nation: U.S. Congressional Documents and Debates, 1774–1875*, memory.loc.gov/cgi-bin/ampage?collId=llcg&fileName=050/llcg050.db&recNum=227. John Parker Hale served in the United States Senate from 1847 to 1853 and again from 1855 to 1865. Initially a Democrat, he helped establish the anti-slavery Free Soil Party and eventually joined the Republican Party.

9. Ableman v. Booth, 62 U.S. (21 How.) 506, 515–516 (1859), reversing In re Booth, 3 Wis. 1 (1854).

10. The arrest, trial, and conviction of Thomas, aka Mason Thomas, aka Mason Spaulding were carried in many newspapers (*Brooklyn Daily Eagle*, April 9, 1858, 2, April 10, 1858, 2; *Richmond Dispatch*, April 12, 1858, 1; *Baltimore Sun*, April 13, 1858, 4; *New York Times*, May 24, 1858, 4, May 25, 1858, 2; *Woods County Reporter*, June 2, 1858, 2). The news reached the Glasgow, Scotland, *Daily Herald* of April 23, 1858, 4. Judge (Recorder) George G. Bernard imposed the

sentence in New York Court of General Sessions on May 22, 1858, after his lengthy dissertation on the law following a motion in arrest of judgment by Thomas's attorney. *New York Times*, May 24, 1858, 3.

11. Charles S. Spencer, *An Appeal for Freedom: Made in the Assembly of the State of New York, March 7th, 1859* (Albany: Weed, Parsons, 1859).

12. *Holmes County Republican*, September 8, 1859, 1.

13. "A Plea for Captain John Brown by Henry David Thoreau; October 30, 1859," *The Avalon Project*, Yale Law School, avalon.law.yale.edu/19th_century/thoreau_001.asp.

14. Emerson's speech at Tremont Temple in Boston, as reported in *The Liberator* (Boston, MA) of November 22, 1859. See also John J. McDonald, "Emerson and John Brown," *New England Quarterly* 44, no. 3 (1971): 377–396.

15. Thomas Wentworth Higginson, *Henry Wadsworth Longfellow* (Boston: Houghton, Mifflin and Company, 1902), 271.

16. *New York Daily Herald*, December 20, 1859, 3. Charles O'Conor's speech, at the Academy of Music in New York City on December 19, 1859, is online at archive.org/details/campaignof1860c00linc/page/n13/mode/2up.

17. For example, *Yorkville Enquirer*, January 26, 1860, 2; *Sugar Planter*, December 31, 1859; *The Greenville Enterprise*, January 26, 1860, 2.

18. O'Conor's Letter to a Committee of Merchants, December 20, 1859, is online at archive.org/details/campaignof1860c00linc/page/n21/mode/2up.

19. "Speech of John Cochrane on the Impending Crisis," *New York Daily Herald*, December 21, 1859, 1; *Buffalo Courier*, January 27, 1860, 1.

20. *Congressional Globe*, January 18, 1860, 510–511.

Chapter 12

1. For the parties' written submissions, see *Lemmon v. People*, 20 N.Y. 562 (1860).

2. There were eight judges on the court during that era, an unusual number that made no sense juridically, given the possibility of a tie vote. The number resulted from a political compromise in which the Legislature thought it wise to have half the judges chosen at large and the other half from among trial judges, rotating in and out. This oddity was later amended, with the court composed of seven judges, as it is today.

3. The oral arguments of Charles O'Conor, William Evarts, and Joseph Blunt are in New York Court of Appeals, *Report of the Lemmon Slave Case*, 12–13. Courts no longer permit attorneys' orations that last for hours or days. Over the decades, the time allocated for oral argument has been reduced as judges rely more on written briefs before hearing the case. Oral argument no longer involves uninterrupted oratory by the advocates, but has increasingly involved exchanges

marked by brisk and frequent questions from the bench to the lawyers. For a history of this development, see Terry Skolnik, "Hot Bench: A Theory of Appellate Adjudication," *Boston College Law Review* 61, no. 4 (2020): 1271–1321; Marshall L. Davidson III, "Oral Argument: Transformation, Troubles, and Trends," *Belmont Law Review* 5 (2018): 203–218; Louis J. Sirico Jr., "Opening an Oral Argument Before the Supreme Court: The Decline of Narrative's Role," *The Review of Litigation, The Brief* 36, no. 1 (2016): 1–18.

4. "The Lemmon Slave Case," *New York Herald*, January 27, 1860, 2.

5. This and the following quotes from his written submission in the official reports, cited as *Lemmon v. People*, 20 N.Y. 562 (1860).

6. For the converse, see Mitchell v. Wells, 37 Miss. 235 (1859), in which Mississippi refused to recognize Ohio law in a manumission case. See also Paul Finkelman, *An Imperfect Union: Slavery, Federalism, and Comity* (Chapel Hill: University of North Carolina Press, 1981), 285–312; Seth Kreimer, "The Law of Choice and Choice of Law: Abortion, the Right to Travel, and Extraterritorial Regulation in American Federalism," *New York University Law Review* 67, no. 3 (June 1992): 467; Louise Weinberg, "Methodological Interventions and the Slavery Cases; or, Night-Thoughts of a Legal Realist," *Maryland Law Review* 56, no. 4 (1997): 1345. See also Anthony J. Sebok, "Judging the Fugitive Slave Acts," *Yale Law Journal* 100, no. 6 (1991): 1847, discussing the constitutional challenges to the Fugitive Slave Act of 1850 as violating the principle of comity by forcing free states to adopt the legal premises of slave states.

7. The *Buffalo Commercial* of January 26, 1860, reported that Blunt told the court that Justice Taney was in ill health, portending a change in the Supreme Court's membership. This does not appear in the record of the oral argument, and we do not know whether the scribe thought it inappropriate to include it in the official record. Whether language in the Dred Scott case was or was not dictum has generated academic writing; see, e.g., Barry Friedman, "The History of the Countermajoritarian Difficulty, Part One: The Road to Judicial Supremacy," *New York University Law Review* 73, no. 333 (May, 1988): 421; Mark A. Graber, "Desperately Ducking Slavery: Dred Scott and Contemporary Constitutional Theory," *Constitutional Commentary* 14, no. 2 (Summer 1997): 276.

8. For the parties' written submissions, see Lemmon v. People, 20 N.Y. 562 (1860).

9. *New York Daily Herald*, January 26, 1860, 4.

Chapter 13

1. *Semi-Weekly Mississippian*, February 10, 1860, 2.

2. Ann D. Gordon, ed., *The Selected Papers of Elizabeth Cady Stanton and Susan B. Anthony, Volume 1: In the School of Anti-Slavery, 1840–1866* (New Brunswick, NJ: Rutgers University Press, 1997), 386.

3. William D. Murphy, *Biographical Sketches of the State Officers and Legislators of the State of New York, in 1854* (Albany: C. Van Benthuysen, 1859), 212. His biography can be found online at "Hon. Shotwell Powell," *Find a Grave*, June 10, 2011, www.findagrave.com/memorial/71136281/shotwell_hon_-powell.

4. [Hiram Smith, Shotwell Powell, James Savage]; [New York (State) Legislature], *Report of the Select Committee on the Petitions to Prevent Slave Hunting in the State of New York* (Albany: C. Van Benthuysen, 1860), babel.hathitrust.org/cgi/pt?id=umn.31951002119455y&view=1up&seq=4.

5. *New-York Tribune*, February 14, 1860, 8; *Liberator*, February 24, 1860, 1. See also Morris, *Free Men Tell All*, 192–193. For commentary on the bill, see *The Liberator*, February 10, 1860, 3.

6. Speech of Hon. Theophilus Callicot, March 14, 1860, in Albany. Callicot had gone to Yale Law School before taking up residence in Brooklyn. In later years, he was convicted and served prison time for illegal traffic in liquor (see In re Callicot, 4 F. Cas. 1075 (1870)), after which he became editor of an Albany newspaper.

7. "Speech of Hon. Theophilus C. Callicot, of Kings County, against Granting Equal Suffrage to Men of Color," *Brooklyn Daily Eagle*, February 14, 1860, 1.

8. *Liberator*, April 20, 1860, 1. Barna R. Johnson's speech is online at digital.library.cornell.edu/catalog/may853214. For his biography, see Murphy, *Biographical Sketches of the State Officers and Legislators of the State of New York, in 1854*. Another biography can be found at G. W. Bungay, *Pen and Ink Portraits of the Senators, Assemblymen, and State Officers, of the State of New York* (Albany: J. Munsell, 1857), babel.hathitrust.org/cgi/pt?id=coo.31924064123056&view=1up&seq=39.

9. Lincoln's Cooper Union speech of February 27, 1860, can be found online at "Cooper Union Address," *Abraham Lincoln Online*, www.abrahamlincolnonline.org/lincoln/speeches/cooper.htm.

10. Lincoln's reference to the Lemmon case can be found at Abraham Lincoln, *Collected Works of Abraham Lincoln*, vol. 3, ed. Roy P. Basler, Marion Dolores Pratt, and Lloyd A. Dunlap (New Brunswick: Rutgers University Press, 1953), quod.lib.umich.edu/l/lincoln/lincoln3/1:199?rgn=div1;submit=Go;subview=detail;type=simple;view=fulltext;q1=548. See also Harold Holzer, *Lincoln at Cooper Union: The Speech that Made Abraham Lincoln President* (New York: Simon & Schuster, 2004), 281, n. 36, 283, n. 38; Eric Foner, *The Fiery Trial: Abraham Lincoln and American Slavery* (New York: W. W. Norton, 2010), 101–102; Finkelman, *An Imperfect Union*, 12; Richard Lawrence Miller, *Lincoln and His World, Volume 4: The Path to the Presidency, 1854–1860* (Jefferson: McFarland & Company, 2012), 231. As to Lincoln referring to the prospect of the Lemmon case becoming a "second Dred Scott decision," see the *Chicago Tribune* of April 10, 1860, 2, and May 24, 1860, 2. See also Edward J. Erler, "The Progressive Transposition of Judicial Power," in *The Progressive Revolution in Politics and Political Science: Transforming the American Regime*, ed. John Marini and Ken Masugi (Lanham,

MD: Rowman & Littlefield, 2005), 197–198; Louise Weinberg, "Dred Scott and the Crisis of 1860," *Chicago-Kent Law Review* 82, no. 97 (2007): 139. As to Lincoln's warning that the Supreme Court's next step would be to decide that a state could not exclude slavery within its borders, see William E. Nelson, "The Impact of Antislavery Movement upon Styles of Judicial Reasoning in Nineteenth Century America," *Harvard Law Review* 87 (1974): 547.

11. *Brooklyn Evening Star*, March 28, 1860, 2; *New York Times*, March 28, 1860, 4; *Racine Journal*, April 11, 1860, 2.

12. *Congressional Globe*, April 6, 1860, 1584, 1586, babel.hathitrust.org/cgi/pt?id=chi.20667294&view=1up&seq=724. Welles was from Ithaca, New York, where he had been District Attorney and County Judge of Tompkins County.

Chapter 14

1. Lemmon v. People, 20 N.Y. 562, 644 (1860). Technically speaking it affirmed the first-level appeals court, which in turn had affirmed Judge Paine's ruling.

2. For an interesting discussion of the Privileges and Immunities Clause as it relates to the Lemmon case, in the majority and dissenting opinions, see Douglas G. Smith, "The Privileges and Immunities Clause of Article IV, Section 2: Precursor of Section 1 of the Fourteenth Amendment," *San Diego Law Review* 34, no. 2 (May/June 1997): 846–851. As to the arguments on this issue in the Lemmon case, and its treatment by the Court of Appeals, particularly by Judge Denio, see also David R. Upham, "The Meanings of the 'Privileges and Immunities of Citizens' on the Eve of the Civil War," *Notre Dame Law Review* 91, no. 3 (March 2016): 1117.

In slave states, there was of course no issue concerning transit with slaves. For example, see Julia v. McKinney, 3 Mo. 193, 194 (1833). In border states, the issue was debatable. In 1843, the Illinois Supreme Court said that slaveowners do have a right of passage through Illinois based on the Privileges and Immunities Clause of the Constitution. Willard v. People, 5 Ill. (4 Scam.) 461 (1843).

Illinois was in a different position, geographically, than states in the Northeast, considering that Illinois would be traversed in travel between Kentucky and Missouri, both slave states. See Fehrenbacher, *The Dred Scott Case*, 680, pointing out that Willard was decided in 1843 and that by the 1850s, the Illinois judiciary's attitude was changing, citing Rodney v. Ill. C. R. Co., 19 Ill. 42 (1857). That is an apt observation considering that New York's attitude changed when, in 1841, it repealed the nine-month allowance for sojourning.

In 1860 the Judges of the New York Court of Appeals were elected, a selection process that did not change until 1977. Judge Denio was the Democratic party nominee in 1857. At the time, the Republican party, and not the Democratic party, was anti-slavery. Some newspapers favored Timothy Jenkins, whom they saw as a predictable anti-slavery vote if elected. For example, see the *Buffalo Morning Express* and *Illustrated Buffalo Express*, October 2, 1857, 2; *Anti-Slavery Bugle*, Lisbon, Ohio, October 24, 1857, 1. Evidently, the Republicans were considering cross-endorsing Denio, based on his eminence as a highly respected jurist. The *New York Tribune*, September 21, 1857, 4, thought it a bad idea, fearing that as the Democratic party nominee, Denio would be inclined to rule with slave power if elected. He was elected, but his vote for freedom made it a 5–3 majority vote in the Lemmon case.

3. A commentator has pointed out that the Lemmon case majority's treatment of comity has emerged as a primary precedent for applying the rule. Kurt T. Lash, "The Enumerated-Rights Reading of the Privileges or Immunities Clause: A Response to Barnett and Bernick," *Notre Dame Law Review* 95, no. 2 (December 2019): 599.

4. As I write this, over a century and a half later, it is tempting to imagine that Judge Wright had a wry sense of humor, in citing Prigg, no less, in support of freedom, and in later citing an 1815 Virginia case, Butt v. Rachel, 18 Va. 209, also in support of his decision to free the slaves. There is a short biography of him, written by Erik Goergen, who quotes a source saying of Wright: "In a memorial address honoring Judge William B. Wright, poet and lawyer Alfred B. Street said of him: 'His taste was cultured by much and varied reading, and he twined the fresh roses of literature with the dry lichens of the law. As a writer, his style was beautifully concise and clear, his ideas showing through the clearness like objects through crystal water.'" From In Memoriam, 37 N.Y. 693 (1868). For the biography, see "William B. Wright," *Historical Society of the New York Courts*, history.nycourts.gov/biography/william-b-wright/, republished from *The Judges of the New York Court of Appeals: A Biographical History*, ed. Albert M. Rosenblatt (New York: Fordham University Press, 2007).

5. Citing Somerset's case, Lofft's R, 1; S.C., 20; Howell's State Trials, 2. For Prigg, see, Prigg v. Pennsylvania, 41 U.S. 539 (1842).

6. 4 Munford's R., 209; 2 Hen. & Munford, 149. The citation translates into Burr v. Rachel, 18 Va. 209 (1814).

7. Benjamin R. Curtis, *A Memoir of Benjamin Robbins Curtis, LL.D.* (Boston: Little, Brown and Co., 1857), 197–198, archive.org/details/cu31924018765002/page/n219/mode/2up, as to Dred Scott being obiter. See also Jack B. Weinstein, "Limits on Judges' Learning, Speaking, and Acting: Part II Speaking and Part III Acting," *Dayton Law Review* 20, no. 1 (Fall 1994): 27. See also the decision of the Supreme Court in Downes v. Bidwell, 182 U.S. 244, 272–275, as to the dicta in Dred Scott.

8. Several writers have discussed Judge Clerke's dissent. See Douglas G. Smith, "Natural Law, Article IV, and Section One of the Fourteenth Amendment," *American University Law Review* 47, no. 2 (December 1997): 359. See also Douglas G. Smith, "The Privileges and Immunities Clause of Article IV, Section 2: Precursor of Section 1 of the Fourteenth Amendment," *San Diego Law Review*

34, no. 2 (May/June 1997): 850–851, discussing Judge Clerke's dissent resting on the Privileges and Immunities Clause. As to Judge Clerke's dissent involving a discussion of choice of laws and the extraterritorial application of Virginia law, see Tobias Barrington Wolff, "The Thirteenth Amendment and Slavery in the Global Economy," *Columbia Law Review* 102 (May 2002): 1005 (the author also notes the resistance of the New York Court of Appeals majority in Lemmon to the Dred Scott decision; to the latter effect, see also Kurt T. Lash, "The Origins of the Privileges or Immunities Clause, Part I: 'Privileges and Immunities' as an Antebellum Term of Art," *Georgetown Law Journal* 98 (2010): 1279); Jeffrey M. Schmitt, "Constitutional Limitations on Extraterritorial State Power: State Regulation, Choice of Law, and Slavery," *Mississippi Law Journal* 83, no. 1 (2014): 105; Suzanna Sherry, "State Constitutional Law: Doing the Right Thing," *Rutgers Law Journal* 25 (1994): 939–940. One writer has pointed out that in dissent, as an argument in favor of an owner's right to travel with their slaves, Judge Clerke said that prior to the Constitution, the Articles of Confederation protected "the removal of property imported into any state," but that the quoted phrase never made it into the Constitution. This came as a disappointment to Southerners Charles Pinckney and George Mason, the writer said, in that without the stipulation, Mason believed, slaveowners might lose their freedom to travel the country with their slaves. See Sean Wilentz, *No Property in Man: Slavery and Antislavery at the Nation's Founding* (Cambridge, MA: Harvard University Press, 2018), 102. There is an obituary for Judge Clerke in *The New York Times*, December 16, 1885, 5.

9. *Cleveland Morning Leader*, April 18, 1860, 2; *Aurora of the Valley*, Newbury, VT, April 21, 1860, 2, which spoke also of the dangers and intentions of the Democratic Party and of its supporters like Charles O'Conor. See also *Randolph Journal*, May 3, 1860, 2; *Anti-Slavery Bugle*, May 5, 1860, 1; *Perrysburg Journal*, May 10, 1860, 2; Sandra L. Rierson, "The Thirteenth Amendment as a Model for Revolution," *Vermont Law Review* 35, no. 4 (Summer 2011): 765.

10. Speech of Hon. James M. Ashley, of Ohio, "Success of the Calhoun Revolution: The Constitution Changed and Slavery Nationalized by the Usurpations of the Supreme Court," US House of Representatives, May 29, 1860 (Washington D.C.: Buell & Blanchard, Printers, 1860), digital.library.cornell.edu/catalog/may851117; *Congressional Globe*, 36th Congress, 1st Session, appendix, 368 (1860), babel.hathitrust.org/cgi/pt?id=ucl.c109461180&view=1up&seq=950. After the war, Ashley advocated for passage of the 13th Amendment, ending slavery in the United States. He served as Governor of the Montana Territory.

11. William G. Bean, "John Letcher and the Slavery Issue in Virginia's Gubernatorial Contest of 1858–1859," *Journal of Southern History* 20, no. 1 (1954): 22–49; William G. Bean, "The Ruffner Pamphlet of 1847: An Anti-Slavery Aspect of Virginia Sectionalism," *Virginia Magazine of History and Biography* 61, no. 3 (July 1953): 260–282.

12. *New York Times*, January 11, 1860, 1; *Wheeling Intelligencer*, January 12, 1860, 1, describing Letcher's inaugural message to the Virginia Assembly. In

November 1860, several months after the New York Court of Appeals ruled against Virginia, Letcher engaged in an exchange of lengthy letters over the Fugitive Slave Act, which Letcher vigorously defended, but said nothing about *Lemmon*. In my research, I have found no instance in which Letcher commented at all about the Lemmon case to anyone, in any capacity. The exchange was with Lewis D. Vail of Philadelphia, and is online at digital.library.cornell.edu/catalog/may921701. The *Wheeling Intelligencer* of January 12, 1860, 2, ran an article questioning Letcher's conversion as a slavery advocate. As for Letcher's earlier anti-slavery stance, his vulnerability on the issue, and the enmity between Letcher and Wise, see William S. Hitchcock, "The Limits of Southern Unionism: Virginia Conservatives and the Gubernatorial Election of 1859," *Journal of Southern History* 47, no. 1 (1981): 57–72 (enmity at 66).

13. *Richmond Dispatch*, February 21, 1861.

14. In his April 28, 2017 email to me, Robert Ellis, Archivist, Federal Judicial Records, said there is no record of an appeal to the Supreme Court in the Lemmon case. In an email of the same date to me, Jennifer Huff, Reference Department Coordinator of the Virginia Historical Society, said she found no reference to the Lemmon case in the papers of then–Virginia Governor John Letcher. It would be fascinating to learn otherwise, but no scholar or historian has found any trace of an appeal. See also Finkelman, *An Imperfect Union*, 313, note 1, who has found none.

15. *New York Herald*, April 23, 1860, 6; *Yorkville Enquirer*, April 26, 1860, 2.

16. *The Register*, May 10, 1860, 2; *Nashville Union and American*, May 5, 1860, 3, as to Hunter and O'Conor. Hunter (1809–1887), a Virginia lawyer, politician, and plantation owner during the Civil War, became the Confederate States' Secretary of State (1861–1862) and then a Confederate Senator (1862–1865). See *The Bossier Banner*, May 11, 1860, 2, as to Davis and O'Conor. The news had even reached England; see *The Standard Banner*, May 17, 1860, 5.

17. *New York Times*, July 19, 1860, 1; *Weekly Advertiser*, August 1, 1860, 4; *Charleston Daily Courier*, July 25, 1860 (effectively praising the letter). For an interesting article on Breckenridge, see Meredith Hindley, "The Man Who Came in Second: How John Breckenridge and the Democratic Party lost the 1860 Presidential Election," *Humanities: The Magazine of the National Endowment for the Humanities* 31, no. 6 (November/December 2010), www.neh.gov/humanities/2011/novemberdecember/feature/the-man-who-came-in-second.

18. *Syracuse Daily Courier and Union*, October 18, 1860, 2, referring to O'Conor's letter of October 4, 1860.

19. *Newbern Weekly Progress*, November 27, 1860, 1.

20. South Carolina's declaration of secession is available online at avalon.law.yale.edu/19th_century/csa_scarsec.asp.

21. Constitution of the Confederate States, Art. IV, Sec. 2, (I), March 11, 1861, avalon.law.yale.edu/19th_century/csa_csa.asp.

Index

Gardiner, Alexander, 80, 81
Gay, Sydney Howard, 26, 27f, 37
God and slavery, 122–23, 134, 135.
    See also Christianity

habeas corpus, writ of, 90–91, 108
    Erastus Culver and, 28, 29, 33, 36
    John Jay II and, 36, 37, 39
    Louis Napoleon and, 28, 29, 33, 81,
        129f
    New York and, 28, 29, 33, 37, 39,
        59–60, 129f, 144
Hale, John Parker, 130, 226n8
Ham, curse of, 122, 123, 224n18
Hambley, Thomas, 68
Hamlet, James, 80–81
Hargrave, James, 11
Harper, William, 96
Harpers Ferry, John Brown's raid on,
    132
Henry, William "Jerry," 74, 75
higher law, xv, 76. See also natural
    law/law of nature
Hillyer, Abraham Y., 107
Hoffman, Josiah, 30
Horsmanden, Daniel, 193n7
Hughes, Willis H., 82
Hulsebosch, Daniel J., 191n14
Hunt, Washington, 75

intermarriage, racial, 10
international law. See nations, law of
interstate commerce. See commerce

Jack v. Martin, 30
Jay, John (grandfather of John Jay II),
    35, 50, 57
Jay, John, II, 153, 225–26nn3–6
    common law and, 37, 43, 46
    Erastus Culver and, 35–36, 40, 43,
        46, 50, 97, 102–3, 106–9, 122
    family, 35, 57

Fugitive Slave Act of 1793 and, 39,
    66
George Kirk and, 37, 189n7
Horace Preston and, 35–36
James Snowden and, 75
John Edmonds and, 37–39
John King and, 127, 128, 225n6
Joseph Belt and, 38–39
Louis Napoleon and, 37
natural law, natural rights, and, 46,
    122
overview, xviii, 35
Paine and, 40
writ of habeas corpus and, 36, 37,
    39
Jay, Peter Augustus, 57
Jay, William, 35, 36f
Jerry Rescue (William Henry), 74, 75
Johnson, Barna R., 150
Johnson, Joseph (Virginia Governor),
    106
Johnson, Nancy, 10, 12, 100, 177n5
    children, xvii, 3, 13
    duties, 4, 5, 21
    Emeline Johnson and, 215n27
    family, 9, 177n5, 187n13
    finances, 98, 100
    freedom and, 22, 33, 40–41, 98
    Juliet Lemmon and, 40–41
    Lemmon family and, 4–6
    Lemmon v. New York and, xiv, 41
    name, 9, 177n5
    overview, xvii
    ownership, 3–5
    Richard Johnson and, 215n27
Johnson, Richard (formerly "Levi"),
    xviii, 99, 168, 215n27
judges
    silence regarding Dred Scott v.
        Sandford, 119–20, 143, 146, 156

Kent, James, 89

New York *Journal of Commerce*, 28,
41, 45, 75, 101–3, 216n32
New York legislation, 47–49, 63, 88,
142, 147. *See also* Constitution of
New York
1817 emancipation law, 43, 56, 60,
96, 121, 143, 157
amended in 1841, 43, 96, 118,
121, 123, 137, 143, 230n2
"An Act to Protect the Rights and
Liberties of the Citizens of the
State of New York," 131
anti-slavery statute, 77
Constitutional Ratification
Convention, 53
New York Act for Regulating Slaves
(1702), 47
regarding punishing slaves, 47–48,
193n6
slave code (1702), 47
writ of habeas corpus and, 59–60
New York legislature, 128
Charles O'Conor and, 117
criticism of, 72–73, 157
Dred Scott and, 113
Fugitive Slave Act of 1850 and,
72–73, 149
Joint Committee of the Senate and
Assembly, 113
racism in, 149–50
Shotwell Powell and, 149
Virginia legislature, William
Seward, and, 76–77
New York Slave Revolt of 1712, 49
New York Slave Revolt of 1741/
New York Conspiracy of 1741,
49, 50f
New York State Assembly, 147, 149
New York Superior Court. *See*
Superior Court of the City of
New York

New York Supreme Court, 60, 93f.
See also Blunt, Joseph; Evarts,
William; O'Conor, Charles
General Term, 115, 220n3, 225n6
Supreme Court of Judicature, 55
Norfolk, Virginia, 18–21

Oberlin–Wellington Rescue, 131, 131f
O'Conor, Charles, 117, 128, 130, 135,
139, 141–43, 145, 153, 160–61
on comity, 118–19, 123, 142
Dred Scott and, 119–20, 143, 145,
146
Foot Report, Foot resolution, and,
118, 142–43
Jefferson Davis and, 167
Joseph Blunt and, 120, 123, 139, 145
letters, 134, 159, 159f
Lincoln and, 153, 162
"Negro Slavery Not Unjust"
(speech), 132, 133f, 134
opening statement, 117–20
overview, xviii, 115
Paine and, 117, 118, 122, 141–42
portrait of, 140f, 167
"privileges and immunities"
argument, 119, 123–24, 143,
155–56
racism, 115, 122, 141
secession and, 134, 162
William Evarts and, 120, 121, 123,
139, 145, 167
Ohio, codifying the Lemmon
decision, 115
O'Neall, John B., 94

Paine, Elijah, Jr., 41, 45, 76, 97,
185n6, 216n30
background, 31, 32
Charles O'Conor and, 117, 118,
122, 141–42

runaway slaves. *See* fugitive slaves